Where Three Ways Meet

D0029019

John A. T. Robinson

Where Three Ways Meet

ABINGDON PRESS / Nashville

WHERE THREE WAYS MEET

Copyright © 1987 by The Estate of John A. T. Robinson
First published 1987 by SCM Press Ltd., 26-30 Tottenham
Road, London

This book is printed on acid-free paper.

Cover design by F. S. Davis

Library of Congress Cataloging-in-Publication Data

Robinson, John A. T. (John Arthur Thomas), 1919–
    Where three ways meet / John A. T. Robinson.
      p.   cm.
    Reprint. Originally published: London: SCM Press,
    1987.
    "A bibliography of the writings of John A. T. Robinson":
    p.
    Bibliography: p.
    ISBN 0-687-45178-7 (alk. paper)
    1. Theology. 2. Church of England—Sermons. 3. Angli-
can Communion—Sermons. 4. Sermons, English. I. Title.
BR50.R63   1989
230'.3—dc19   88-34143
                                  CIP

U. S. Edition published in 1989 by Abingdon Press
201 Eighth Ave., South, Nashville, Tennessee

MANUFACTURED BY THE PARTHENON PRESS AT
NASHVILLE, TENNESSEE, UNITED STATES OF AMERICA

Contents

CONTENTS

Preface

Much of what I should write in this Preface, I have already included in my biography of John.[1]

I explained, for instance, in the Preface to the biography:

> It was in September 1977 that Bishop John Robinson asked me to be his literary executor. It seemed a somewhat pretentious title for what it then involved. He would phone me before he went away on a long journey, and tell me where his will was, and in what state – and where – his latest writings were. He would phone again as soon as he got back, to report his safe return. It was at the end of May 1983 that he phoned one day and, after listening to my troubles for quite a time, said: 'Well, now I have some news for you: I have inoperable cancer.' My role and responsibility assumed then a sudden importance I had hoped it would never need to be given.

In fact, few great decisions have fallen to me in relation to this book; for, as John describes in his Introduction, he quickly got to work on preparing for publication two volumes. The first, *Twelve More New Testament Studies*, was published posthumously in 1984, and the second volume of ' "relicts" which might or might not be deemed to be publishable' he assembled and handed to me in a file when I had my last meeting with him at Arncliffe in mid-August 1983.

After John died, it became clear that the title of this second book should not be what he had suggested – *The End of All Our Exploring* – not least because Monica Furlong had written a book with that title. But John himself had given a clue to what an alternative title might be. At that last Arncliffe meeting he had shyly produced two quarto pages on which he had written enigmatically: 'Where Three Ways Meet', and underneath had listed all the major books he had written, divided into the 'three ways'. John had been doing some self-analysis (of his mind, not his psyche), apparently fairly recently (he had used the results at the College of Preachers in Washington that May), and wanted any future biographer to have the benefit of it. It is probably best simply set down as John wrote it:

WHERE THREE WAYS MEET

The way of theological exploration

Thou Who Art
In the End God
Honest to God
The Honest to God Debate
But That I Can't Believe!
Exploration into God
The Human Face of God
Truth is Two-Eyed

The way of biblical interrogation

The Body
Jesus and His Coming
Twelve New Testament Studies
Redating the New Testament
Can we Trust the New Testament?
Wrestling with Romans
The Priority of John
Twelve More New Testament Studies

The way of social responsibility

On Being the Church in the World
Liturgy Coming to Life
Christian Morals Today
The New Reformation?
Christian Freedom in a Permissive Society
The Difference in Being a Christian Today
The Roots of a Radical
The Church's Most Urgent Priority in Today's World

Themes

The Church and the Kingdom
Centre and Edges
Roots and Fruits
Both-And rather than Either-Or

Rooted in order to be radical
Paul to Romans. . .
Four Makers of Contemporary
    Theology: Pattern in writings
    and concerns
Fall into 3 classes
Three trajectories, constantly
    criss-crossing
A person where 3 ways meet
Lines on which all of us are
    travelling in our ministries
Must in different ways and
    different proportions hold
    them together
    if we are going to be
    whole in our response
Which first – arbitrary: no
    before or after in this trinity

1   *The way of theological exploration*
Constantly pushing out; questioning accepted doctrine; stripping away; cutting to the heart; revisioning, re-interpreting; being stretched; never resting content; pressing out from edges.

2   *The way of biblical interrogation*
Digging to roots; probing; compelling the scriptures to give up their message for us now; going behind received interpretations; refusing to accept stock answers; return to source; centre; rooted to be radical.

3   *The way of social responsibility*
Responding to what God is saying to us through his world of people; the call of the kingdom and the claims of love; reading the signs of the times; forcing us out into the world.

All three journeys, trajectories, must illumine, challenge and correct each other, driving us to the new questions. Constantly shifting kaleidoscope; to be at the point of obedience which will differ for each one of us, and from month to month and year to year.

Books waymarks reflecting my responses. Never left behind. Wouldn't want to un-say anything I've written, but wouldn't want to say it like that now. Return in new forms.

'Where Three Ways Meet' is of course a classical quotation referring to the crossroads where Oedipus met and unwittingly slew his father.

It ought to be added that, probably some time after he had drawn up this gnomic composition, John himself had written a series of additional comments not all of which are decipherable. Against *Truth is Two-Eyed*, for example: 'Stretching. Uniqueness of Christ in a pluralistic world. One-eyed defined, not confined – a bigger, not exclusive, focus and first-fruits.' And against *Can We Trust the New Testament?*: 'Cynicism of Foolish; scepticism of wise; fundamentalism of fearful; conservatism of the committed.' Several of his book titles had a cluster of abbreviated comments alongside. It is not impossible that although John was handing over these pages to a future biographer – and it is obviously an important document for understanding how he saw himself – it was conceived as the outline sketch of another fairly autobiographical book which he hoped to have written had he lived: a sequel to *The Roots of a Radical*.

So here is *Where Three Ways Meet*. It does not contain all John assembled which 'might or might not be deemed publishable'; and it contains some material which John did not include. Although he applied himself to the work of selection and revision, there is good reason to think that he would not have made the precise selection he did had he not heard Time's Winged Chariot hurrying so near.

All the papers in Part One are what John suggested; he also suggested the Bibliography of his writings to conclude the book. The selection of sermons and addresses is different from his. It seemed clear that all the sermons and addresses in *this* book should be those preached to university and college congregations and should characterize his preaching as 'scholar, pastor and prophet' in his last years. (There are, of course, many of his sermons 'parochial and plain' that are as yet unpublished.)

A book which contained some of John's last sermons but did not include his very last and most memorable 'Learning from Cancer' would be greatly lacking. It seemed right, therefore, to include it in this volume as well as in John's biography.

Ruth has described how 'On Monday afternoon 5th December (1983) John was very ill again. . . Stephen received the precise whispered instructions about the wording and dating of the Preface to the posthumous essays!' So it is that John's signature to what is now called the Introduction is dated the very day of his death.

Eric James
Corpus Christi 1987

Acknowledgments

I am grateful to the publishers of the papers in this volume who in each case have given permission for them to be reprinted; to the Oxford and Cambridge University Presses for permission to quote from *The Revelation of John* from the *New English Bible* © 1970; to Collins Publishers for permission to quote extensively from *Incognito* by Petru Dumitriu and from *A Life of Bishop John A. T. Robinson: Scholar: Pastor: Prophet*; to André Deutsch Ltd for permission to quote from *Equus*, by Peter Shaffer; and to the Revd Don Cupitt for permission to reproduce his dialogue with Bishop John Robinson.

I am also grateful to the staff of SCM Press, whose care in publishing writings posthumously has been particularily needed and generously given.

Finally, as Director of Christian Action I wish to acknowledge the generosity of Ruth Robinson in giving all the royalties from this book to Christian Action, which her husband had generously supported over many years.

Eric James

Introduction:
Six Months in Retrospect

When, on 5 June 1983 my specialist gave me six, or possibly nine, months to live, it meant that I had to sort out the choices and priorities available to me in what, after the initial shock, seemed quite a remission. For one could do a good deal in that time. In what follows I am deliberately concentrating only on what I could seek to get written in that period – though there were clearly other more important priorities.

The first thing was what I was going to do about the Bampton Lectures which I had been appointed to deliver at Oxford in the four Sunday mornings of February and the four of May 1984. Owing to the two terms' sabbatical study I had been granted the year before, I had got the big book on *The Priority of John*, due to come out of these, finished to the extent that my material could if necessary be edited for publication by others. And, thanks to the confidence I had in Charlie Moule and Chip Coakley who were immediately gracious enough to promise they would see to this, I was able to put further work on it temporarily out of my mind. Such editing, I was well aware, was no light task, but one which I could implicitly trust them to do with the most meticulous care and judgment and with the help of my secretary Stella Haughton, who has learnt to cope with my scribbles and tapes! But it was nothing to transforming the book into the eight half-hour lecture-sermons as which under the ancient foundation they had to be delivered from the pulpit of St Mary's. I had intended to compose these, starting from scratch, during the summer; but this was now obviously impossible. Later I thought I should be able to give them priority as soon as I had recovered from the operation, or, as it turned out, two. But this too was evidently going to be beyond my concentration. So, in order not to let Oxford down, I asked Charlie Moule whether he would also not only deliver the lectures but write them from my material for them. This was a most onerous request, but he most graciously and promptly agreed, so this left me free to give myself to more limited and attainable targets. While I was in hospital I started (on tape) what I rather pretentiously simply called for a family record 'A Journey of a Second Life', but I gave it up when I came out.

Meanwhile there were quite a number of items of unfinished agenda. The last thing I did before my illness was diagnosed, though the symptoms of what they thought at the time to be a duodenal ulcer were there, was the Presidential Address to the Cambridge Theological Society on 12 May, which I called 'The Last Tabu: The Self-Consciousness of Jesus'. This had been postponed because only the previous week I was at the College of Preachers in Washington DC, for two nights, talking most of the time (and eating the most expensive meal I had ever been taken out to at one of the Watergate restaurants). So I could not have been too bad. This and various other pieces, both published and unpublished, led me to consider whether there might not be the material to hand for a collection of posthumous (?) essays, which I thought I should like to have some part in pre-selecting. I doubted whether there was enough, but surprised myself to discover that there might in fact be sufficient not only for one but for two collections. After one or two abortive shots at sorting them out I came to the conclusion that they fell most naturally into two.

The first was a set of scholarly articles on the New Testament which would complement my *Twelve New Testament Studies*, published in 1962 and long since out of print, under the title *Twelve More New Testament Studies*. Because I alone could revise and where necessary rewrite these I decided to give them priority, since most of them required only limited work. As I had the copy-editing help of Jean Cunningham, who on her retirement from SCM Press actually wanted to rot her brain not only in doing this for *The Priority of John*, as she had done for *Redating the New Testament*, but also for the collection of studies, there was every reason for getting on with them as quickly as possible and having them published before the Bamptons. This meant I could also refer back to them as working papers for the latter.

Some, as I said, had already appeared in printed form. But a number required extra work. This applied in particular to an old piece on 'Hosea and the Virgin Birth' which I more than doubled in length in the light of reflection on the issues in my later writings.

Then, though I did not realize what labour it would involve at the time, I decided to recast in written form material on the Lord's Prayer which I had originally given as lectures in Cambridge. It simply showed how tedious it is to get into satisfying literary style what is first prepared for speaking and how hard the right word in the right place comes, for me at any rate. Let no one imagine that I write (as some evidently do) with facility! It also encouraged me, against the natural tendency in such circumstances, not instinctively to decline requests for additional work, and I decided to expand what was merely going to be a footnote to the Bamptons into a contribution, under the title 'The Fourth Gospel and the Church's Doctrine of the Trinity' I had been asked to make to the Festschrift for George Caird.

Besides these more technical New Testament studies I found I had a number of pieces which fell more into the series of essays composed on the side that I had had published at ten-year intervals – *On Being the Church in the World* (1960), *Christian Freedom in a Permissive Society* (1970), *The Roots of a Radical* (1980). I certainly had no intention of handing them over for publication myself yet – after all they were not 'due' till 1990! But only, if need be, to aid my literary executor, I thought there was no harm in assembling some 'relicts' which might or might not be deemed to be publishable. Again some had already been printed, but in the case of others I was stimulated to respond positively to requests which I might otherwise actually have got out of or declined. This applied to a piece on 'Religion in The Third Wave', which began life some time ago in very different circumstances but which, it occurred to me, might well adapt as a contribution for which I had been asked to a volume honouring a 'fellow heretic', Lloyd Geering of New Zealand. Once more I decided, again with some labour, to put into publishable form four lectures on interpreting the Book of Revelation today, which also started as lectures in more popular form at Cambridge and elsewhere. And finally I wrote for our friends a reflection on 'Learning from Cancer' which in various recensions sought to share at greater depth what had come to me from the experience I had been through. So altogether, with such further revision of *The Priority of John* as lack of library facilities allowed, I seem to have managed in the limited working day available before I tired quite a bit in the six months – thanks to the provision of sick-leave by Trinity which permitted me remission of my teaching load. Indeed I can scarcely recall a period when I have been able to pack so much in – and there is no doubt that it has also helped to keep me going. So the warning received has given me much for which to be grateful.

John A. T. Robinson
5 December 1983

PART ONE

Where Three Ways Meet

The Way of Theological
Exploration

What Future for a Unique Christ?

A Lecture delivered on the annual Divinity Day, October 1982, to the Divinity College, McMaster University, Hamilton, Ontario, Canada

What future for a unique Christ? It is a surprisingly modern question. It's safe to say that even when I was an undergraduate it would not have rated in the top ten. It was something that if you were a Christian you simply tended to take for granted. We weren't still quite with Fielding's Pastor Thwackum and his splendid simplicities. 'When I speak of religion,' he said, 'I mean the Christian religion. And when I speak of the Christian religion, I mean the Protestant religion. And when I speak of the Protestant religion, I mean the Church of England.' But in practice one got away with talking about 'our incomparable religion' (or 'liturgy', or whatever) because in ignorance it never received comparison or in insolence was placed beyond it.

But now the situation is very different. In fact even to claim that Jesus Christ is unique or final sounds arrogant, and most young people, I suppose, would begin by assuming the opposite. Indeed many Christians seriously wonder in what sense, if any, they should even try to defend it.

There has been a challenge on at least two fronts. First, and most obviously, from other religions. Unlike our fathers we now actually live in a multi-faith society, and in many cities in Britain we have to take this into account in our educational syllabus. Hindus and Buddhists, Sikhs and Moslems, are our neighbours, and every variety of Eastern wisdom is on offer in the underground. Gurus come and gurus go, and even our Divinity Faculties are not confined to Christian theology. We cannot go on talking about Christ as in the days when Christians and humanists had it to themselves.

The other challenge is more subtle, but if anything more profound.

Jungian psychology, for instance, which is the most sympathetic to religion, speaks very positively of the Christ-figure as an archetypal image of the self. Yet why confine this to Jesus or tie it to that particular bit of history? If I were born in India or China I would image it very differently. Man has developed a rich store of symbols. That of the Christ crucified and risen may, as Jung says, be a very profound one. But why make it exclusive? For many other images, of the mandala or the lotus, will speak more compellingly.

In what sense, if any, should a thoughtful Christian want to maintain that Jesus was unique?

First of all, here are two senses which I think we can rule out.

1. The weak sense in which each and every one of us is unique, an unrepeatable individual. That is very mysterious but not very significant, though it is important to say this of Jesus against some forms of traditional Christian doctrine which have stressed that he was man at the expense of his being genuinely and in every sense a man.

2. The opposite extreme is to say that he was absolutely unique in kind. He after all was the Son of God. He may have lived like a man, he may have been like us in every respect (except sin), but he entered our human scene from without, like a cuckoo born into a human nest. He was an anomalous exception – a heavenly being becoming a man rather than a regular product of the evolutionary process like every other member of the species *homo sapiens*.

Now one can dress up this claim in all sorts of ways, and it is at the heart of what many Christians would say was of the essence of the Christian faith, but I don't think you can get round the conclusion that this is presenting a Christ who was unique because he was abnormal. And the corollary of this, if you press it, is that he is of very doubtful relevance for the rest of us. He didn't start where we start. I believe in fact that this undermines the gospel rather than defends it. If this is what is meant by the uniqueness of Jesus as the Christ then I think it is rightly under question and it is healthy that both from inside and outside the church traditional presentations of the doctrine of the Incarnation and person of Christ should have come under examination. To quote the titles of two recent English symposia, if *The Myth of God Incarnate* had done it better and if its answer *The Truth of God Incarnate* had even heard the question (and not assumed that truth was simply the opposite of myth), some useful clearing of the ground might have been effected; instead I fear both sides have queered the pitch. (Though a third volume, *Incarnation and Myth: The Debate Continued*, has since put some constructive things together out of the rubble.)[1]

Let me state the only sense in which I would want to defend the uniqueness of Christ. This is that Jesus is unique because he alone of all mankind of whom we have any external evidence or internal experience was truly normal. He was *the* son of man, *the* son of God, the Proper Man, who lived in a relation to God and his fellow men in which we are all called to live but fail to live. This does not mean that he had everything or was everything (you mention it, he had it), but that here was a man who uniquely embodied the relationship with God for which man was created. In this man God was reflected, as St John puts it in a simile from family life, as in an only son of his father – he who had seen him had seen the Father. Or as St Paul puts it, he was the image of the invisible God, the perfect reproduction, as opposed to the distorting mirror, of his fullness, his glory.

Unlike the contributors to *The Myth* volume, I would want strongly to retain and insist upon the category of 'incarnation'. For in this man, the Christian gospel dares to assert, we see the Word, the Logos, the self-expressive activity of God in all nature and history, what God was and is, enmanned as far as human nature can contain it in an actual historical individual who is bone of our bone, flesh of our flesh – the only truly normal son of man and son of God. And I would equally want to insist, strongly, with the New Testament witness that '*God* was in Christ reconciling the world to himself'. In Christ God was doing something for us that we could never do for ourselves. That is the emphasis that those on the inside of Christian theological discourse want to hold to who would cling to substitutionary language, though I would prefer with the great weight of the New Testament witness to stress the *hyper*, on behalf of, rather than the *anti*, instead of; for Christ died not in order that we should not have to die, but precisely so that we could die, to sin rather than because of sin. He died as our representative, not our replacement. And he could do this only as a man who was totally and utterly one of us. Yet his act was God's act. To adapt a distinction of Austin Farrer's, he was not a man doing human things divinely, but a man doing divine things humanly. He was doing something distinctive in kind, something finally that God alone could do. That is what the older apologetic sought to safeguard, unhappily I believe, by saying that he *was* different in kind from us, thus cutting the ground from his solidarity with us. And this is, again, what it sought to express by insisting that in order to save us he must *be* God. But the New Testament does not say that God was Christ, or that Christ was God, *simpliciter*. It says that God was *in* Christ, acting redemptively and conclusively, doing (as we might put it) his 'own thing', through one who perfectly embodied who he was and what he was about.

That is in all conscience a tremendous claim. But before going on to say how I would defend it, let me refine it further against misunderstanding.

To believe that God is best defined in Jesus is not to believe that God is confined to Jesus. On the contrary, as St John makes clear in his prologue, the life and the light focussed in this man is the life with which everything is alive and the light which enlightens every man coming into the world. Jesus is not the exclusive revelation or act of God. The Bible itself insists that he has not left himself without witness anywhere, that at sundry times and in divers manners he has been speaking to his world. As a Jewish writer so beautifully put it of the divine Wisdom, well before the birth of Jesus, 'age after age she enters into holy souls and makes them God's friends and prophets'. The many-faceted splendour and the strange and often dark shapes under which God has been apprehended and worshipped are becoming more familiar to us the more we know both of comparative religion and depth psychology. The Christ-image is infinitely bigger and richer – and more disturbing – than what Christians under the influence both of Catholic triumphalism and of Protestant particularism have made of it, by drawing a tight little circle round the historical Jesus (or rather, their image of him) and calling it the whole of God. Being honest to Christ today, which means being honest to what the whole Bible and the whole church and the whole man, under the continuing revelation of the Spirit, sees in him, means being open to the fact that Christ is bigger than Jesus and God is bigger than Christ. And the fact that most laymen – and let's face it, most ministers and most of us – find that, initially at any rate, threatening is an indication of how blinkered and one-eyed our education has been.

The very term 'Christ' is in the first instance, of course, not Christian but Jewish. It soon became a proper name for Jesus, but it remains a title like 'the Buddha'. The Christ figure, like the Logos, is much wider than Jesus. It stands for whatever reveals, mediates, embodies the invisible, timeless mystery of *theos* in the finite, temporal and human. The Christ is God with us, or God in us, the manifestation of the divine in the human, or, as Jung put it, the God-image in us, consubstantial with God and man. The Christ in this sense covers a concern as wide as humanity, though the actual word 'Christ' may appear to exclude the Hindu or Moslem, just as the actual word 'God' may appear to exclude the Buddhist.

The New Testament message is that the Christ has appeared in Jesus, that in him the universal light of the Logos has been focussed as in the burning-glass of a single historical human being. But even as a proper name Christ includes more than Jesus or anything limited to thirty years of this man's historical existence. It embraces the cosmic Christ, the heavenly Christ, the Christ incognito in the least of these, the Christ that is to be. Indeed half the New Testament message of the Christ is of the Parousia, which in effect says 'You ain't seen nothing yet.' Moreover, this Logos, decisively disclosed in Jesus, is perceived by the New Testament writers as the light and life of *every* man. In his light we are enabled to see the light of God everywhere: it is not that outside him there is no light.

The New Testament message is that Jesus is the Christ, that the Christ you have been looking for, or, as Jung might have put, the Christ of the collective unconscious, is to be recognized in this man. But I believe that today we are being forced to state more carefully what we mean by this 'is'. Let me give an analogy I have used before. According to traditional Roman Catholic teaching the Roman Catholic Church was quite simply the Holy Catholic Church and *vice versa*. The rest of us were 'out', our orders 'null and void'. Vatican II rephrased it more carefully. The two are not to be conjoined by a simple *'est'*, 'is'. It is not that the Holy Catholic Church *consists of* the Roman Catholic Church but that it *subsists in* the Roman Catholic Church – the true church is in it but also beyond it. Similarly I believe we must say that the Christ subsists in Jesus, not that the Christ consists of Jesus. To believe that God is best defined in Christ is not to believe that God is confined to Christ. Or, to use a distinction familiar to theologians, Jesus is *totus Christus* – the Christ through and through: his whole being is an open window into God. But he is not *totum Christi*, all of Christ, the entire manifestation of the Christ-figure. Similarly Christ is *totus deus*. As Michael Ramsey has put it, 'God is Christlike and in him there is no unChristlikeness at all.' But he is not *totum dei*, all there is of God to

13

be seen in the world. This leaves me free to say as a Christian that he is for me the focus, the definitive revelation of all the scattered light of God reflected and refracted in many other images, that, as Paul put it, he is *the* image of the invisible God, in whom all my experience is given coherence and integration as in no other. But it does not require or indeed allow me to say that he is this exclusively, that there are no other faces or foci of the Christ except that which I have seen in Jesus nor other faces of God except the human face of God in Christ. No other task, I believe, is more urgent for the church today than to learn how to restate its conviction of the centrality of Christ both in relation to other faiths and in relation to insights of modern psychology without on the one hand being imperialistic and triumphalist (which, let us face it, we were when in the period of Christendom we had it to ourselves) or lapsing into a helpless syncretism, in which all religions and all insights are as good as each other or can be regarded ultimately as saying the same thing (which they are not). This is one of the points at which we must be both humble and honest and at which a true theology must give us the tools of discrimination. And we shall not find them without engaging in the risk of genuine inter-faith and what Raymond Panikkar in his latest title calls *Intra-religious Dialogue*. But I need not pursue this further because I have tried to spell it out in my *Truth is Two-Eyed*, in particular in the chapter on the uniqueness of Christ.

As St Paul puts it again, in the magnificent words that form the motto of this Divinity College, *ta panta*, not just all things, but the whole sum and structure of the universe, everything within and without, *en auto(i) synesteken*, in him coheres and hangs together. In the title of a book on Indian Christian theology, which has had to face this question more urgently than most, he is 'unique *and* universal'.

I would call myself a Christian because I would in all humility dare to make the same claim. It is not because I don't see any light or anything of God in all these other figures or images: on the contrary I am more aware, especially since my visit to the East, of how one-eyed and blinkered we have allowed ourselves to become. I need these other figures and images to complete, clarify and correct, to use Reinhold Niebuhr's formula, what comes to me through my own tradition. It is rather that what I see in Jesus as the Christ, and not only in the thirty years of his earthly life but in what Augustine called the *Totus Christus* filling and reconciling the entire cosmos, incorporates and integrates more of my experience than any of the other focal figures or archetypal images.

Since I have mentioned Jung let me use a category of his that I think provides a crucial test of this claim – the 'shadow'. This stands for all those elements in experience that are not in themselves evil but which we would rather not have to live with or acknowledge; the things about ourselves or our world that we repress or project on to others – all the dark aspects of life we would rather reject than integrate. Maturity, wholeness, individuation, he said, comes from being able to incorporate and integrate the shadow. But what we are tempted to do is disown it and to project images of God or the Christ-figure from which these aspects of reality, without us or within, are hived off on to some antibody, like the Devil or Anti-Christ. And Christians, said Jung, have been as guilty of this as anyone, leaving themselves with a God or Christ-figure that rejects so much in experience – the suffering, the absurd, the impersonal and, in the case of chauvinist males, the feminine – instead of taking it up and creatively dealing with it. That is why 'the unacceptable face of Christianity', to be seen so often in church history, constantly stands in need of completing, clarifying and correcting by the truth that can come through the dialogue with other religions and indeed with psychology and humanism and Marxism and light from any other source.

In fact I become more and more convinced that the Christ, in the broad sense of the image of the invisible, unconditional reality of *theos* in the visible and conditional, is far bigger than what E. M. Forster called 'poor little talkative Christianity'. He can and must be seen to wear other clothes, just as the first Council of Jerusalem was stretched to see that he could not be confined to wearing Jewish clothes. Indeed we may even have to be prepared to sit light to the name Christ, or to the word God, if they have over-identified the unconditional with the conditional and seemed to equate rather than locate the Beyond in the midst.

But when all has been said that has to be said – and even Jesus himself, as the writer to the Hebrews boldly asserts, had to be perfected, made whole by the things that he suffered – I am still persuaded, or I wouldn't call myself a Christian, that this particular model of the Christ incorporates the shadow, enables the antinomies of experience to cohere and hang together, more creatively than any other. Thus in its central and distinctive mystery of the cross and resurrection Christianity integrates and transfigures the light and the dark sides, I believe, more profoundly than in the coexistence, for instance, within Hinduism of Krishna and Kali, the figures of dalliance and destruction; it deals with the problems of suffering, and above all of sin, more radically and dynamically than the impassive serenity of the Buddha, however moving; and, for all its sanctioning especially in Protestantism of the great white male upon the throne and its current rejection in Catholicism of women priests, it incorporates the feminine more fully than the patriarchal religions of either Judaism or (especially) Islam.

I make this claim with great humility and open-endedness – without presuming to say that it must look like this to others. Yet for all that I receive and still more need to receive from elsewhere I would not be honest to my apprehension of the truth if I did not also want to insist that for me the revelation of God as Father in the cross of Jesus and the disclosure of man's destiny, as one of the early Christian Fathers put it, 'as in a son', represents the interpretation of the less than personal by the personal in a manner and to a degree that I do not see anywhere else. And I would echo the testimony of a Christian theologian who has reflected on these questions as deeply and as long as any of our generation, now a neighbour of mine in Cambridge, Norman Pittenger:

> For myself I believe that the finality of Christ is nothing other than his decisive disclosure that God is suffering, saving and ecstatic love. Surely you cannot get anything more final than that. But there may be many different approaches to this, many different intimations, adumbrations and preparations.

Yet for the New Testament itself Jesus, and his resurrection, is but the firstfruits of the harvest to come, the 'leading shoot', in Pierre Teilhard de Chardin's term, of the new humanity. Indeed in the words of an Indian Christian theologian, which echo the old church father Irenaeus, 'the Incarnation is as much about what man is to become as what God has become'. The finality of Christ avoids being a misleading phrase only if we remember that for St Paul 'the perfect man', like 'the last Adam', is a description not of the historical Jesus but of that new spiritual humanity into which mankind has but begun to be built. If for Christians Jesus is of unique and definitive significance (a less misleading word than final), it is not because he is the last word beyond which it is impossible to say anything, or some static norm like the standard metre against which every other has for

ever to be lined up, but because they believe as I believe that he offers
the best clue we inhabitants of planet earth have been given to what
Blake called 'the human form divine', or Tennyson 'the Christ that is
to be'.

2

A Tale of Two Cities: The World to Come

A Dialogue between The Revd Don Cupitt, Dean of Emmanuel College and The Rt Revd John A. T. Robinson, Dean of Chapel, Trinity College, held in Great St Mary's, Cambridge on Sunday 25 April 1982. The introduction by Don Cupitt was scripted and everything thereafter extempore.

Galatians 5.1: 'For freedom Christ has set us free; stand fast therefore, and do not submit again to a yoke of slavery.'

The New Testament epistles often make a contrast between two kinds of religion. There is a religion of the letter and a religion of the Spirit. There is a religion of milk fed to babes in Christ, and there is a religion of meat for adults who are old enough to think and act for themselves. There is a religion for schoolboys who are under the discipline of an external authority, and there is a religion for sons who have come of age and entered upon their inheritance. There is a religion of external commandments and there is an inward religion of freedom. Sometimes St Paul is contrasting the Old Covenant with the New, and sometimes he is making a distinction between two stages in the personal development of each Christian believer. It was evidently very important to him that Christians should be satisfied with nothing less than the full maturity and freedom of the gospel, and should not allow siren voices to lure them back into immature and authoritarian styles of religion.

The issue St Paul raises is still alive. Through all the history of the church the battle for the full freedom of the gospel has had to be waged ceaselessly and has never been decisively won. The struggle for change and renewal has continued, but it has always been opposed by the forces of tradition which seek to restore pre-Christian structures and ways of thinking.

On the one hand, it is an obvious historical fact that Christianity lives by continual change. The gospel is not something that can be passed from one person to another unexamined, like an unopened parcel. On the contrary, the very nature of religious truth is that it must be continually rediscovered and reminted. The gospel is not a static ideology, but a life that continually renews itself. Each believer must discover it for the first time, and each theologian must begin all over again. The pattern is that each succeeding Christian thinker and innovator frames his position and constructs some sort of pedigree for it by means of which he ties it into the received tradition. In this way the Christian tradition accumulates like a string of onions. Nothing runs the whole length of the string, but the continual fresh starts, each duly tied in to the chain, produce an impression of continuity. It is only when you look closely that you realize that the tradition is entirely made up of fresh starts that have subsequently been woven together to create the effect of an unbroken line.

But, on the other hand, this task of continual recreation and renewal always runs into opposition, and has to be undertaken in the teeth of a good deal of misunderstanding. The reason is that people find it hard to accept that Christianity lives by continual death and rebirth. They keep falling back upon a pre-Christian conception of faith as concerned with what is fixed, authoritative and unchanging. They need at least an illusion of immutability. So there is a constant popular pressure for immobilism and unthinking dogmatism.

This pressure for immobility can be very damaging. To take a minor illustration of it, out in the parishes the laity often tend to have very fixed role-expectations about the behaviour of the clergyman. They require him to behave and to speak in prescribed ways, and profess to be very shocked and indignant if he does not act in just the way that their expectations dictate. This pressure can be psychologically very damaging, and from a Christian point of view can destroy all spontaneity, humanity and freedom. It is important not to allow oneself to succumb to it.

In a rather similar way, theologians may be pressed by people's expectations to think certain things and to speak in certain ways. In this case, the reason is that people's perception of religious meanings tends to be very fixed and unquestioned. However, the task of the creative theologian is to attempt to bring about appropriate changes in people's perception of religious meanings, and this is inevitably a very difficult thing to do. Any shift in religious meanings is felt to be very threatening. People feel that they are losing something old and familiar, and neither understand nor welcome what they are being offered in its place. So there is trouble. Especially since 1830, almost all creative theologians have attracted criticism in both the Roman Catholic and the Protestant traditions. The same public controversies have been replayed over and over again.

In some cases, progress does seem to be made. In 1860 a modest and rather boring symposium called *Essays and Reviews* was published. It was a very moderate plea for liberalism in theology. The essayists were accused of atheism and of moral dishonesty in retaining their Orders, and there was an immense outcry and a series of court cases which continued for several years. Yet one of the essayists survived to become, thirty years later, Archbishop of Canterbury. This was one of those cases where the heresy of one generation became the orthodoxy of the next, the sort of case that Jesus described as 'whitewashing the tombs of the prophets'.

So progress can slowly be made, but meanwhile the pressure towards conformity and immobility remains strong. One must continue to struggle against it, because otherwise – as one of the 1860 essayists said – the church will 'die from the top'. In the past, Christian faith has always lived by the law of death and rebirth, and has struggled to renew itself in each succeeding period. Even today the same task must be attempted. We must try to articulate Christian faith in a fully modern idiom for our own age.

But the difficulties are very great today, because of the wholly exceptional magnitude and rapidity of cultural change in the modern period. If faith is to become fully contemporary and to engage with the spiritual life of our own age, it must undergo yet another mutation. Only, this time, because there is so much ground to make up, the personal cost of winning one's way through to a truly contemporary faith will be greater than ever before, and the opposition will be correspondingly sharper.

For in the modern period the gap between established Christian ways of thinking and the surrounding secular culture has become very wide. Look at it first from within the circle of faith, and we see that for nearly three centuries most major Christian movements have been neo-conservative. The movements that have most lastingly entered into the life of the churches have been, for example, in the eighteenth century, Pietism, Methodism and Evangelicalism; in the nineteenth century, Anglo-Catholicism and Roman Catholic Ultramontanism; and in the twentieth century, Fundamentalism, Pente-costalism and various other neo-conservative movements. Faced with external criticism, the tendency has been to strengthen the defences, reaffirm traditional language, and retreat into a ghetto of the mind. Of course there have been liberalizing and modernizing movements too, and they have enjoyed some successes, but their permanent influence in the church has not been so great as the influence of the neo-conservative movements.

The result, as everyone knows, has been that there has been a widening of the gap between Christian and secular ways of thinking. One consequence of this is that there is a danger of Christian language becoming evacuated of meaning, and being reduced to a series of shibboleths. For example, in the recently-publicized ARCIC conver-sations, it transpired that many Anglicans feel that there is not enough scriptural evidence for the corporal assumption into heaven of the Blessed Virgin Mary. The question was discussed as if we knew what is meant by a corporal assumption into heaven, and the only issue is whether we have enough evidence for the proposition. But to an educated modern person who is used to examining closely the meanings of words, the real difficulty is that he cannot see what can be meant by an apotheosis, an ascension, or a corporal assumption into heaven. A human body is a spatially extended object. If it moves, it must move along a continuous track through space and time, and for it to remain alive its physical environment must remain stable within very narrow limits. I can go so far as to imagine, I suppose, that Mary's body might suddenly vanish; but I cannot imagine by what means and to what place it is supposed to be transported, or how it lives when it gets there. Of course, by study of the history of religions I can learn about other similar ideas that have been held in various other cultures. I can learn how these ideas worked, and I can produce a sort of sociological interpretation of the function of such beliefs. However, if I conclude that *that* must be the meaning of the doctrine, I am told that my interpretation is heretical. So I am defeated. The language appears to me to be meaningless, except on the basis of cosmological and scientific beliefs that appear to be plainly untenable. The debate between believers who do accept and believers who do not accept the corporal assumption of Mary into heaven thus seems to me to be a meaningless debate, conducted within a sub-culture on the basis of presuppositions that became untenable many centuries ago. I can't take sides, when neither side is saying anything intelligible.

Here, then, is just one example of how religious language, maintained unchanged within the circle of faith, threatens to become quite meaningless. And it shows us why religious conservatism fails. It tries to maintain the integrity of faith uncorrupted by worldly modernizing ways of thinking, and the upshot is that it falls into meaninglessness. The language deteriorates into a series of empty passwords. People go on using these passwords to prove their orthodoxy to each other, but the passwords have in fact become nothing more than empty sounds. And my fear is that by today a very great deal of Christian language has suffered this fate. To quote another example, I receive many letters exhorting me to get acquainted with certain very important invisible persons. But in our world today it is very hard to see how to understand and put to use the idea of an invisible person. Christian language presents so many puzzles that a demanding spiritual quest must now be undertaken if we are to remint Christian meanings. If people tell me that there is a perfectly intelligible and satisfactory orthodox faith and they see no problem with it, then I can only reply, good luck to you; but unfortunately to me it seems that the deterioration of Christian language has now gone so far that I am compelled to go back to square one and try to think it all out again for myself.

For consider now what has been happening outside the walls of the church during all these years. The whole idea of absolute and unquestionable truth, coming down from above and backed by the power of social authority, has gone and has been replaced by a new conception of knowledge. In our culture the only knowledge now recognized is man-made, provisional and critically-established. The only way to truth is by free enquiry. Theories are put forward and tested publicly against evidence not under their control; and they are maintained only until they are falsified or shown to need re-formulating. A theory is of interest only in so far as it is formulated precisely and open to some kind of testing. There is no dogmatic knowledge at all any more, for we have found by experience that such real truth as it is given to human beings to attain can be found only by constantly and habitually seeking out and testing all concealed assumptions. The knowledge we get in this way is admittedly merely human, socially constructed, and subject to continual revision, but it is all we have. Nowadays a sceptical presumption pervades all our knowledge, testing it all the time and keeping it continually on the edge of breakdown. Yet this sceptical presumption is also the basis of a new and odd kind of strength. To a traditional dogmatist, used to living with a solid structure, the critical way of life seems intolerable. Living with no fixed framework at all, the critical thinker seems to be a sort of footloose vagrant. Yet critical thinking has produced the fabulously rich and complex world of modern science and all the other structures of knowledge with which a modern university is concerned. Yes, they are fluid and insubstantial by traditional dogmatic standards, yet they are also very beautiful and in their own way very powerful creations.

Now it seems to me that a fully modern Christian faith has to come to terms with the critical spirit. For me that means that modern faith must be pilgrim faith, faith in the open air, faith unprotected by any fixed dogmatic framework, faith that lives by a continual death and rebirth, and is completely open to change. Its course is guided, not by fixed points in the past, but by future ideals that are aimed at. The resources of Christian language and tradition are used not in a dogmatic way, but instrumentally as tools for the furtherance of the spiritual life.

Traditional faith perceives the universe as like a great house with rules laid down and with various tasks to be performed. Finding your vocation meant discovering what function had from all eternity been assigned to you, for you to perform as your contribution to the running of the whole household. With such a world-view, people drew their sense of life's meaning and purpose from above. Religious values and life-tasks were ready-made. You needed only to fit in and to find your pre-ordained place in the whole scheme of things.

That view of the world, typical of a traditional society, has now wholly passed away. We are now in a world where we can no longer be mere passive recipients of meaning, but where we have to create meaning. For we now know that all meanings are human constructions, as in Niels Bohr's quantum physics, where the world is no more than a system of probabilities until theory-guided human observations make it determinate. Or, to take a very different example, different languages and different societies construct reality in different ways. To those who study many religions it is obvious that religion is a facet of culture, a changing social construction, a way of shaping human life. It is only in the modern period that we have come to see how profoundly human activity shapes reality; but once we do realize it then our understanding of faith must become creative. God himself must be thought of, not as a metaphysical being, but rather as the ideal goal of the spiritual life, and the Christian task is to bring into being a world in which people have become fully conscious and liberated creators of religious meaning and value – the world that Jesus called the kingdom of God. If I could summarize the view that I have come to in one sentence, it might go something like this: all the many worlds that human beings have inhabited are now understood to be human social constructions; Christian faith is a corporate commitment to attempt to bring into being the new world proclaimed by the earthly Jesus and symbolized by the exalted Jesus Christ.

In the past it has been common for people to see the religious quest as a quest for a sort of metaphysical underpinning for the present order of things. Religion was concerned with validating authority, and providing cosmological backing for institutions. These ideas are still popular even today, when we see the Pope surrounded by the same sort of ideology as the Pharaoh of Egypt and the Inca of Peru. Sacred authority descends from the heavens through the earthly representative of God, and is then diffused through the various ranks beneath him to the common people. Such ways of thinking are at least five thousand years old, and are evidently still influential: but to my mind they are not really tenable today. For me Christian faith is a project for a new humanity in a new world. It is a spirituality, a way of inner transformation for each believer; and it is a social ethic. It is primarily a religion of redemption. The old realist metaphysical theologies were mainly concerned to guarantee and to validate. Their interest was fundamentally political rather than truly religious. I want to replace that kind of theology with what you might call a theology of ideals, or a theology of hope. The object is not to mobilize religious sentiment around the *status quo* or to seek cosmic reassurance, but to mobilize Christian aspiration after the new humanity and the new world promised in Jesus Christ.

On Saturday next I have a new book appearing called *The World to Come.*[1] It is a fairly tough book, though I hope a little easier to read than the last one. It is mainly concerned with how we are to make the difficult transition from the traditional realist faith to the new fully voluntary and creative kind of faith that I am groping after.

For make no mistake: the transition is difficult, at any rate for most of us, and especially for those of us who have been strongly committed to a realist theology and have felt it slipping away from us in the last twenty years. For us – I mean, for people like me – the new kind of faith can only be reached by passing through the fire.

On the other hand, I do know some people who have taken to the new point of view easily and without difficulty. They have never been strongly committed to a metaphysical theology, nor have they suffered from the various psychological hang-ups associated with realist faith. They have always seen religious ideas as symbolic projections that vary from one culture to another, and are to be used simply as tools. They have always regarded Christianity as primarily an ethical and spiritual path, and a project for the renewal of human nature. I've been surprised to find them already living at their ease in a territory which I have been able to reach only after a more arduous journey than I care to recall.

So although *The World to Come* is almost apocalyptically strenuous, I am hopeful that a time may come when the struggle to get free of dogmatic Christianity will be no more than a memory. Christian faith will be intellectually and psychologically purified, and will simply address itself to the task of bringing into being the new age of which we have a promise and a foretaste in our Lord and Saviour Jesus Christ.

JOHN ROBINSON Thank you, Don, very much for that most engaging and lucid introduction. I think we should all be grateful to Don Cupitt for his clarity, for his transparent sincerity, the rigour of his thinking and, I would add, for his courtesy, which is not always characteristic of even Christian debate. Reading his earlier book *Taking Leave of God*[2] (a quotation I would remind you not from an atheist but Meister Eckhardt, the Christian mystic) was for me something of a purgative experience. I reviewed it with a great deal more sympathy than many of my colleagues, and I would want strongly to uphold his right to say it within the church and I appreciate his desire to stay in. In fact I found myself saying to Michael Green last term, who was being dismissive, 'Michael, you *must* listen to him. He is trying to do the sort of thing that Kierkegaard did for the church of his day a hundred years ago.' And I wholly applaud his critical faith. But now let me try to sharpen up some differences for the sake of dialogue, not debate. Let me start first with what he has just said this evening. Then I would like to go on to where he seems to me to be going in his new book *The World to Come* – which I have the advantage over you of having read, albeit in snatches in most unpropitious circumstances. I certainly do not want to come to any final judgment on it.

25

Let me fasten on a polarization which seems to run through all he says and appears to me distorted, for I don't actually find myself at either pole. He sets up two religious worlds, the first (corresponding to the yoke of slavery of his text) is a house of dogmatic truths and given norms and codes. And he illustrated that from what he called the dominant, neo-conservative movements of the past three hundred years. Incidentally, I am not altogether sure that their influence has been the most enduring. After all, the conservatives did not win the religion and science debates of the last century: they were routed, whatever bits they picked up afterwards. Nor am I sure that the gap between Christian and secular ways of thinking is widening. On science and religion, even on sexual morals, I would say that they were probably closer. The battle of the old dogmatisms is out, except in the ecclesiastical 'sunbelt' and the Festival of Light; but most modern theologians would wholeheartedly agree that truth, as he says, can only be found by 'constantly and habitually seeking out and testing all concealed assumptions'. This was a point that William Temple made a generation ago. There are only truths, human truths, hypotheses, theories, constantly inadequate and revisable statements about revelation, seen as encounter with that which is most deeply true about our environment at the level, as the Bible would put it, not simply of flesh but of spirit.

There is, I believe, a real parallel, rather than antithesis, with scientific truths. Of course the body of scientific knowledge is a human construction, in which the contribution of the observing subject is being recognized as more and more vital. But such knowledge is falsifiable and therefore scientific to the extent that it is not purely subjective, simply creating our meanings, imposing our interpretations. Well, equally, religious truth is not objective knowledge of invisible metaphysical entities, as the old science claimed to be of physical entities. Indeed, I want to demythologize as much as anyone, which does not mean to debunk, but precisely to say what the profound language of myth, to which every human discipline is driven beyond a certain point (think for instance of Freud's use of the Oedipus myth), to say what that language is really about: namely to describe and respond to realities too deep for mathematical or quantifiable formulae, realities as 'real' as love or freedom or trust of another person. And in my judgment the words 'respond-to' are vital. Religious statements are descriptive not simply of our ideals, spiritualities, ethical attitudes or resolves, but of that level of reality to which these represent a creative and, in the deepest sense, rational response.

Take, for instance, a typically religious assertion like Augustine's: 'Thou hast made us for thyself and our hearts are restless till they find their rest in Thee.' Religion is the appropriate, indeed inescapable, response to that which will not let us go. Or take the biblical statement: 'Herein in love, not that we loved God but that he first loved us.' Now it seems to me, Don, that you are saying: 'Herein is love that we love God', the personification of our ideal. Indeed, in your new book you quote Spinoza: 'He who loves God must not expect to be loved in return', and you ask 'Can we learn that?'; and you add Goethe's comment on Spinoza's saying: 'If I love you, is that your concern?' and say 'Can we learn that?' Well, I cannot actually believe anyone in love saying to his girl: 'If I love you, is that your concern?' Love is essentially reciprocal, even if Christian love tells us that we must go on loving even if we do not get any response. Let me stop at that point and see what response I *do* get.

DON CUPITT I'll take up one or two points, but I mustn't let my tongue run away with me because I'm sure John has a lot more things to fire at me. I think there is some truth in his charge that I polarize, that I overstate the contrast between the objectified, ideological dogmatic view of Christianity and the one I am seeking to put in its place because, after all, Christians have always known that doctrines are meant to shape conduct. And it is that conduct-shaping, that regulative, side of doctrine, on which I lay chief emphasis – and I am not saying something wholly new there. Perhaps I do polarize the difference between traditional dogmatic Christianity and the voluntary or spontaneous faith with which I try to replace it. But I have to do that for strategic reasons. If you describe too fully all the fine shades of opinion on the spectrum, you won't succeed in making the contrast between the two ends sharp enough.

On the quotation from Spinoza at the end, I think I was there raising the question of disinterestedness. I could perhaps introduce that like this: I think the demythologizing of the ancient religions and everything else that people have traditionally lived by, which has occurred in this century, has reduced us to the sort of spiritual condition that Samuel Beckett has described in his plays. We are utterly at a loss, and I say it is in that condition of loss, when you reach this point, there is no alternative but for faith to become creative, for religious values and meanings which are no longer to be found in the way the world runs have now to come *from within* yourself. You have got to create them. And so I laid very strong emphasis in the first book on learning disinterestedness, and in the second book on learning to make faith, to make love, to create religious value, because it is no longer laid on for us by the way the world is built in the way that it was when, say, this church building was erected.

People up to Darwin's time still thought that they lived in a universe which had a moral order built into it, which was itself almost a kind of cathedral. The cathedral was the image of the cosmos: the cosmos of a cathedral. When people lost all that, and they were aware that they had lost it by the end of the nineteenth century, there was a mood of nihilism and deep pessimism. Now what I am trying to do in my new book is take the reader through that experience, to the new kind of faith on the far side of it; and I link it with the way in which Jesus prophesied the end of traditional social order and religion of Israel and led his followers through his death to the birth of the Christian faith. So the idea of the end of the world links for me, it is the basic analogy by which the preaching of Jesus is related to, and bears upon, our own spiritual condition.

But now I would like to come back to you, John, because I think there is a difference here. I think at heart you are a liberal and I'm a radical. I would like to come back and ask you what you made of that theme in the book. You see, I have always been fascinated by the image of Jesus as a preacher of the end of all things, the image Albert Schweitzer made prominent at the beginning of this century, and I have been struggling for years to come to a satisfactory interpretation of that side of his message. That was one of the main things that I was trying to do in this book: to show the relevance for our time of Jesus' message, about the changeover from an external law, a heteronomous kind of religion, to the kingdom-faith in which God is poured out into the hearts of each believer, and in which the tablets of stone are exchanged for a law written in one's own heart. I wonder what you made of it, John, or whether that is simply not a way of doing theology that's congenial to you?

JOHN ROBINSON No, no. I find all sorts of very significant insights in the kind of thing you were saying, but I would like in fact to lead on to one or two other remarks about your whole picture of Jesus and the presuppositions you bring to it. But, just before we get on to that, you didn't actually take up either of my quotations of St Augustine or St John and I cannot actually see that the truth of those convictions, that there is a disturbing sort of claim upon our lives, is affected in the slightest by anything that (say) modern cosmology tells us about the universe. Obviously the setting in which we have to respond is quite different. Also the threat to meaning and the kind of world through which we are all living makes for the most enormously different questions; but I simply do not feel that they put us at the point of saying we have got to whistle to keep up our courage in the dark, we have got to throw our own meaning into the universe, because nothing, as it were, is coming at us.

DON CUPITT What you said there sounded to me like poetry. You were using language like 'interpreting reality at its deepest level': you were using language in a poetic and expressive way. Well, my way of thinking accounts for that. I say that indeed religious language is poetic and expressive, but would you say that your way of doing theology is subject to tests of truth? Or is it a sort of fixing religious labels to moral virtues?

JOHN ROBINSON No, I think it is trying to be articulate about things that I find will not let me go, and there are all sorts of things in the Christian religion that I would much rather run away from and escape from, yet there are things that constantly, as it were, claim me and make me wrestle, and one has always to be trying to refine one's language; and I think theology is constantly going through this process. But I don't think we are left in a totally bleak and barren world.

I actually want to go on to two other areas. May we turn to the question you raised about Jesus because this, for me, was all part of a more general thing that seemed to me to be present in the book, where you always write as if the word 'critical' is the opposite of the word 'conservative'. Now it seems to me that one can be critical and still come to conservative conclusions. Being critical means being absolutely open to follow the argument wherever it leads, and the conclusions will be determined by the evidence. You always seem to me to use the word 'critical' interchangeably with the word 'sceptical'. But one can also, I think, be uncritically sceptical, and I would say that by now you have embraced a quite excessive and uncritical scepticism, for example, about the historical Jesus, which I believe needs challenging. For instance, you say with uncharacteristic dogmatism that Jesus could not have said: 'This is my body, this is my blood', because the words presuppose that Jesus' death has already occurred. Well, I would say that this is not sufficiently critical scholarship, and as a New Testament man I want to come back on all sorts of points. I think you say some very true things, but by the end your picture of the historical Jesus seems to be so reduced to a figure of irony, an eschatological prophet who puts all sorts of questions to us – very real ones – but I would want to say a great deal more and I think that I'm being just as critical as you are.

DON CUPITT Well, I've been criticized by other people who have read this book in the proof stage for not going far enough, but I still do attempt to tie Christianity back to Jesus! So you're always attacked on both sides here: on the more radical side, people will say that what we know of Jesus is so very little, and it can never be more than probable, so how can it be right to suppose that Christianity can in perpetuity be tied to the historical Jesus? Well, the way I have tried to do it is to show how, in his ways of teaching, he introduces the idea of two value scales which imply two different worlds, the old and the new; the world in which ordinary worldly people live their lives, and the new, absolute perspective upon human affairs that he calls the kingdom of God. And I've tried to show in the tradition of Jesus' teaching this rather annihilating new perspective upon human life that is being introduced. But over the last five or six years I have become gradually more cautious about the historical Jesus under pressure of recent movements in biblical criticism. I was rather conservative until about six or seven years ago, but I have gradually been brought up-to-date by friends.

JOHN ROBINSON Well, you read the wrong people!

DON CUPITT Well, yes, but you see the trouble is that I am impressed by the point that Professor Dennis Nineham makes about the enormous difference between the world in which Jesus lived and our own – not only the prominence of the supernatural but also the fact, for example, that his titles just have no parallel in our culture. The general world-view within which his teaching is set is profoundly different from ours. So it is not easy to find any creative and religiously productive analogy between him in his setting and us in ours. The one that impresses me most profoundly is the idea of an old world and a new, the passing away of an old world and the coming of a new, the idea of a kind of clash of value-scales; and that was what I sought to bring out in talking about the historical Jesus. Even if more could be said, I am not sure that more could be said that would be religiously useful and relevant today.

JOHN ROBINSON Maybe we could get to the sort of world that

you described in terms of Samuel Beckett, though I do not actually remember you quoting him in the book, where we now are. In fact you start your new book with a splendid chapter, called 'Hyperborean Faith' and for those of you who don't know who the Hyperboreans were, they were people according to Herodotus who lived beyond the North Wind and still managed to survive; and in your introduction tonight you described your book as almost apocalyptically strenuous. In fact, my first reaction was to feel that it was so far out as to be a sort of religion for South Georgia, and Maggie might like to send out some copies as comfort for the troops for the long winter evenings!

In your earlier book you described your position as a sort of Christian Buddhism and I found that strangely attractive, even if not finally satisfying. And the book was dominated in its quotations by the men of enlightenment, especially Kant and Kierkegaard. Well, Kierkegaard is still there, but the rationalists have now been quite overtaken by Nietzsche, and this you seem to be saying is where it all leads: if not to Christian nihilism at any rate to a faith that can only live the other side of nihilism. And the air is very rarefied here, living on a diet of what you call the four guiding principles of truth, disinterestedness, creativity and love, of which God is the symbolic personification and Jesus the teacher and embodiment. And you urge that the appropriate attitude now is 'to wait upon the ultimate truth of the human condition with a quiet and unflinching gaze like a traditional monk meditating upon a skull until all egoistic illusions have been burned out of him'. Well, that is magnificent, but is it religion for more than what Kierkegaard called, and in his last words came to see himself as, *the exception*? My fear is that you may have put yourself so far out that you cannot speak to the general, and that I think would be a great pity; and indeed, can you yourself stay there – and what's the next move after that?

DON CUPITT Well, if we accept, as I think we must, the new secular world-picture that has been built up by the scientific method of my critical thinking, then Christian supernatural beliefs present a problem. As I said, it is not so much that we lack evidence for their truth. It is rather that we find it very hard to say what they mean or to put them to use, to see how we can fit them in to our general picture of the world. For example, what is the use of prayers for rain in the context of modern meteorology, prayers for good harvest in the context of modern agriculture, prayers for the sick in the context of modern medicine, and so forth? It is all familiar enough. So some sort of drastic re-interpretation or even surgery is inevitable, and the question is what form shall it take? Well, I start from nothing in a way, like a character in a Samuel Beckett play, and I think I have done quite a lot constructively if I have done something in *Taking Leave of God* to save the essentials of Christian spirituality, and in *The World to Come* to save something of the Christian doctrine of redemption, the old hope for a better world, and Christian ethics. So I rather congratulate myself on how constructive I have been!

It depends what point of view you're looking at. I think you are assuming that much more can be saved than can be. The crucial point is: can religious faith become conscious of itself? Now an example of this is all those battles over myth that I discuss in the book. The increase in consciousness, when one's thinking becomes fully critical and one becomes aware of one's own theory, is very alarming and presents a great challenge to faith. The object is to wake up religious belief and make it fully conscious of itself and responsible for itself. Religious belief has to become fully voluntary and creative and it has to come to terms with the modern knowledge that myths are myths. Now *The World to Come* is tough because it is written from the point of view of a person like myself who has had to make a very tough spiritual journey. But a lot of other people, as I said earlier, are already at the sort of point that I am trying to reach. So I do not think my point of view is actually far out in relation to where the real world and real people are now. It is only as it were within the context of the politics of faith, within the church context, that my views seem far out. If we looked at it in a larger context, I hope what I am doing would be regarded as constructive.

(From this point in the dialogue there were questions from the floor which both speakers answered, but it was not possible to transcribe these.)

The Way of Biblical
Interrogation

3

Interpreting the Book of Revelation

When I first thought of unpublished material that I might write up, my inclination was to include this, if at all, in my collection of *Twelve More New Testament Studies*. For that is where by subject matter it would seem naturally to fit. But I soon realized that it belonged to a different category and level. Those *Studies* were intended to push out the frontiers in the area of New Testament scholarship, to respond to fresh questions, if not to come up with original answers.

But this represented a different exercise. It was originally prepared – in the 1950s – as an introduction to the subject for students at Cambridge, and subsequently revised and repeated for lay audiences in different parts of the world. It was addressed not to scholars, who will find little new here, but to men and women in the contemporary church who have seldom given their minds to this apparently remote and largely irrelevant appendix to their Bibles.

The Book of Revelation seems to belong to a world apart, which even New Testament scholars tend to treat in isolation. The area of apocalyptic, Jewish and Christian, of which it forms part is an area inhabited largely by specialists in a thought-world that lives by rules of its own. It is noticeable that those who write commentaries on Revelation do so on little else, and scholars who range freely in the rest of the New Testament tend to steer off the Apocalypse. A notable example of the latter was C. H. Dodd, who never uttered anything in print on the book except to say that he thought that it was a sub-Christian work. Indeed, when, late in the day, it came to deciding under his chairmanship who should do the first draft for the New English Bible, he was only too happy to unload it on to me as the most junior member of the panel! And as far as lay people are concerned, apart from certain purple passages, like the vision of the new heaven and the new earth on which it closes, they are prepared to leave its thick undergrowth and strange symbolism to the religious fanatics. It seems to have little to do with the secular world in which they have to live their lives.

I hope to show that paradoxically it is more particularly addressed to making sense of that world than any other book in the Bible. But it clearly cannot do that without some kind of a key, and this depends on trying first to enter sympathetically into the world in which and for which it was written. From the purely historical aspect I have sought to place it where I now believe it belongs, in the chapter on it in my *Redating the New Testament* (1976), and to this I must refer the reader who wishes to pursue the question in closer detail. I would set its writing in the period of chaos in the Roman empire that succeeded upon the suicide of Nero in AD 68, and I am increasingly convinced that this makes sense of the situation to and for which the writer is speaking. But I must warn the reader that most scholars do not agree with me, though this was the view shared by all shades of opinion, conservative and radical, a hundred years ago. They placed it in *c.* AD 95, at the end of the reign of the emperor Domitian. The best statement of the case for the earlier date is still, I believe, that of the great Cambridge scholar F. J. A. Hort, the contemporary of Westcott and Lightfoot, who unfortunately never succeeded in finishing more than an Introduction and Commentary on the first three chapters, which was published posthumously in 1908. By 1920, when the still standard commentary on the Greek text written by R. H. Charles was published in the International Critical Commentary series, it received no mention at all! But then Charles, who ended up as Archdeacon of Westminster, was one of the brood whose entire scholarly life was lived in the strange world of apocalyptic and his erudition constantly tended to exceed his judgment. Two other now largely forgotten books which appeared at much the same time seem to me far more balanced, the commentary by the American I. B. Beckwith and the study by A. S. Peake[1] who, so far from being isolated in his interests to this book, is best known for his one-volume commentary on the entire Bible. Finally, I would mention four other valuable aids. The first two are on the opening letters to the Seven Churches, which provide a vital and vivid geographical and historical background to the book, that by Sir William Ramsay and more popularly by William Barclay.[2] The others are two modern commentaries intended for laymen, by Ronald Preston and Anthony Hanson, and more recently by John Sweet.[3] The Torch series must have the unique distinction of having the Book of Revelation as the *first* commentary to appear in it, and as an attempt to bridge the gulf between the ancient and modern worlds confronted by an equally cataclysmic situation, still seems to me the most exciting way into its message for today.

But let us start where our author, whoever he is, takes his stand.

The Book of Revelation strikes the twentieth-century reader as the strangest and most remote in the New Testament. In fact it is in many ways the most modern. Our traditional way of reading the Bible (for instance in church) is to begin with the pre-Christian Old Testament and move from that to the Gospel. But this is not to start from where *we* are, which is in a post-Christian world in which most things appear to go on as if Christ had never been.

And this is where the Seer of Revelation starts – in the Roman empire in the second half of the first century we call AD, in which it looked as if all that Christ had meant had gone for nothing. How can one work *back* to the Gospel from that world? That is his problem.

But our problem is more complex. For if we are to see what he has to say to our world, we must first stand in his world. Unless we discipline ourselves to do this, we are likely to get what he is saying wildly out of context and hopelessly distorted. And this, of course, is what has happened to this book of the Bible above all others. It has been used as a quarry for any construction, however crazy.

C. H. Dodd once wrote a little-known book of childrens' stories entitled *There and Back Again*. He might have used this as the title of his inaugural lecture as Professor at Cambridge in which he said that the ideal interpreter of the New Testament must make two journeys. First he must go *there*, to the now strange world of the New Testament, and really enter into it and see what its writers are trying to see and to say through their eyes. But then he must come *back* again, to our world, to reinterpret what that message meant in that context to a world that thinks and feels very differently. For this he needs two very different sets of interpretative skills, which brought together made Dodd such an ideal choice as Director of the New English Bible.

In the first two sections of what follows we shall seek to make the journey 'there' and in the second two the journey 'back again'. We shall ask 1. Who is this man? 2. What is this book? 3. How should we place it today? and 4. What has it to say to us?

1. *Who is this man?*

In all the ancient tradition of the church it was ascribed to the same author as the Fourth Gospel and the Johannine Epistles, namely John the apostle, the son of Zebedee. Certainly there are more connections for the rest of the Johannine corpus than with any other part of the New Testament, both from the external attestation and to a lesser degree from the internal evidence. Indeed, until modern times the ascription to its single author has been the dominant tradition and is still the official doctrine of the Roman Catholic Church. In antiquity this was seriously challenged only by Dionysius of Alexandria, in a remarkable anticipation of modern literary criticism, and he was supported by the church historian Eusebius. And in modern times common authorship has been supported not only by first-rate conservative scholars like Lightfoot, Westcott and Hort, but, with various qualifications, by a remarkable number who would not really be classified as conservative at all. Even when one thinks the case must have been knocked out it seems very reluctant to lie down.

And after all the book does claim to be by John – four times (1.1, 4, 9; 22.8). But this very fact sets it apart: for this is precisely what neither the Gospel nor the Epistles of John do. There is a likeness and an unlikeness which meets us at every point and which makes the problem of the relation between the Apocalypse on the one hand and the Gospel and Epistle of John on the other a far from simple one.

Let us briefly run through some of these points of contact.

(a) *The external evidence* The external attestation of the Book of Revelation as the work of John the apostle is excellent, and in fact better than that for the Gospel. Justin Martyr, who lived in Ephesus, the centre of the region to which the book is addressed, and that at a time (*c.* AD 135) when the generation for which Irenaeus thought it was written had not passed, declared that it is by 'John, one of the apostles of Christ' (*Dial.* I.81), an explicit statement which neither he nor anyone else till almost half-a-century later makes of the Fourth Gospel. Irenaeus, who speaks in about AD 180 of a number of copies known to him 'all good and *ancient*' and who also came originally from that area, likewise had no doubt in ascribing the Apocalypse with the rest of the Johannine literature to 'John the disciple of the Lord', by whom he clearly meant the Apostle. The same view is shared by Tertullian, Hippolytus and Origen, who explicitly ascribes it to the son of Zebedee (*In Joh.* 1.14). But Origen's pupil, Dionysius,

Bishop of Alexandria (died in 265) could not share this view and his reasons (preserved and endorsed by Eusebius, *HE* 7.25. 7–27) are worthy of record, since they anticipated by 1500 years so much that modern criticism has restated more scientifically. They are summarized by R. H. Charles in his commentary as follows: 1. The evangelist does not prefix his name nor mention it subsequently either in the Gospel or the Epistle, whereas the writer of the Apocalypse definitely declares himself by name from the outset. That it was a John who wrote the Apocalypse he admits, but this John did not claim to be the Beloved Disciple, nor the one who leaned on his breast, nor the brother of James. 2. There is a large body of expressions of the same complexion and character in the Gospel and in I John which are wholly absent from the Apocalypse. Indeed, with some exaggeration, he claims that the latter 'does not contain a syllable in common' with the former two. 3. The Greek is quite different. The former two are written in faultless Greek and it would be difficult to discover in them any barbarism or solecism. But the dialect and language of the Apocalypse is inaccurate Greek, characterized by barbarous idioms and uncouth solecisms.

Dionysius appealed from the external evidence to the internal; and we must do the same.

(*b*) *The internal evidence* Dionysius' first point – the lack of anonymity – we have already mentioned. And an apocalypse is, if anywhere, where you would expect anonymity – or a hiding behind some fictitious name of the past, like Daniel or Enoch. In fact I think it is true to say that this is the first apocalypse, Jewish or Christian, we know which ever bore the name of its writer. And this tradition of anonymity or pseudonymity was to be continued in the church, and most of the subsequent Christian apocalypses are in the names of others, though now not of patriarchs and other Old Testament characters but of apostles. This of course raises the question whether our Apocalypse may not be pseudonymous, i.e. claiming to be written in the name and character and authority of the apostle John (as the Apocalypse of Peter seeks to perpetuate the authority and aegis of the apostle after his death). But against it stand two objections: 1. According to tradition the apostle John was still alive at the latest likely date for its composition (*c.* AD 95). And at this point impersonation becomes imposture. 2. There is no evidence at all that the seer is seeking the aegis of apostolic authority for his views. He is clearly speaking on his own authority as a Christian prophet under the direct inspiration of Jesus Christ (1.1). He never claims to be an apostle, nor like the author of II Peter, which many would think pseudonymous, does he claim to be an eye-witness (as the author or authors of John and I John clearly do). Indeed, as Charles puts it, he appears to look upon the apostles 'retrospectively and from without' (21.14; cf. 18.20). This I do not think is decisive against apostolic authorship (I personally believe Ephesians is by Paul, who makes a comparable reference to 'his holy apostles and prophets' in 3.5); but I think it is fairly decisive evidence against a man whose authority rests in a deliberate but bogus claim to be an apostle.

Secondly, there is the general situation, which contains both fascinating similarities and differences.

In the Johannine Epistles and in the letters to the seven churches we have pastoral letters probably written about the same time and to much the same area (the Roman province of Asia, or what is now the west coast of Turkey) by a man who in each case appears to exercise a wide-ranging authority born of extended knowledge of their Christian history. There is the same reference as in the Johannine Epistles back to what was true of their faith 'at first' (2.4f.). The situation to which the author of the Apocalypse writes is indeed very different. It is now one of persecution, already sharp but likely to get both more severe and more general (e.g. 2.10, 13; 3.10); but it could perfectly well be said that it is the circumstances that have changed, not the author. Again, the heresies attacked have similar more antinomian (2.14) and gnosticizing (2.24) tendencies. But, despite the similarities, the dangers assailed are only superficially the same. There is no hint of the docetic christology which lay at the heart of the errors combatted in the Johannine Epistles. Moreover, what is put in their place is different: if the heart of what the John of the Epistles has to offer is the conviction that God is love and that Jesus Christ has really come in the flesh, in the Apocalypse there is no emphasis upon the love of God (the noun is never used of God and the verb only twice of Christ) and the stress is entirely upon the risen not the incarnate Jesus.

Thirdly, this brings us to the doctrinal differences and parallels.

In christology the Gospel of John and the Apocalypse are the only New Testament books which describe Christ as both the Word of God and as the Lamb of God (though for the latter cf. I Peter 1.19). In Rev. 7.17 the Lamb is also 'to be their shepherd', a designation especially characteristic of John 10. He is also to be the substitute for the Temple (see 21.22), teaching to be found also in John 2.19–22 and 4.21 and nowhere else (but cf. Matt. 'a greater than the temple is here'). In John 19.37 and Rev. 1.7 both refer to looking on the pierced body of Christ (not elsewhere referred to), and agree in quoting Zech. 12.10 in a form different from the Septuagint, though it is a literal translation of the Hebrew, from which both could have taken it independently. But while there are significant parallels it is to be noted 1. that while the Gospel uses the title Logos absolutely in a quasi-metaphysical sense, the Apocalypse uses it only in the Old Testament phrase 'the Word of God' and that as a conquering Messianic title. 2. Conversely, in the Apocalypse 'the Lamb' is used absolutely, in the Gospel it is, on both occasions, 'the Lamb of God' (1.29, 36) – and more significantly in the Gospel it is *amnos*, in the Apocalypse always *arnion*. 3. Jesus is not in fact called 'the Shepherd' in Revelation (contrast Hebrews and I Peter where he is): only the *verb* 'to shepherd' is used, which is *not* applied to Jesus in the Gospel. Here as always the parallels are never exact enough to demand identity of authorship, and against them must be set much greater doctrinal differences.

The Christ of the Apocalypse, the mighty one, who rules the nations with a rod of iron, is not very obviously the Good Shepherd who lays down his life for the sheep. Nor is the Father who so loved the world that he gave his only Son immediately identifiable as the almighty Creator of the Apocalypse, enthroned apart in majesty, judging the nations in his wrath. True, 'the wrath of God' is there in the Gospel (John 3.36) and judgment is committed to the Son of man (5.22, 27), but the whole feel is different. The Apocalypse is dominated by a thirst for vengeance, or at any rate for righteous retribution, quite foreign to the Gospel. *Thymos* or fury of God so characteristic of the Apocalypse (seven times) is inconceivable in the Gospel or Epistles of John. In the same way, signs of apocalyptic eschatology are present in the Gospel ('The hour is coming when all who are in the tombs will hear the voice of the Son of man to come forth, those who have done good, to the resurrection of life, and those who have done evil to the resurrection of judgment', 5.28f.) and even more in the Epistles (e.g., *parousia* and Anti-christ, though neither phrase is in the Apocalypse). But it is almost incredible that the writer least influenced by apocalyptic in the whole New Testament should so quickly have become so whole-heartedly steeped in it. It is the fact that he enters into it so unreservedly and full-bloodedly which is the real difficulty; there is no suggestion of any need for demythologizing such as one finds in I John, the Antichrist identified with false teachers.

Other features which lie on the borderline between doctrine and diction are:

1. The use of the Old Testament. In the Fourth Gospel this occurs in clear citations and in the Epistles not at all. Except when he is quoting, John is using his own language. In the Apocalypse we have exactly the reverse situation. There are *no* Old Testament quotations, but equally hardly a verse which does not contain echoes or snatches of Old Testament phraseology. The use is utterly different, though it is only fair to say that the use in Revelation is typical of the allusive style of apocalypses, which tend to be a pastiche of Old Testament phrases. Paul falls into this usage in I Thess. 1, 8–10, as do the Gospel apocalypses, especially in Mark 13.25f. and parallels.

2. The use of number symbolism. This is patent in the Apocalypse where every number is symbolic (which is again typical of apocalypses). In John, apart from the twelve baskets at the feeding of the five thousand, common to all the Evangelists, there is, as far as I can see, no number symbolism (not even, to my conviction, in the 153 fishes). Though the Gospel of John is frequently said to be constructed in sevens (signs, I am's, witnesses, etc.) this is far from certain – a good deal of stretching and juggling is necessary – and significantly, of all the numbers between one and eight, seven is the only one that never occurs (the adjective occurs once in the phrase 'at the seventh hour the fever left him', but I defy even the most ingenious symbolist to extort any convincing symbolism from that). In Revelation, of course, the number seven occurs countless times.

3. Diction. Again we have the same situation – intriguing similarities, but just as great difficulties. Apart from the doctrinal expressions already mentioned like the Logos and the Lamb, there is a common use of such imagery as the water of life (and indeed of the word 'life' in general), springs of water, God dwelling or tabernacling among men (cf. Rev. 7.15, 'he who sits on the throne will dwell with them', and John 1.14, 'the Word became flesh; he came to dwell among us', though both of these go back to the Old Testament and to the Jewish notion of the *shekinah*, with which the consonants of the Greek *eskēnōsen* coincide). There is the same contrast between truth and falsehood (*alēthinos* is common to both, though in a subtly

different sense – in the Apocalypse veridical as opposed to real: *alētheia* (truth) and *alēthēs* (true) are not in the Apocalypse at all), similarly concerned with *martyria* (witness), the same use of *nikan* for victory over the world, and such phrases in common as '*tērein*', commandments, 'keeping the word', 'hearing my voice', etc. But over against these must be set (*a*) the fact that the Apocalypse uses different Greek words for the same things: *arnion* (the Apocalypse) – *amnos* (the Gospel) or lamb, *Ierousalem* (the Apocalypse) – *Ierosolyma* (the Gospel for Jerusalem), *ho Kaloumenos* (the apocalypse) – *ho Legomenos* (the Gospel) for the one who is called; (*b*) the fact that the really characteristic and distinctive vocabulary in each case is quite different. Thus Beckwith in his commentary lists what he calls twenty-four favourite words of the Apocalyptist which by their distribution betray his hand throughout the book (both Revelation and John have a distinctive and uniform diction throughout). Of these twenty-four only two (*anabainō*, go up, and *hydōr*, water) could be called characteristically Johannine, and *anabainō* has nothing of the pregnant doctrinal sense in the Apocalypse which it has in the Gospel. Conversely, of the lists given by Law[4] of typical Johannine words echoed in the Epistles, few could be said to be characteristic of the theology of the Apocalypse (e.g. the dualism between light and darkness: *phōs*, light, only occurs three times and that literally, in the Apocalypse *skotia*, darkness, never).

4. Grammar. This is probably the most decisive point of all, and is regarded by Charles as sufficient in itself to refute identity of authorship. Yet there is also the usual common ground. Charles describes the author of the Apocalypse as 'a Palestinian Jew who immigrated to Asia Minor when probably advanced in years'. Like the Evangelist, his first language was Aramaic or Hebrew and not Greek, though unlike the Evangelist he regularly used the Hebrew Bible in preference to the Septuagint. But there the similarities end. For as Dionysius saw very clearly – and Greek was his own language – while the author of the Gospel and Epistles wrote perfectly *good* Greek, the Apocalyptist wrote barbaric Greek. It is the difference between the refugee who comes across in youth and old age. The Apocalyptist never mastered Greek. As Charles says, in devoting over fifty pages of his Commentary to 'A Short Grammar of the Apocalypse', the indebtedness of which to F. S. Marsh is insufficiently acknowledged, 'his Greek . . . is unlike Greek that was ever penned by mortal man. No Greek document exhibits such a vast

multitude of solecisms and unparallelled idiosyncrasies. Most writers on John the Apocalypticist have been struck with the unbridled licence of his Greek constructions. But in reality there is no such licence. The Greek, though with parallel elsewhere, proceeds according to certain rules of the author's own devising.' Indeed, his instrument, crude as it is, is extraordinarily effective. What he wants to say is almost always clear; but he just uses a pidgin Greek of his own, which is certainly not that of the Gospels or Epistles of John. Incidentally, too, his vocabulary is a good deal wider and more colourful, whereas that of the Evangelist is far flatter and more limited.

The only ways of harmonizing the two are to say: 1. the Greek of the Revelation was John's own style – the correct but limited Greek of the rest of the Johannine literature is that of an amanuensis. This might account for the grammar, but hardly for the whole style and cast of mind which make Revelation, like the Gospel of John, quite unmistakable to listen to. 2. The language of Revelation is that of a trance (but there is no evidence that he actually *wrote* in a trance or even that psychedelic drugs have this effect) or in a style deliberately put on for this kind of writing (there is no answer to this: criticism stands silent). 3. The two writings reflect different stages in his mastery of the language (so Westcott, Hort, etc.). But this would force us to put the Apocalypse much earlier – and there are no other grounds for this. Moreover, the grammar of the Apocalypse does not sound like the Greek of a man who is trying to write Greek, making mistakes, but not beyond considerable improvement. It is much more the language of a man who has settled down to his own level and style of speaking, finds it adequate, and could not care less if other people do not speak it as he does. No schoolmaster writing a report on his prose would discern much hope for improvement!

We are bound, I think, to conclude that the Revelation is not by the same hand as the Gospel and Epistles of John, nor by the same mind, even if he had got someone else to write it for him. Nevertheless, it clearly has contacts with the Johannine circle – though so it has also with the Synoptic tradition, especially in the apocalyptic portions of the latter – though Charles' conclusion that the author knew and used a number of our New Testament books as they stand is as precarious as most of his other judgments. It is impossible not to believe that the Seer moved in much more apocalyptic circles in Palestine than the Evangelist or his disciples ever did. If he did cross to Asia Minor relatively late in life, he must already have soaked himself in the apocalyptic parts of the Hebrew Old Testament and Pseudepigrapha, let alone in the Christian apocalyptic tradition. The evidence is perfectly compatible with his only having come into contact with the distinctively Johannine tradition after his arrival in Asia Minor. The contacts are of language and terminology rather than of deep-set presuppositions, and many of the similarities appear to derive from the situation addressed (including in that the terminology his readers were already used to) rather than any basic similarity in the mind addressing him. We must even be cautious about equating the pastoral situation too closely. The churches the Seer is addressing were in the area of the Lycus valley which Paul had evangelized. The Johannine Epistles presuppose no Pauline influence, nor indeed do they really allow for any previous Christian history but that which the recipients had experienced under the writer himself.

Moreover, it is not clear that the two documents (the Apocalypse and the Epistles) are written with the same pastoral authority. One of the arguments for identity of authorship is the difficulty of supposing there were two persons apparently in much the same area both of whom seem to sound uncommonly like primitive archbishops. But on closer inspection the type of authority with which they speak is subtly different. The John of the Apocalypse speaks, as indeed he claims, with the voice of direct inspiration. He is a prophet, or, if we like, *the* prophet, of the churches of Asia in the latter part of the first century. Though the two types of authority appear similar, his sanction is in fact different from that of the Elder disclosed to us in III John. The latter pronounces with the authority of his own person: 'If I come, I will bring up the things he is doing' (III John 10) – and that will be that! The Seer never suggests that he in his own person has any such authority. He always speaks simply of the mouthpiece of the Spirit or the living Christ: 'If you do not repent, I (Christ) shall come and remove your lamp from its place' (2.5; cf. 2.16, 22; 3.3, 11, 20). That is the prophet speaking, not the bishop. There is in fact no real evidence that the writer of Revelation exercised any administrative or apostolic oversight over the churches to which he writes or that he had personally known them from the beginning: he only represents Christ as having done so 'though obviously the Seer speaks out of a real personal knowledge of each church's situation and has introduced a considerable amount of local colour. But he does not claim to have been their apostle, nor to have begotten them in the faith. Nor does he show any signs of an apostle, above all the testimony of an eye-witness, such as is claimed in the Gospel and first Epistle. That he came to be identified with John the Apostle is natural from his name, his situation, and the authority of Christ with which he claims to speak; and indeed the traditions about the two (especially in Clement of Alexandria) are so mixed up that it is difficult to be sure which of the two – if there were two – it is to which reference is being made. But this identification is natural, I submit, only if there *was* an apostle of that name in that area at that time with whom he could be confused. To that extent the external evidence for the Apocalypse, even if unconvincing for the Apocalypse, supports the tradition that John the Apostle was *the* figure in those parts at that time.

2. *What is this book?*

We have focussed so far on the author of this strange book. I want now to look at its purpose in the context of the situation for which he was writing, and then in the last two sections to try to bring it out of the first century into the twentieth, to show in modern terms what it is seeking to say and how it is relevant to our situation. Obviously this is the book above all in the New Testament that stands in need of interpretation, of re-translation not merely out of its exotic Greek but even more out of its strange thought-forms. But equally clearly the history of its interpretation shows how disastrous it is simply to reinterpret it of each new situation in the world or the church without first asking to what and to whom it was originally meant to apply. Like all prophecy it had a historical context, and what it means can only be ascertained by reference to that context. It may have an enduring meaning, in so far as it says things to that context which are true of all contexts, but we shall never with any objectivity be able to know what it is really saying to us in our situation till we take the trouble to find out what it first said to its own.

What then was the original aim and destination of the book? There is no sentence beginning, as in the Fourth Gospel or the First Epistle of John: 'These things are written' or 'I write this, that . . .'. But there are other statements which go some way to clarify the purpose. In 1.1 we read 'This is the revelation given by God to Jesus Christ. It was given to him so that he might show his servants what must shortly happen. He made it known by sending his angel to his servant John', and subsequently in 1.11 John is told, 'Write down what you see on a scroll and send it to the seven churches: to Ephesus, Smyrna, Pergamum, Thyatira, Sardis, Philadelphia, and Laodicea', and the book is frequently described as a book of 'prophecy' (1.3; 2.7, 9, 18).

We must first clear our minds of the idea that prophecy simply means prediction, clairvoyance. Of course, it includes this; but a large part of the trouble is that the Book of Revelation (popularly known as 'Revelations'!) has been treated as if its primary object were to be a sort of celestial Old Moore's Almanac. But apocalypse simply means unveiling – and certainly not only of the future – and prophecy means, for the Bible, speaking under the inspiration of God, whether about God or the present or the future. And in fact the content of the Book of Revelation is defined precisely in these three ways: 'Write down what you have seen, what is now, and what will be hereafter' (1.19). The probable reference of these words is 1. to the vision of the living Christ in chapter 1, 2. to the present situation of the seven churches in chapters 2 and 3, and 3. to the future design of God. That is to say, in the light of his vision of Christ the Seer is enabled to do two things; first, to speak with prophetic insight into the present needs of the church on earth, and, secondly, to penetrate 'behind or beyond the headlines' to that level of reality where history is shaped and the things that must be have their origin in the things that are.

It is relevant to notice at this point that this two-fold division between the earthly and the heavenly correspond to the two-fold division of the book of Daniel, the canonical model of all apocalyptic writings. The first part of Daniel is not indeed letters but stories, stories of the past dealings of God with his people in time of persecution to encourage them under the terrors of Antiochus Epiphanes in the second century BC; the second half (chapters 7 to the end) takes the reader behind the headlines to give him a vision, as it were, from the heavenlies, from the end, of where earthly history, with its apparently meaningless succession of world empires, each worse than the first, is really going and what must be its outcome. The first part of the prophet's function is *speaking to* the situation, insisting that despite appearances God is *in* it for power and for judgment; and the second part is *interpreting* the situation, disclosing that, despite appearances, God is *behind* it, seeing it through to his invincible ends.

In Revelation there is this same pattern but a different proportion. The interpretation occupies chapters 4 to 22, the direct address to the empirical situation only chapters 2 and 3. But a tremendous amount is packed into the two chapters. They are the tersest letters in the New Testament. Each one is highly stylized, highly allusive, and sharply pointed. The author is clearly not concerned to waste words, and though his allusions are often lost on us, it is clear that he knows exactly where the cap fits. It seems highly improbable that these letters ever stood alone or that they were actually sent as genuine letters. They are too condensed for that. Their introductions are built out of the vision of the living Christ described in chapter 1, and they frequently end with phrases, such as the tree of life, the second death, the new Jerusalem, whose symbolism is intelligible only in terms of the subsequent apocalypse. The letters are clearly to be pored over in the light of the book as a whole and in the light of each other. Sir William Ramsay showed, and more recently William Barclay popularized in his *Letters to the Seven Churches*, that they gain much point when read in the light of the local conditions as we know them, and doubtless far more in the light of what *they* knew.

Of the situation addressed in general it is to be observed that the actual state of affairs is not in fact nearly as catastrophic as it is defined in the visions that follow, nor was the immediate historical outcome anything like as fierce or as widespread as the writer feared. As a matter of fact, in the letters it is only in 3.10 that he speaks of 'the ordeal' as falling 'upon the whole world'. In 2.10 he envisages a sharp persecution which will involve a ten days' imprisonment. Despite the suggestion in the apocalypse that follows that pretty well every faithful Christian will be martyred, the only actual martyrdom referred to is that of 'Antipas, my faithful one' in 2.13 at Pergamum. Since this city is styled the place where Satan's throne is and is known later to have been a centre of emperor worship, it may be that the imperial cult was the occasion of conflict. But it must be admitted that there is very little in the seven letters to suggest that this was the great enemy it is portrayed as being in the visions of the Beast and the Scarlet Woman that follows. The immediate dangers to the churches seem to come not from the imperial power but from Jewish opposition (2.9 and 3.9) and from the general dissolute life of a Levantine city, rationalized into the systems of teaching which doubtless said that for a truly spiritual man these things did not matter. Whoever the Nicolaitans were (2.6, 15) and the woman

Jezebel 'who claims to be a prophetess' and 'by her teaching lures my servants into fornication and into eating food sacrificed to idols' (2.20), it looks as if they were apostate Jews or Christians caught up in gnosticizing mystery cults ('the deep secrets of Satan': 2.24), rather than agents of the imperial power.

But when the Seer turns, as it were, to trace the pattern underlying these sporadic outbursts and this whole mixed-up situation, in which there are no clear blacks and whites and in which the real danger is in being neither hot nor cold (3.15f.), he goes behind everything to the might of the imperial power, which he sees bestriding the world like a colossus. Though the demonic character might not yet be fully apparent, he sees that this is the real incarnation of evil with which the church must fight her final war.

Let us then take, as a specimen of how Revelation must be interpreted against its historical background, the passages in which he depicts this evil power and its outworking in history, chapters 13 and 17. They are typical of his whole cast of mind and will introduce us to much of his peculiar symbolism and to the principles of its interpretation.

First, chapter 13:

1 Then out of the sea I saw a beast rising. It had ten horns and seven heads. On its horns were ten diadems, and on each head a
2 blasphemous name. The beast I saw was like a leopard, but its feet were like a bear's and its mouth like a lion's mouth. The dragon conferred upon it his power and rule, and great
3 authority. One of its heads appeared to have received a death-blow; but the mortal wound was healed. The whole world went
4 after the beast in wondering admiration. Men worshipped the dragon because he had conferred his authority upon the beast; they worshipped the beast also, and chanted, 'Who is like the Beast? Who can fight against it?'
5 The beast was allowed to mouth bombast and blasphemy,
6 and was given the right to reign for forty-two months. It opened its mouth in blasphemy against God, reviling his name and his
7 heavenly dwelling. It was also allowed to wage war on God's people and to defeat them, and was granted authority over every
8 tribe and people, language and nation. All on earth will worship it, except those whose names the Lamb that was slain keeps in his roll of the living, written there since the world was made.

9, 10　　Hear, you who have ears to hear! Whoever is meant for prison, to prison he goes. Whoever takes the sword to kill, by the sword he is bound to be killed. Here the fortitude and faithfulness of God's people have their place.

11　　Then I saw another beast, which came up out of the earth; it had
12　two horns like a lamb's, but spoke like a dragon. It wielded all the authority of the first beast in its presence, and made the earth and its inhabitants worship this first beast, whose mortal wound had
13　been healed. It worked great miracles, even making fire come
14　down from heaven to earth before men's eyes. By the miracles it was allowed to perform in the presence of the beast it deluded the inhabitants of the earth, and made them erect an image in honour
15　of the beast that had been wounded by the sword and yet lived. It was allowed to give breath to the image of the beast, so that it could speak, and could cause all who would not worship the
16　image to be put to death. Moreover, it caused everyone, great and small, rich and poor, slave and free, to be branded with a mark on
17　his right hand or forehead, and no one was allowed to buy or sell
18　unless he bore this beast's mark, either name or number. (Here is the key; and anyone who has intelligence may work out the number of the beast. The number represents a man's name, and the numerical value of its letters is six hundred and sixty-six.)

We may comment briefly on the following verses:

v. 1. The beast out of the sea. In Daniel 7.3 'four great beasts came up out of the sea'. The beast is a recognized symbol for a world power of evil; and the sea, with the myth of the leviathan, of the abode of evil powers. But there is also the fact that from Ephesus or Patmos the power of Rome is a maritime power exercised across the sea (later the great whore is 'enthroned above the ocean'). Ten horns is the characteristic of the fourth and worst beast in Daniel. Horns mean power, and ten horns, with diadems, complete sway and sovereign power. The seven heads are interpreted later as seven Roman emperors, but also with the implication that the beast now had its full complement: it was at the zenith of its imperial might. The blasphemous names on the heads refer probably to the title *divus* attached to the emperors, arrogating to themselves the prerogatives of God.

v. 2 It has the characteristics of each of the first three beasts of Daniel 7, which are identified as leopard, bear and lion, and with its ten horns the attributes also of the fourth. It embodies and recapitulates all world empires that preceded it. But any power it has is 'given' to it by the dragon, i.e. Satan. It is not autonomous.

v. 3 One of its heads appears to have received a death-blow, but the mortal wound was healed. Chapter 17 will make it clear that this refers to one of the emperors, Nero, who was already dead but was due to come back before the end, according to popular expectation.

v. 4 This refers to the despair it engenders. Who can compete with the beast? Men give up in face of totalitarian power. Resistance seems useless.

v. 5 This alludes to the bombastic claims of tyrannical power, the Reich that will last for a thousand years. In fact it is allowed to last for forty-two months, alias 1260 days, alias 'a time, times, and half a time' (derived from Dan. 7.25, etc.), i.e. three-and-a-half years, which is the stock apocalyptic period for the reign of evil. It is half the perfect number, but perhaps derived in the first instance from the actual duration of the persecution under Antiochus Epiphanes.

vv. 7f. The beast exercises a world dominion, claiming and getting the worship and adulation of all who are not true members of the church, which it persecutes relentlessly.

Incidentally, the phrase in verse 8 'before the foundation of the world' is to be connected not with 'slain' but with 'written', as in the parallel words in 17.8, 'whose names have not been written in the book of life from the foundation of the world'. Predestination from the foundation of the world is predicated of Christians in Eph. 1.4 and Matt. 25.34 and of Christ in I Peter 1.19f., but the idea that he was slain from the beginning is quite unparalleled and indeed contrary to New Testament doctrine of the decisive new event, once and for all, of the death of Christ.

v. 10 Captivity and death are inevitable. Only endurance, not escape, can avail.

vv. 11ff. Here we have another beast completely dependent on the first beast and exercising its power only by delegation. Its object is to make men worship the first beast. It is usually taken to refer to the local agents of the imperial power, especially those engaged in enforcing the imperial cult. It comes out of the earth, locally, not from across the sea – and it does not look too bad. In fact it looks like a lamb (a caricature of the church), and it has only a two-horn power, but its words have the deceptive lure of the very serpent itself. Its power is derived from its capacity to deceive men (14) to confuse the moral issue, which was so characteristic of the Nazis. It calls down fire from heaven, leading men to think that its sacrifices have the approval of God (13) – in the way that the 'German Christians' had the blessing of Hitler. And the representation of the beast which it provides is so life-like that men worship it as a living power (15). But it exercises complete stranglehold over the social, political and economic order (16f.): without the mark of the beast you can do nothing; it is the brand that signifies complete ownership and slavery. The parallel with what the Nazis enforced upon the Jews is so close that one can hardly credit that they did not see it. And much the same conditions for engaging in business or getting a university education obtain in Eastern Europe today.

v. 18 Then comes the clue for identifying the whole evil set-up. We are told that it is the name of a man – that is to say the Beast and one of its heads (i.e. the empire and one of its emperors) can be regarded for practical purposes as identical. There is one head which is so representative that it can stand for the whole. The clue is the number 666. On purely *a priori* grounds, the existence of the legend of Nero *redivivus*, there is a strong possibility that the number represents the sum of the numerical value of the letters of his name (Hebrew and Greek did not have figures, which we derive from the Arabs, but use the letters of the alphabet instead (a´ = 1 etc.). *Gematria*, as it was called, provided a great game, matching the letters of a person's name with the number it represented. In this case it does not work in Greek, but it does in Hebrew, which shows that this is the language in which the Seer really thought and worked. Neron Caesar = 666. This also had the advantage that if one took the Latin form of the name Nero Caesar and translated it into Hebrew characters it yields 616, which is a variant reading. This is confirmed by Suetonius, the Roman historian, who tells us that such a cryptogram on Nero's name was actually current in his life-time. In Greek the letters add up to 1005, and this fits the jingle he quotes:

> Count the numerical values
> Of the letters in Nero's name,
> And in 'murdered his own mother':
> You will find their sum is the same.
>
> (Suetonius, *Nero* 39)

It looks as if Rev. 13.18 is the Christian version of a familiar game. This I believe is certainly the most probable of an enormous number of ingenious guesses, and should be sufficient to put out of court all subsequent identifications (the Pope, Luther, etc.).

Then we have chapter 17,

1 Then one of the seven angels that held the seven bowls came and spoke to me and said, 'Come, and I will show you the judgment
2 on the great whore, enthroned above the ocean. The kings of the earth have committed fornication with her, and on the wine of her fornication men all over the world have made themselves
3 drunk.' In the Spirit he carried me away into the wilds, and there I saw a woman mounted on a scarlet beast which was covered with blasphemous names and had seven heads and ten horns.
4 The woman was clothed in purple and scarlet and bedizened with gold and jewels and pearls. In her hand she held a gold cup, full of obscenities and the foulness of her fornication; and
5 written on her forehead was a name with a secret meaning: 'Babylon the great, the mother of whores and of every obscenity
6 on earth.' The woman, I saw, was drunk with the blood of God's people and with the blood of those who had borne their testimony to Jesus.
7 As I looked at her I was greatly astonished. But the angel said to me, 'Why are you so astonished? I will tell you the secret of the woman and of the beast she rides, with the seven heads and the
8 ten horns. The beast you have seen is he who once was alive, and is alive no longer, but has yet to ascend out of the abyss before going to perdition. Those on earth whose names have not been inscribed in the roll of the living ever since the world was made will all be astonished to see the beast; for he once was alive, and is alive no longer, and has still to appear.
9 'But here is the clue for those who can interpret it. The seven
10 heads are seven hills on which the woman sits. They represent also seven kings, of whom five have already fallen, one is now reigning, and the other has yet to come; and when he does come
11 he is only to last for a little while. As for the beast that once was alive and is alive no longer, he is an eighth – and yet he is one of
12 the seven, and he is going to perdition. The ten horns you saw are ten kings who have not yet begun to reign, but who for one hour are to share with the beast the exercise of royal authority; for
13 they have but a single purpose among them and will confer their
14 power and authority upon the beast. They will wage war upon

the Lamb, but the Lamb will defeat them, for he is Lord of lords and King of kings, and his victory will be shared by his followers, called and chosen and faithful.'

15   Then he said to me, 'The ocean you saw, where the great whore sat, is an ocean of peoples and populations, nations and
16   languages. As for the ten horns you saw, they together with the beast will come to hate the whore; they will strip her naked and leave her desolate, they will batten on her flesh and burn her to
17   ashes. For God has put it into their heads to carry out his purpose, by making common cause and conferring their sovereignty upon the beast until all that God has spoken is
18   fulfilled. The woman you saw is the great city that holds sway over the kings of the earth.'

Here we have the vision of the woman on the beast, who with its seven heads and ten horns is the same beast as in chapter 13. Arrayed in the royal purple and scarlet, the woman represents the personifica-tion of the imperial power (cf. Britannia), and her name is identified as Babylon (as in I Peter 5.13) = the great city which has kingdom over the kings of the earth (v. 18) = Rome. Harlotry is the stock Old Testament figure for idolatry and godlessness.

vv. 8ff. Clearly again Nero *redivivus* is equated with the beast as such. He is one of the seven Roman emperors (10f.) yet is to return as an eighth before going to perdition.

This passage I believe gives the clue to the debate and setting of the book. I must not get diverted into what is essentially a historical argument which does not make all that difference to the interpreta-tion, and I have provided the evidence in my *Redating the New Testament* chapter VIII. Traditionally (from Irenaeus onwards) the book has been regarded as coming from the end of the reign of the Emperor Domitian, who died in AD 96. But I have come increasingly to question this. Verse 10 says specifically that the sixth emperor is now reigning. The first five were Augustus, Tiberias, Caligula, Claudius and Nero. The sixth, Galba, only lasted seven months from June 68 to January 69, and I believe this fits the date of the book well. The temple in Jerusalem, which was destroyed in 70, is apparently still standing in 11.1–13, though the city is under siege, and if it had already been razed to the ground it is incredible that the worst judgment visualized for it should be a violent earthquake (rather than enemy action) in which one-tenth of the city fell. The persecution of Christians under Nero in 65, who were fastened on as scapegoats for the fire of Rome in July 64 after he could not scotch the rumours that he himself had started it for his own advantage, was, from the lurid account in Tacitus (*Ann.* 15.44.2–8), quite sufficient to have triggered off the fear that this might be the end in a total blood-bath or what the Nazis called a 'final solution'. Persecution under Domitian, as Tertullian says, was very small beer in comparison, and does not seem to have been directed against the church as such but against noblemen of influence whom the emperor feared. The main argument (apart from the external tradition) for a late date is that the imperial cult had not by then assumed such proportions. But already in the city of Rome according to Sulpicius Severus (*Chronica* 2. 29.3), an edict was publicly published under Nero that 'no one must profess Christianity', after which Paul was beheaded and Peter crucified. I believe that the vision of the Apocalypse is not describing the situation in Asia Minor then, or indeed at any other time, but projecting (like Daniel in his day) the pogrom in Rome on to the clouds of heaven and the end of time. The apparent dissolution of all stable authority after the suicide of Nero, when in fact there were three emperors in one year, may well have encouraged the hope that the end of Babylon could not be long delayed. There is, the writer fully believes, only one more king to go and he will have a very short span, before the final fight with Antichrist represented by Nero *redivivus*.

vv. 12ff. The ten horns who are ten kings who have not yet received royal power are probably not ten later Roman emperors, but represent the totality of the powers of the earth who at the end will merge their authority in that of the beast to form a single world state. Evil comes to a head in the final battle with the Lamb and his forces – and this is actually part of the providence of God, the workings of his purpose. For ultimately the whore will perish by the internecine forces of self-destruction (the ten horns and the beast who come to hate the whore): Rome will be destroyed at the hands of Nero and his hordes, expected to return from the East with such a host to avenge himself on the imperial city. On the timing and manner of the fall of Rome the Seer was clearly wrong, but no one can deny that spiritually, and even politically, he was very near the mark.

But this raises the question, after we have tried to see his intention against his own time, of how the book is legitimately to be interpreted today.

3. How should we place it today?

I want to devote these last two sections to the question that really interests and perplexes us about the Apocalypse. This is not, unless we are born with an insatiable and perverse curiosity, what is the clue to the historical allusions, what is the key to the number of the beast, but what relevance it has to present-day Christianity and to the world in which we live. We can easily see enough the kind of relevance it does not have, the relevance seen in it by what Isaiah called 'the astrologers, the star-gazers and the monthly prognosticators' (they are now weekly). The sects, the Seventh Day Adventists, Jehovah's Witnesses, the British Israelites, and the rest have no doubt that it is the key to what is now happening in the world. What relevance has it to one who takes biblical theology and historical criticism seriously? Did its relevance disappear when Nero failed to materialize with his Parthian hordes?

Let us begin by asking in modern terms what the Apocalypse set out to be and to do. It set out, as its name implies, to be an 'unveiling'. From one point of view it corresponds to what in the modern newspaper would still be called 'the revelations of our special correspondent' or might feature in a column headed 'Cassandra speaks' or 'Behind the headlines'. For what the Seer is doing is inviting his readers to go behind or rather beyond the headlines, to discern what is really happening 'beneath' the surface of current events. But that is our way of expressing it. The Hebrew mind, or indeed almost every age until our own would have said 'above' the surface of current events. But we tend to locate truth, 'profundity', in the depths rather than the heights, and so much of the biblical imagery can suddenly be made a good deal more relevant and acceptable to our time by the simple device of reading 'depths' for 'heights'. Depth psychology sounds a good deal more scientific than 'spiritual wickedness in high places'! (See Paul Tillich's sermon 'The Deep Things of God' – a title derived from this book – in *The Shaking of the Foundations*.)[5]

But let us return to the contemporary counterpart of the Apocalypse. From another point of view this is the political cartoon, with its immediately recognizable symbols and disguises (including animals like the bear for Russia or the elephant for the Republican Party of the United States), or the underground newspaper of the resistance movement. Apocalypses, it must be remembered, essentially belonged to the category of seditious (and ephemeral) literature, and this explains why they were usually anonymous and always cryptic, just as Swift had to wrap up his political pamphlet in the innocent guise of *Gulliver's Travels*. Of the draft of the New English Bible I noted with pleasure that the Book of Revelation alone had been marked on the cover 'Confidential'. That exactly gets the note of it. It was for private circulation only – in the proper quarters. And it was not for mass production: it was to be read out (1.3; 22.18) and the reader was where necessary to elucidate what it was not safe to spell out in black and white (cf. Mark 13.14: 'Let him that reads understand'). From one point of view, it is quite frankly a political pamphlet. It sets out to take those who listen to it behind the headlines of what was happening and must happen in the power-politics of the contemporary Roman empire.

To be cryptic and mysterious is part of the essence of the matter. But it is also an exposé (an *apocalypsis* or 'unveiling'). Its modern equivalent is the underground newspaper, or rather the broadsheet of the underground church. The style of this class of literature has remained remarkably the same. The technique is that of the cartoonist, the surrealist artist, the space-fiction writer, the psychedelic visionary, the transcendental meditationist and the Jungian or Freudian interpreter of dreams rolled into one. One might compare Genet's *Balcony*, which is a series of psycho-sexual fantasies of power – represented by the blown-up figures of the bishop, the judge, the general, the police-chief, all set in a brothel, the 'house of illusions' – against a backdrop of a revolutionary *coup d'état*. Another parallel is the kind of painting by which children or psychotics are encouraged to expose depths of their psyche which they cannot possibly put into words. And its symbolism is certainly no more difficult than that in any exhibition of contemporary art – or for that matter of Hieronymus Bosch or William Blake, who have perhaps got closer to its heart than anyone else.

But the difference – and the reason why the Book of Revelation is in the Bible, whereas *Gulliver's Travels* or Giles or Peanuts are not – lies in what its writer saw 'behind the headlines'. What you expect from 'the revelations' of our contemporary columnists (especially on the Lord's Day) is hardly likely to be very penetrating and you can be quite certain that their door will not be open on to heaven. But that is the depth at which the Seer sets out to interpret events. What he is interested in is not prediction for its own sake, like the crystal-gazer on the end of the pier (though because he can see the pattern he can see the inevitability of the course of events). What he is concerned with, rather, is the spiritual depth of what is taking place in the world around him. He is seeing history as it were in 3-D, uncovering a dimension in which the surface of events takes on a new significance and a new urgency.

Consider, he is saying to us, the conflicts and tensions of this world's order. Take whatever happens to be hitting the headlines at the moment, penetrate beneath the surface of the cold war or the arms-race, the terrorism or the coups, and you will see nations and races and groups of men and women under the sway of -ologies and -isms, economic bogeys and deep-seated psychological forces over which they seem to have no control. This is the level depicted by the beast with its horns, or the ghoulish locusts with their heads like horses and their hair like women – all the irrational drives in history that surge up from the pit of the collective unconscious, and, as Butterfield put it in his *Meaning of History*, 'mix everything we do in a lot of dirt'. But however much we may expose by probing into the psycho-sexual depths and taking the lid off the political scene (and the yellow press has nothing here over the Book of Revelation with its scarlet woman and her gold cup 'full of obscenities and the foulness of her fornication'), there are still, says the Seer, deeper levels to be taken into account which any purely political or psychological interpretation must fail to discern. The beast receives his power only from the dragon, and the dragon is the force of the demonic. The whole of history is seen through into heaven – is at bottom, or at top – a spiritual conflict, 'the Devil and his angels fighting against Michael and his angels', and at the heart of that conflict, and victorious in it, stands the Lamb, bearing upon it the marks of its slaughter, to whom all power has been given in earth and heaven.

But if all power has been given to him, if in Christ all things have been reconciled in heaven and earth and under the earth, why in heaven's name do things go on as they do? That is the real question, the agonizing question, to which the Seer addresses himself. Why, why, why? How long, O Lord? These are the sort of questions that always rise to the surface in the churches of the persecution, and not only now in the churches of the persecution. In the world of the H-bomb, and even in a world after the H-bomb has been let off, or in the face of ecological Armageddon, is any interpretation of the meaning of history still possible in terms of Christ and the love of the cross?

That, in terms of his day, with the inevitable prospect, as far as he could see, of universal martyrdom, of the church humanly speaking being wiped out, was the problem confronting the Seer. Many would say that in fact he has not succeeded, that for all its majesty his interpretation is frankly sub-Christian. It is an exegesis of history not in terms of suffering love, but of something less – of vindictive power, however refined by justice. And, when every allowance has been made for what he is trying to do and what he is not, one is bound to admit that in his final answer to the problem of evil he does fall short of the highest insights of the New Testament. But there is also an important sense in which one can say that the Christian gospel is assumed and assimilated more completely in this book than in any other biblical writing. It is not concerned like the Gospels with setting forth the distinctive Christian message; it is not, like the Epistles, concerned with explicating its theology or expounding the way of life which follows from it; it is not like Acts concerned with the history of the church, the carrier of this life. The intention of all these other books is to focus attention upon the decisive divine move in the chess match of history. They are out to show how the events of the life, death and resurrection of Jesus Christ constitute the winning stroke, which has precluded any other outcome, though the game has yet to work itself out to the final checkmate and the opposition has yet to resign.

The Book of Revelation, on the other hand, is not directly concerned with this winning move. It presupposes from first to last that it has taken place and that it is utterly decisive. 'The sovereignty of the world has passed to our Lord and his Christ' (11.15); 'Thou hast taken thy great power into thy hands and entered upon thy reign' (11.17). Nowhere else in the New Testament, even in the Epistle to the Hebrews, do we get quite the same impression of utter and abiding finality, as of a will and testament proved and settled long ago and now in incontrovertible operation. The Christ of the Revelation is the Lamb 'with the marks of slaughter upon it' (5.6), the pluperfect tense of the verb expressing as nothing else could the continuing efficacy of an act of God accomplished once and for all in history.

Yet this abiding reality is everywhere presupposed rather than expounded. For the concern of the Seer is not primarily with the great move which has won the game: it is with the moves which the opposition continues to make after it has taken place. What is the significance of secularism in a redeemed world? How are these moves to be understood? Are they random? If not, what of the pattern of their development, and how does it fit into the pattern of victory already disclosed in what, in every sense of the word, was God's *coup de grâce*? Is there some sort of dialectic by which they can be interpreted and even predicted; and above all how do they continue to work out, despite their contrary character, to the checkmate already made inevitable by the decisive move?

These are the questions with which this book, and, with the exception of isolated passages elsewhere, this book alone in the New Testament, is attempting to deal. It was the first essay in supplying what we should now recognize as a Christian theology of power. Such a thing had been tried before for the pre-Christian world in Jewish prophecy and apocalyptic. The Book of Daniel, for instance, was an essay in the theology of power; a rather naive one (with Nebuchadnezzar being put out to grass), but a serious attempt. The Book of Revelation was the first essay in coming to terms with the post-Christian situation, with the incredible assertion that the *telos*, the goal, of history had already taken place and that in consequence everything was henceforth different.

The instrument and medium of interpretation adopted by its author was the familiar old one of prophecy and apocalyptic. This was a peculiarly Jewish instrument. It corresponded with what the Greeks sought to do by philosophy, the orientals by mysticism and the modern world by science. It attempted to penetrate behind the moving images on the screen of history to discover the abiding principles by which the flux of phenomena could be understood, explained and justified. What was peculiar to it was the underlying conviction that the ultimate truth about the universe must find its expression in final fact. This conviction of an ultimate correspondence between truth and events, expressing itself in the peculiarly Hebraic virtue of hope, derived from the fact that at bottom their God was a God of history and not simply a God of nature. The last word about God must also be the last word about history. Consequently, while the Greek expressed his ultimate certainties in terms of timeless truths, or the modern in mathematical formulae, the Jew necessarily cast his in the form of future events. If God is God, these things must be. The interest of the prophets and apocalyptists was not in the future for its own sake: they were concerned with interpreting the present, but their convictions of what was the deepest truth about the present necessarily found expression in statements about the age to come. If you wanted the clue to the will that controlled the present, look, they said, not to timeless laws or eternal values, but to the end of history, to the state of the universe when that will would finally out. And this state they pictured, as they pictured their vision of creation and man as God originally meant them, in the language of myth, in which alone the inexpressible could be conveyed in pictures and stories and images.

So much for the Jews. But the Christian apocalyptist was confronted by the astonishing fact that in a real sense the day of the Lord, the *telos* of history, had already come. 'You have seen the end of the Lord', says the Epistle of James. Did that mean that the whole task of the apocalypticists was now superseded?

The answer given by the Book of Revelation is, No. But the entire perspective has been altered. The Christian apocalypticist is no longer simply looking 'to the end': rather, he is looking out on the world 'from the end'. He is writing after the decisive move has taken place. 'Then he who sat on the throne said, "Behold! I am making all things new!" And he said to me, "Write this down; for these words are trustworthy and true. Indeed", he said, "They are already fulfilled"' (21.5f.). They have been true since Easter morning. In Christ, as Paul said, 'there is a new world; the old order has gone and a new order has already begun' (II Cor. 5.17).

Nevertheless, the Seer is writing to a world in which none of these things seems to be true in the very least. The game continues as if nothing decisive had happened at all. It is only if a man is 'in Christ' that he can view it like this. To the person who knows the world only 'after the flesh', from a human point of view, it looks just like the same old round of battle, murder and sudden death; and in the eyes of the 'mockers', 'all things continue as they were from the beginning of the creation' (II Peter 3.4).

And here it is that the place of apocalypse, of 'unveiling', is still to be found. It is now no longer the speculative unveiling of divine counsels lying hidden in the future. It is the 'dis-covery', the laying bare to the eye of faith, of what already is the veriest truth of the present world-situation, as it has been since the resurrection of Jesus Christ. For the transfiguration of history has already begun, for those on the mount. 'Henceforth' says Jesus to the Sanhedrin – from this very moment onwards (in Matthew *ap' arti*, and in Luke *apo tou nun*) – 'you will see the Son of man seated at the right hand of the power and coming on the clouds of heaven' (Matt. 26.64). For the Synoptists, as for John, the exaltation and coming of the Son of man is a continuous process initiated by the events of the passion and resurrection. That process has indeed yet to be consummated, the end-term or outcome of it being pictured in the traditional language of the myth, as the great 'day' when all will be made light, the final 'apocalypse' or 'epiphany' of Jesus Christ: 'Behold, he is coming with the clouds. Every eye shall see him, among them those who pierced him; and all the peoples of the world shall lament in remorse' (Rev. 1.7).

But the manifestation does not simply wait till then. 'The apocalypse of history', to use Eugene Lampert's phrase, is already on. After all, there is a sense in which Jesus predicted that even the high priest and his associates would see the Son of man in glory and the kingdom coming in power. They could not escape it. Come it must; and if it came, not for them in redemption, it must come in judgment – in their supersession by the Christian church and in the destruction of the Temple and all that they stood for. And they would see it and lament, even if they did not see him as he is.

So it is that John the Seer sets out to interpret post-resurrection history. His canvas is as broad as it can be; not merely the history of the Jews, though that comes in, but the history of civilization itself, represented in the figure of the great city Babylon, standing at that time for imperial Rome. He writes 'in the Spirit, on the Lord's day' (1.10), taking his stand, that is to say, as a Christian in that 'element of the last days' as Oscar Cullmann called the Spirit on the church's anticipation of the day of the Lord, and looking out from the End. He is told to record 'What you have seen, what is now and what will be hereafter' (1.19).

'What you have seen', as I have said, refers to his opening vision of the Son of man, the First and the Last and the Living One, in the midst of the seven golden candlesticks (1.12–18), that is to say, the risen Christ reigning in his completed church. This is the ultimate truth, the great resurrection reality, in the light of which the whole course of history has now to be interpreted. 'What is now' refers to the description which follows in the Letters to the Churches in chapters 2 and 3 of the empirical state of Christ's church on earth. And there is no pretence that this is spotless, infallible or anything else. Indeed judgment cannot but begin at the house of God, and the whole church, represented by the number seven, is in this age a *corpus permixtum* – the tares grow together with the wheat. Nevertheless it should be aware of what is happening, for it holds the clue to the present events. And this is its privilege and its responsibility. 'What will be hereafter' is the theme of the book from 4.1 onwards. These things are set in the future, because it is only in the unrolling of history that they will become manifest for what they are. They concern God's judgment on the non-Christian world, which does not yet see his coming. It must be for them line upon line, precept upon precept, here a little, there a little. What the Seer is doing is foreshortening this process, whose outcome to the Christian, looking at it from the End, is already certain. Just as Jesus weeps over Jerusalem, so John, with the mind of Christ, laments already over civilization: 'If thou hadst known, thou in this thy day, the things that belong to thy peace! But now they are hid from thine eyes . . . Behold, thy house is left unto thee desolate.' Jerusalem might not fall for forty years, Rome for nearer four hundred: that was immaterial. The heart of prophecy is not a forecast; it is not concerned with the details of the moves, which are matters of freedom. The heart of prophecy is to know the things that are, which make the things that shall be the things that must be.

The secret of this knowledge is not the peering of second sight, as if the clue to things long in the future, but 'a door opened into heaven' (4.1). To the Christian there is another whole dimension to living, in the light of which the true heights and depths of present existence are disclosed. The world is not just the flat-land mapped by the psychologist or the sociologist. Looking at things from the End the Christian descries not simply, as the earth-bound man does, the clash of classes and ideologies and the dialectical pattern of economic laws. Implicated in every event are great and mysterious forces of good and evil, Michael and his angels locked in mortal conflict with the devil and his angels. The Christian knows that there is 'war in heaven' (12.7); and he knows that not as something that is only going to take place at the end of history, after everything else, nor as some fray in regions far remote from this; but as the reality, perceived in all its spiritual, eschatological depth, of what meets him in the tensions and clashes of the historical scene. He can face the world for what it truly is. The events of the End are nothing other than the course of history since the resurrection, the lurid colours and grotesque shapes of apocalyptic serving simply to project them on to the clouds of heaven, like some giant Brocken spectre, the final issues of life and death introduced into even the most mundane and parochial events by the coming of Christ.

It is with this apparatus that the Seer of Revelation comes to interpret the secular history of his time. He insists that this is not the closed universe which the secularists would like to consider it. It is open to dimensions of activity and interpretation of which he suspects nothing. And this impression is skilfully conveyed by John's dramatic technique. His method throughout is subtly indirect, impressionistic, even surrealistic. He is a master at suggesting overtones of meaning by teasing allusion, and touching off trains of association by evoking archetypal images deep-rooted in the human consciousness. The very archaism of style which he affects – an impossible kind of Hebrew thinking in Greek letters – seems deliberately intended to waft the reader back into the dream world of Ezekiel, Zechariah and Daniel. No other book is so soaked with Old Testament quotation, but, as I said, he never cites a single verse *in toto* – always the memory of a phrase which frees the image to suggest much more than the original context contains. There is the constant and bewildering alternation between heaven and earth, the sudden introduction of refrains of worship or of woe, the rude interruption of otherwise connected scenes with isolated occurrences, as, to quote Preston and Hanson's commentary, 'a star falls from heaven; a millstone is hurled into the sea; an angel flies in mid-heaven; a voice cries, "A measure of wheat for a penny"'. It is the technique of *Hellzapoppin'* or Thornton Wilder's play *The Skin of our Teeth* sub-titled, if I remember rightly, 'the story of civilization in comic strip'. And all through there is a cataract of sounds and colours. Vivid images are simply splashed across the canvas – scarlets and golds and dazzling whites, trumpets and thunders, hails and earthquakes and voices, stars falling like windfall figs shaken down by a storm (6.13) or swept by the tail of the dragon and flung upon the earth (12.4).

It is history in wide-screen, 3-D, glorious technicolour, and stereo. Cecil B. de Mille really missed the climax to his career, though I doubt whether, if the film was honest, as opposed to Hollywood 'epic', it would even get an X certificate either for sex or violence.

So much for his literary form and artistic technique. What is he actually saying through it all?

4 *What has it to say to us?*

Let us begin by taking a specimen passage which is fairly typical of the whole and try to analyse and interpret it. Read chapter 6, verses 1 to 8:

1 Then I watched as the Lamb broke the first of the seven seals; and I heard one of the four living creatures say in a voice like
2 thunder, 'Come!' And there before my eyes was a white horse, and its rider held a bow. He was given a crown, and he rode forth, conquering and to conquer.

3 When the Lamb broke the second seal, I heard the second
4 creature say, 'Come!' And out came another horse, all red. To its rider was given power to take peace from the earth and make men slaughter one another; and he was given a great sword.

5 When he broke the third seal, I heard the third creature say, 'Come!' And there, as I looked, was a black horse; and its rider
6 held in his hand a pair of scales. And I heard what sounded like a voice from the midst of the living creatures, which said, 'A whole day's wage for a quart of flour, a whole day's wage for three quarts of barley-meal! But spare the olive and the vine.'

7 When he broke the fourth seal, I heard the voice of the fourth
8 creature say, 'Come!' And there, as I looked, was another horse, sickly pale; and its rider's name was Death, and Hades came close behind. To him was given power over a quarter of the earth, with the right to kill by sword and by famine, by pestilence and wild beasts.

These pictures of 'the four horsemen of the Apocalypse' have been described as four brilliant little vignettes of the way God's judgment works itself out in history (Preston and Hanson). They are attempting to give some kind of theology of power and to fit into the eternal victory of Christ the processes of politics and economics which appear entirely unrelated to it.

The first thing to note is that power is something which is regarded as created and given by God. The crown and the sword – the very symbols of power-politics – are *given* to the horsemen. This is a very different theology of power from that of many Christians today who regard the processes of power-politics as what supervene in history precisely when God is *not* present and of some pacifists who would start from the position that force is of itself evil (a version of the old

Manichaean heresy that matter is evil, for power, as atomic power shows, *is* matter). But these things are given by God: power in its various manifestations has been locked up in the universe by its creator. The forms of destruction it assumes are still his: what *he* wills to supervene when men forsake him, not what is left when he forsakes the world.

The first vignette depicts what happens in the political order in these circumstances, when the state becomes all-powerful and its creeping might advances conquering and to conquer. The second describes the military consequences of this world-conflict; the red horse and in the hands of its rider a great sword with which to take peace from the earth and cause men to slaughter one another. The third depicts the results in the economic order; an economy of scarcity and inflated prices and rationing: a black horse of austerity and its rider with a pair of scales. In the proclamation that follows a penny represents a day's wage, the measure (a choenix) just enough to keep body and soul together. Perhaps one could try putting this horseman in modern dress. 'And the third cartoon was of a black-coated figure, a civil servant, and in his hand he held a ration book, and underneath was the official announcement: "An ounce of butter a week and three ounces of sugar. Cooking fats and milk at present unrationed".' The fourth picture is the most terrible of all; the nihilistic revolution of destruction, death and hell, in which the whole process ends. After two world wars (without imagining what would be let loose by a third) it is not so difficult for our generation to read meaning into the words: 'And power was given to them (Death and Hades) over a quarter of the earth, with the right to kill by sword and by famine, by pestilence and wild beasts.' Again, it is not difficult to translate into terms of nuclear radiation or biological warfare – or for that matter psychotic breakdown – the ghastly picture of the locusts which rise from the pit in chapter 9:

1 Then the fifth angel blew his trumpet; and I saw a star that had fallen to the earth, and the star was given the key of the shaft of
2 the abyss. With this he opened the shaft of the abyss; and from the shaft smoke rose like smoke from a great furnace, and the
3 sun and the air were darkened by the smoke from the shaft. Then over the earth, out of the smoke, came locusts, and they were
4 given the powers that earthly scorpions have. They were told to do no injury to the grass or to any plant or tree, but only to those

men who had not received the seal of God on their foreheads.

5 These they were allowed to torment for five months, with torment like a scorpion's sting; but they were not to kill them.

6 During that time these men will seek death, but they will not find it; they will long to die, but death will elude them.

7 In appearance the locusts were like horses equipped for battle. On their heads were what looked like golden crowns; their faces

8, 9 were like human faces and their hair like women's hair; they had teeth like lions' teeth, and wore breastplates like iron; the sound of their wings was like the noise of horses and chariots rushing to

10 battle; they had tails like scorpions, with stings in them, and in their tails lay their power to plague mankind for five months.

11 They had for their king the angel of the abyss, whose name, in Hebrew, is Abaddon, and in Greek, Apollyon, or the Destroyer.

But though it may not be difficult to make these things relevant and contemporary, still what is all this about these things being 'given', and what is the nature of the God who apparently wills them? This leads us directly to the central problem of the Apocalypse. Just what is its doctrine of God, with all this language of wrath and blood, destruction and revenge? Can it possibly be the God and Father of our Lord Jesus Christ? This is what has led so many from the earliest times, down to such distinguished Christians as C. H. Dodd in our own day, regretfully to dismiss the book as frankly sub-Christian.

But at least before we judge let us try to understand. Two factors have to be taken into account.

1. It does not say that these ghastly consequences are the direct creation and will of God. The locusts like the beast rise out of the abyss, the opposite pole to heaven: they represent spiritual forces in nature and history in rebellion against God. Nevertheless, and this is the biblical doctrine of God as the Lord of history, they do not operate simply against him. He is not at their mercy. Even the forces of destruction he uses and takes up into his own design for victory. Just as Isaiah saw the ravages of the Assyrian as the rod of Yahweh's anger (10.5ff.) – yet the Assyrian himself sees it quite differently; 'for his thought is only to destroy and to wipe out nation after nation' (10.7) – so the Seer of Revelation sees God using the internecine forces of destruction to achieve his ultimate end, by actually causing them to combine in a single monstrous world empire: 'For God has

put it into their heads to carry out his purpose, by making common cause and conferring their sovereignty upon the beast until all that God has spoken is fulfilled' (Rev. 17.17). And just as Isaiah sees that the final destiny of the stout heart of the King of Assyria, for all his use as the divine tool, is the utter consumption of his kingdom so that 'the remnant of the trees in the forest shall be so few that a child may count them' (Isa. 10.19), so the end of Death and Hades is to be 'flung into the lake of fire' (Rev. 20.14). When they are no further use to God they are absolutely disposable. 'There shall be an end to death, and to mourning, and crying and pain; for the old order has passed away' (Rev. 21.4).

2. It is most important to remember that in the greatest part of the Book of Revelation we are dealing with what Luther called 'Christ's strange work', his *opus alienum*, not his *opus proprium*. We are trying to see how the love of God is manifested in the end-moves of the chess match which resist his *coup de grâce*, not with the redemptive act of grace itself. And in these moves the love can be manifested only indirectly – through a glass darkly. In the few passages where the author is directly concerned with the love of God to those who can see it as love, nothing could be more tender than the Book of Revelation: 'Here I stand knocking at the door; if anyone hears my voice and opens the door, I will come in and sit down to supper with him and he with me' (3.20); 'The Lamb who is at the heart of the throne will be their shepherd and will guide them to the springs of the water of life; and God will wipe all tears from their eyes' (7.17). There is nothing there of the rod of iron.

But to the non-Christian world this love can appear only as wrath (*orgē*). It is of great importance to try and understand this great biblical concept. Its constant presence within the pages of scripture, and nowhere more than in the Book of Revelation, represents a resolute refusal to allow that any person or thing or event can ever fall out of the relationship of personal love in and for which it has been created by God. Nothing can ever be merely impersonal in this universe; to say so is a denial of the existence of God. One recalls the sequence of cause and effect listed by the prophet Amos (3.3–6): 'Do two men travel together unless they have agreed? Does a lion roar in the forest if he has no prey? Does a young lion growl in his den if he has caught nothing? Does a bird fall into a trap on the ground if the striker is not set for it? Does a trap spring from the ground and take nothing? If a trumpet sounds the alarm, are not the people scared? If disaster falls on a city, has not the Lord been at work?' Substitute 'love' for 'Lord' and you get the New Testament version of it. The New Testament insists on preserving the recognition that even the most iron laws of cause and effect, physical or moral, must represent ultimately the operation of nothing less than the divine love. And this fact the worst that evil may do cannot finally destroy, because it is a fact grounded in God. That is the ultimate guarantee that this world must remain God's world, and even the most distorted humanity God's humanity. Men may change the wine of God's love so that to them it is drunk as the vinegar of his wrath. But out of this dimension of love-hate man cannot fall. If he did he would cease to be God's man – and God would cease to be God. The divine wrath is ultimately the saving guarantee of the divine compassion, that God will not let man go, that the bands of love will hold on to him, even if they first have to become a halter to hang him. For the wrath is 'the wrath of the Lamb' (Rev. 6.16).

The stress on the wrath of God witnesses to the merciful fact that even the scarlet woman, even the beast, for all its bestial degradation is still God's humanity. The processes of destruction, which moral retribution brings inevitably in its train, are still the expression not only of an iron *karma* or fate, as in Hinduism, but of a personal control. Once that principle of interpretation is abandoned Christianity has no theology of secular history.

Nevertheless it is equally clear that the wrath of God, for all the insistence that it witnesses to the ultimate personal constitution of the universe, does not mean the personal vindictiveness of God. 'The wrath' describes not a state of the divine attitude (still less of a divine emotion), as if that changed with sin, but the condition of man and society which forces the divine love to appear as wrath, yes, as impersonal. Perhaps one could paraphrase thus the succinct statement of Rev. 11.18, 'And the nations were wroth, and thy wrath came' as 'The nations were wroth, and so to them thy love came as wrath.' Sin always depersonalizes, and if men will have it so, God's love must meet them through the channels that sin itself creates, as law rather than as love. Wrath, as Paul insists, means that God 'gives men over' (Rom. 1.24) to the consequences of their own choice. He allows, as it were, society to stew in its own juice – the vinegar it has made of his wine. 'Let the evil-doer go on doing evil and the filthy-minded wallow in his filth' (Rev. 22.11). If that is the cup a man chooses, he must drink it to the dregs, to the last bitter consequences.

Take, for instance, one of the most ghastly passages of the Book of
Revelation (14.9–11):

9 Yet a third angel followed, crying out loud, 'Whoever worships
10 the beast and its image and receives its mark on his forehead or
    hand, he shall drink the wine of God's wrath, poured undiluted
    into the cup of his vengeance. He shall be tormented in
    sulphurous flames before the holy angels and before the Lamb.
11 The smoke of their torment will rise for ever and ever, and there
    will be no respite day or night for those who worship the beast
    and its image or receive the mark of its name.

As Preston and Hanson put it, 'It is not a picture of an angry tyrant
arbitrarily punishing those who have offended him with physical
torture. It is the assertion, by means of traditional symbolism, that
the most terrible thing that can happen to any human being is
deliberately to turn away from the highest Good' . . . 'The sufferings . . . of those who persist in rejecting God's love in Christ are
self-imposed, self-incurred, self-perpetuated'.[6] And they are what
they are precisely because they take place 'in the presence of the holy
angels and in the presence of the Lamb' – hell is 'inescapable
godlessness in inescapable relationship to God' (Paul Althaus). God
will go on treating us as persons – as bound up in relationship to him
– *for ever and ever.*

Yet this is not and cannot be the last word about the wrath of God.
What appears to be merely primitive and destructive is, considered at
its deepest level of all, something strangely, even terrifyingly,
different.

Let us watch. Take what seems to be the most blood-thirsty
passage in the entire work, specifically instanced by Dodd to show
that the Revelation cannot really be considered a Christian book:
14.14–20:

14 Then as I looked there appeared a white cloud, and on the cloud
    sat one like a son of man. He had on his head a crown of gold and
15 in his hand a sharp sickle. Another angel came out of the temple
    and called in a loud voice to him who sat on the cloud: 'Stretch
    out your sickle and reap; for harvest-time has come, and earth's
16 crop is over-ripe.' So he who sat on the cloud put his sickle to the
    earth and its harvest was reaped.
17 Then another angel came out of the heavenly temple, and he

18 also had a sharp sickle. Then from the altar came yet another,
the angel who has authority over fire, and he shouted to the one
with the sharp sickle: 'Stretch out your sickle, and gather in
19 earth's grape-harvest, for its clusters are ripe.' So the angel put
his sickle to the earth and gathered in its grapes, and threw them
20 into the great winepress of God's wrath. The winepress was
trodden outside the city, and for two hundred miles around
blood flowed from the press to the height of the horses' bridles.

On the surface this appears to be the last terrible harvest of the
process of judgment, the final crushing of the grapes of wrath. This is
where the world process has led – one vast blood-bath, universal and
complete. Such is probably the significance of the figure 1600
furlongs. 'Four is the complete number of extent, covering the four
points of the compass (as seven is the complete number of quality);
the square of four indicates entire completeness. It is multiplied by
one hundred as a sign of greatness.'[7] This is indeed essential truth of
the picture that the Seer is portraying. But turn it upside down, like
those comic drawings of heads that lour one way up and beam the
other, and what do we see? In the first place, we notice that the
person who holds the sharp sickle is, as verse 14 indicates, the risen
Christ, 'one like a son of man, seated on a white cloud and wearing a
crown of gold'. This is indeed what we should expect: this is none
other than the work of Christ. But this strange work, this *opus
alienum* par excellence, turns out to be, deep down, none other than
his *opus proprium*, his great work of redemption. The reference to
the winepress is, of course, an allusion to the strange passage in Isa.
63.1–6; 'I have trodden the winepress alone; and of the peoples
there was no man with me; yea I trod them in my anger, and
trampled them in my fury; and their life-blood is sprinkled upon my
garments and I have stained all my raiment'. This image of the winepress is taken up again in Rev. 19.11–16:

11 Then I saw heaven wide open, and there before me was a white
horse; and its rider's name was Faithful and True, for he is just in
12 judgment and just in war. His eyes flamed like fire, and on his
head were many diadems. Written upon him was a name known
13 to none but himself, and he was robed in a garment drenched in
14 blood. He was called the Word of God, and the armies of heaven
followed him on white horses, clothed in fine linen, clean and
15 shining. From his mouth there went a sharp sword with which to

71

smite the nations; for he it is who shall rule them with an iron rod,
and tread the winepress of the wrath and retribution of God the
16 sovereign Lord. And on his robe and on his leg there was written
the name: 'King of kings and Lord of lords.'

Again the blood-bath, but note that it is no longer simply the blood
of his enemies: the life-blood in which his robe is steeped is his own,
just as we have heard earlier that the robes of his followers who ride
behind him have been made white in 'the blood of the lamb' (7.14).
Suddenly the whole thing is transformed (and this is typical of the
author's use of the Old Testament). So we look again at chapter 14 and
notice in verse 20 that the wine-press that was trodden was 'outside
the city' and we are reminded of Heb. 13.12, 'Therefore Jesus also
suffered outside the gate to consecrate the people by his own blood'.
This winepress, the great winepress of the wrath of God, is none other
than the wood of Calvary, and the blood that came out from it, even to
the bridles of the horses, sufficed for the whole world – to the ends of
the earth and the end of time. As Preston and Hanson put it again, 'The
way God judges his enemies is not by killing them but by suffering
death at their hands'.

I would repeat that this is not the only meaning of the passage, nor
its first and obvious meaning. The scene is a picture of judgment – for
the cross *is* 'the judgment of this world' – and the rejection of God
which it represents is a blood-bath, as the Gospel apocalypses,
focussing it historically upon the fall of Jerusalem rather than of
Rome, make equally clear. The sole question is whether this is the only
picture which the passage presents, one of unrelieved and purely
retributive judgment. It may be that it is; and perhaps it is only wishful
thinking to believe that it is not. But, just as in the judgment scenes of
the Fourth Gospel, there are, I think, real enough indications to
suggest that the *double entendre* is there.

Or consider another passage apparently of equally unrelieved
vengeance. This describes one of 'the seven bowls of God's wrath'
(16.1) modelled on the seven plagues of Egypt:

4 The third angel poured his bowl on the rivers and springs, and
they turned to blood.
5 Then I heard the angel of the waters say, 'Just art thou in these
6 thy judgments, thou Holy One who art and wast; for they shed the
blood of thy people and of thy prophets, and thou hast given them
blood to drink.'

72

Judgment and naked retribution it seems, echoing Isa. 63.6: 'I made them drunk in my fury, and I poured out their life-blood on the earth.' And judgment of course it is. But is it only their own blood that is given them to drink, and of which they are judged worthy? Is there not just an echo here, not merely of one who turned water into blood, but of one greater than he who turned water into wine, who said, also in judgment, 'You shall indeed drink my cup' (Matt. 20.23) and who finally 'took a cup with the words, Drink from it, all of you; for this is my blood, the blood of the covenant, shed for many *for the forgiveness of sins*' (Matt. 26.27f.).

No one will pretend that the Book of Revelation contains the whole gospel of the divine compassion, or that the compassion it does contain is always explicit. It was written to fortify a church that was being butchered, not as missionary propaganda. The book does not soar to the heights of Christian truth. But it does not plumb its depths. It does not so much express the gospel as presuppose it. But it presupposes it more thoroughly perhaps than any other. There is nothing in human history or the individual psyche, in the world as it is or the world as it shall be, in heights or depths, that can fall outside the limits of the cosmic Christ, the Alpha and the Omega.

The book ends indeed with the vision, one of great beauty and peace (21.22–22.5), a world order, a secular city, bathed with the light of the Lamb, in which there is no more need of a temple, for God in Christ is Lord of every part. To it all races bring their contribution and the tree of life, with its perpetual fruiting, serves for the healing of nations. The alienation of Eden is overcome. The consummation is as complete as it is still agonizingly awaited.

Nevertheless we should be wrong to look here for the full gospel of reconciliation. That, as I said, is not primarily what the Book of Revelation is about. It is not pleasant reading. A theology of the concentration camp one would hardly expect to be that. But the Christian must have such a theology, unless no Christian is ever to sit on a war crimes tribunal. But the author of the Revelation would have said that Christ sat there. It is indeed his strange work. Enough that even here we can catch a hint that it is not wholly strange.

And even in the terror there is an awful beauty. No one perhaps penetrated to the heart of the Apocalypse more piercingly than that visionary and poet and artist William Blake, and his picture of the living Christ is that of the 'Tiger! Tiger! burning bright in the watches of the night'. 'Who framed', he asked, 'thy awful symmetry?' And as a sample of that terrible beauty I would end with what I believe is in every sense one of the purple passages of literature in the entire Bible, and the superb description of the final fall of Babylon in chapter 18:

1 After this I saw another angel coming down from heaven; he came with great authority and the earth was lit up with his
2 splendour. Then in a mighty voice he proclaimed, 'Fallen, fallen is Babylon the great! She has become a dwelling for demons, a haunt for every unclean spirit, for every foul and loathsome bird.
3 For all nations have drunk deep of the fierce wine of her fornication; the kings of the earth have committed fornication with her, and merchants the world over have grown rich on her bloated wealth.'
4 Then I heard another voice from heaven that said: 'Come out of her, my people, lest you take part in her sins and share in her
5 plagues. For her sins are piled high as heaven, and God has not
6 forgotten her crimes. Pay her back in her own coin, repay her twice over for her deeds! Double for her the strength of the
7 potion she mixed! Mete out grief and torment to match her voluptuous pomp! She says in her heart, "I am a queen on my
8 throne! No mourning for me, no widow's weeds!" Because of this her plagues shall strike her in a single day – pestilence, bereavement, famine, and burning – for mighty is the Lord God who has pronounced her doom!'
9 The kings of the earth who committed fornication with her and wallowed in her luxury will weep and wail over her, as they
10 see the smoke of her conflagration. They will stand at a distance, for horror at her torment, and will say, 'Alas, alas for the great city, the mighty city of Babylon! In a single hour your doom has struck!'
11 The merchants of the earth also will weep and mourn for her,
12 because no one any longer buys their cargoes, cargoes of gold and silver, jewels and pearls, cloths of purple and scarlet, silks and fine linens; all kinds of scented woods, ivories, and every sort of thing made of costly woods, bronze, iron, or marble;
13 cinnamon and spice, incense, perfumes and frankincense; wine, oil, flour and wheat, sheep and cattle, horses, chariots, slaves,
14 and the lives of men. 'The fruit you longed for', they will say, 'is gone from you; all the glitter and the glamour are lost, never to
15 be yours again!' The traders in all these wares, who gained their

16 wealth from her, will stand at a distance for horror at her torment, weeping and mourning and saying, 'Alas, alas for the great city, that was clothed in fine linen and purple and scarlet,

17 bedizened with gold and jewels and pearls! Alas that in one hour so much wealth should be laid waste!'

18 Then all the sea-captains and voyagers, the sailors and those who traded by sea, stood at a distance and cried out as they saw the smoke of her conflagration: 'Was there ever a city like the

19 great city?' They threw dust on their heads, weeping and mourning and saying, 'Alas, alas for the great city, where all who had ships at sea grew rich on her wealth! Alas that in a single hour she should be laid waste!'

20 But let heaven exult over her; exult, apostles and prophets and people of God; for in the judgment against her he has vindicated your cause!

21 Then a mighty angel took up a stone like a great millstone and hurled it into the sea and said, 'Thus shall Babylon, the great

22 city, be sent hurtling down, never to be seen again! No more shall the sound of harpers and minstrels, of flute-players and trumpeters, be heard in you; no more shall craftsmen of any trade be found in you; no more shall the sound of the mill be

23 heard in you; no more shall the light of the lamp be seen in you; no more shall the voice of the bride and bridegroom be heard in you! Your traders were once the merchant princes of the world, and with your sorcery you deceived all the nations.'

24 For the blood of the prophets and of God's people was found in her, the blood of all who had been done to death on earth.

*The Way of Social
Responsibility*

A Christian Response to the Arms Race

A lecture delivered to the University of Newcastle-upon-Tyne in 1981 and first published in Debate on Disarmament *ed M. Clarke and M. Mowlam, Routledge and Kegan Paul 1982.*

When I chose this title it did not occur to me that I should need to justify both parts of it. Yet I could hardly believe my ears when I heard Caspar Weinberger, who with the rest of President Reagan's travelling troupe has been doing more than anyone else to orchestrate the European disarmament movement, say recently on the BBC: 'There is no arms race. There can't be. For you can't have a race with only one entrant – and we've never competed.' Just who do they think we are, to believe that – and actually have the nerve to accuse us of being dupes of Soviet propaganda?

Then in an interview to *The Times* before his Reith lectures Professor Laurence Martin, for whom I have a much greater personal regard, was reported as saying: 'The very phrase "arms race" is a bad metaphor; it is neither fast enough nor competitive enough to be a race, and it is not the heart of the problem.'[1] Just how much faster or more competitive has it got to get? And what goes deeper to the heart of the problem?

But I should like to concentrate on justifying my choice of the first part of the title: 'A Christian response', for I am not claiming to present *the* Christian response. There are, and will continue to be, differences between Christians on this as much as on any other highly technical, as well as deeply moral, issue. This is neither surprising nor shameful. There have always been pacifists and non-pacifists in the church, as today there are both unilateralists and multilateralists. And I would plead strongly, here as elsewhere, for a both/and, not simply for an either/or. For the line between them goes right through the middle of myself.

On the basic moral issue Christians should be completely at one. At every Lambeth conference over the past fifty years the statement has been reaffirmed that 'war as a method of settling international disputes is incompatible with the teaching of our Lord Jesus Christ.' And there would be unanimous agreement among moral theologians that unrestricted nuclear warfare could never be justified under the doctrine of the 'just war' (a doctrine which may still have important things to say about the 'just revolution' and lesser dilemmas); for it can never meet the requirement of proportionality of response. That for me carries the further corollaries, that limited nuclear war could never be justified either, since one can never be sure that it would not lead to the other, and second that all weapons of mass destruction, whether nuclear, biological or chemical, are out, *even* if one does not intend to use them. For to threaten their use for deterrence is equally immoral if you mean it and foolish if you do not. Unlike Mr Francis Pym when he was Minister of Defence, I could not say that I should myself be ready to press the button. And this is no theoretical issue, for we are requiring young men, in our name, to take upon themselves the terrible burden of this decision. We have one young man, still only an undergraduate at my college in Cambridge, who was one of three key-holders on a Polaris submarine, until he got out, scarred by the experience for life.

Yet I do not want to use my time discussing the issue of whether or under what circumstances the use or threat of nuclear weapons could ever be justified. I am more concerned with how we *stop* them being used. And on this the record of Lambeth conferences or Papal encyclicals is about as discouraging as that of disarmament conferences or arms-limitation talks. They seem to make not the slightest difference. All things go on as they have been from the beginning, except that the arms race constantly escalates and proliferates, the doomsday clock ticks nearer to midnight, and the cry goes up, 'How long, O Lord?' Yet the cry is perhaps the most significant thing. For the breaking of the mould is suddenly beginning to look a real possibility, and the perception is dawning that we *need* not go on like this.

As in British politics, what seemed before so set is cracking before our eyes. The mould of the two-party system is breaking up. That in itself does not *solve* anything, nor does it mean that we should all go off and join the equivalent of the SDP. Indeed the noises I hear coming from the SDP on disarmament are still so uncertain that I need to be much more convinced by them on this issue. Nor is fissiparation in itself a good thing. In fact I have said in effect to Tony Benn and Shirley Williams and David Steel 'I love you all. You represent bits of my deepest convictions. Why can't you get together?' But I know that this is politically impossible, and there are deep and genuine divisions. Yet I am all for holding opposites in tension and convinced that truth comes from both ends at once, rather than from an either/or polarization or a soggy centre. In any case the lines of division and polarization are, I believe, largely – and in the time we have got – dangerously irrelevant. And this applies to both the old and the new lines.

The old pacifist/non-pacifist debate has largely been by-passed by recent developments. This does not mean that there are not fundamental issues involved – of how to meet evil or on the place of restraint – on which we shall all come down on different sides at different points. But the old crunch-question of whether to bear arms or accept the draft is increasingly irrelevant. The issue today, I believe, is recognition of the right not to support the arms race with one's taxes. And as a non-pacifist I would want to give my backing to the peace tax campaign, to allow anyone the freedom of conscience, not to evade the burden of taxation, but to divert to a 'peace tax fund' administered under the government for specific peace-making purposes, the proportion of tax allocated to a defence strategy based on nuclear weapons. I believe we must press for this right to be recognized legislatively on the same grounds and with the same safeguards as conscientious objection to military service. It is of course hopeless to expect this present administration to recognize it, and I believe it is a legitimate goal to seek some commitment in this direction from the competing political parties at the next election. And until this freedom is granted it is important to fight for it, and if necessary to go to prison for it, as Bertrand Russell did in the First World War. Yet as a non-pacifist I also want to press for an alternative defence policy that is both credible and usable, which may, initially at least, be no less costly. So again I am split. I will fight for the freedom, but might not wish to go all the way in availing myself of it.

But not only is the old pacifist versus non-pacifist divide anachronistic but increasingly, it seems to me, the new line-up between unilateralists and multilateralists is unreal and distortive. And it allows the establishment to divide and rule, as St Paul played off the Pharisees against the Saducees.

The unilateralists can be labelled 'softies' or neutralists, if not fanatics or freaks, who march with their hearts and not their heads. They can be represented as 'copping out', throwing away the deterrent, upsetting the precarious stability which has preserved the peace, and in effect though not in intention making war more likely. The multilateralists, on the other hand, can be represented as not doing anything till the other side does, as re-arming in order to disarm (alias 'negotiating from strength'), and in effect just fuelling the arms race. So the sterile debate goes on, and no one wins – except the industrial-military complex.

I believe we must all be unilateralists now – and multilateralists. 'Protest and survive' and 'negotiate and survive' are not alternatives. As the latest production of Bradford University's School of Peace Studies, *As Lambs to the Slaughter* (which can certainly not be construed as an argument for doing nothing), insisted, the long patient process of dismantling fears, building up confidence, re-taining a balance stage by stage, cannot be bypassed or despised, *if* the actual object is to get the powers to remove missiles as opposed to making ourselves feel good.[2] In E. P. Thompson's words at the close of the 1981 Hyde Park rally, 'We've won the argument, but we haven't even stopped one missile in its tracks.'

Perhaps I may be allowed to utter a few fraternal home-truths about how unilateralists look to the other side with whom I am also closely in touch, particularly from where I am placed at Cambridge, within both the scientific and the religious establishments. It is so fatally easy to be counter-productive as, for instance in my experi-ence, are the Israelis to almost all visitors from the West, who go with most of their contacts and sympathies on the Jewish side and return with a far greater appreciation of the Palestinian cause. And it only increases the counter-productivity then to be labelled anti-Semitic, which is about as neurotic a reaction as dubbing nuclear disarmers anti-American.

Now the effect, though not of course the intention, of the self-styled Peace Movement is often as alienating. Are those not wearing CND badges *ipso facto* part of the 'war movement'? A letter appeared in *The Guardian* (I am ashamed to say from a department of theology) just after the Hyde Park rally deploring once more 'the deafening silence of the church' and asking where were all the bishops and clerical collars (who would want to wear one in Hyde Park anyhow?).[3] It went on: 'Enough of this armchair soliloquizing! Let the clergy and the leaders of the churches get out of their cloisters and put their feet where their mouths are!' Even if this were a just criticism, and even if putting one's foot in one's mouth were a desirable posture, I would beg those who say such things to realize that they are being about as counter-productive as the Reagan Administration or the Home Office's pamphlet *Protect and Survive* have been on the other side.

The situation is going to be changed – and if we are not in it for this we had better get out – only if the centre of gravity of the great inert body of middle opinion, of leaders and of led, is shifted, albeit marginally. And for that a massive combined operation is going to be necessary, starting at both ends at once. Let me give an illustration which I think is paradigmatic. One of the most successful campaigns of modern times was that which stopped in its tracks the South African cricket tour of England in 1970 – and all such official exchanges since. This was achieved by the combination of two pressure-groups, working from opposite ends. There was the radical action group under Peter Hain threatening to put tin-tacks on the pitch. But there was another group under David Sheppard, then my successor as Bishop of Woolwich, who as a former captain of England and a member of the MCC operated from within the Long Room at Lord's. I don't believe that either alone could have stopped the tour. But together they won the day by giving a decisive tilt to the establishment.

It so happened that just as I was writing this a letter came through my mail asking that 'the teaching staff of the Faculty of Divinity in the University of Cambridge declare their opposition to the presence of all forms of nuclear weapons on British soil and their commitment to a policy of unilateral nuclear disarmament'. Would that most of them individually might; but I had to oppose it as simply bad politics. It is rather like asking the Regius Professor of Divinity or the Archbishop of Canterbury to put tin-tacks on the pitch, and when they won't – or they don't answer – accusing them of 'deafening silence'. It is not only inept but actually sets the cause back. I am all for working on both of these characters, and I am all for the mass demonstrations and the pressures from below which are vital to changing the atmosphere and altering the terms of the debate. For I am appalled by how many of the ecclesiastical and even more of the scientific establishment who are still apparently unappraised of the issue or unsparked by it – though as always in any profession this applies less to the genuinely big men at the top than to the mass of second-class minds, especially when research-grants or contracts are directly or indirectly involved. I believe that a great deal has to be done – as is being done, for instance, within the medical profession – to help scales fall from the eyes; and I can testify to how long it took for me really to *see*.

But let us tackle it with both 'valour and discretion', and above all do not let us wantonly divide or alienate our forces. Let me offer one other example, as an awful warning – the case of Rudi Dutschke, the German student activist of the sixties. He was the victim of a bomb-attack (in church) which all but killed him and stopped him either reading or writing for a long time. With great courage he gradually fought his way back to health and got himself admitted to do a PhD at Cambridge, on the understanding that he was completely out of active politics. But a witch-hunt started for deporting him as a danger to the peace. There was massive protest at this from the university, and, for once in those heady days of student riots, everyone was united from the vice-chancellor down to the students. But what did the students do at their mass-meeting? They called a strike, thus hitting not the government (who in the person of Reginald Maudling as Home Secretary needed all the battering he could get), but the university, thereby gratuitously setting the students against the lecturers. So despite being torn to shreds by Michael Foot in the Commons debate, to which I listened, the government won the vote (though certainly not the argument) and deported him to defenceless Denmark, who were honoured to have him, and where I later met him again before his tragically early death. So let us learn the lesson and draw some conclusions.

First let me say something about ends, and then about means. Let me put the object of the exercise like this. The inexorable appetite of the arms race is fed by a process that starts with the research scientists and the hardware technologists (whose salaries of course are already fed by the process), who scan the frontiers of what it is possible to develop, if they are given the resources. They then talk to the military-industrial complex, who don't need much persuading that it must be developed, to forestall the other side and to maintain employment (and of course profits). So the Pentagon talks to the politicians, or Whitehall to Westminster, or the equivalent within the corridors of the Kremlin, and they quickly discover the current missile gap. Finally the politicians, abetted by the media, persuade the people to elect them when this is necessary, or work away behind closed doors when it is not. So the M-X missiles and the B1 bombers and the neutron warheads and the Chevalines and the Tridents and the cruise and the Pershings and the SS-20s, etc., etc., are designed and delivered, with ever more sophisticated weaponry waiting in the pipe-line to tease the scientists who talk to the military who talk to the politicians who talk to the people who pay for the house that Jack built.

All we have to do (all!) is to reverse that process: to insist that it is the people who instruct the politicians, who instruct the military, who instruct the scientists what *we* want for *our* defence. It is as simple and as seemingly impossible as that.

Now if you want to move the world the first thing you need is a fulcrum: you have got to get some leverage somewhere. And that is why, because no one individual can do everything, I have decided to put my little weight behind the movement for European nuclear disarmament. For Europe is clearly the most sensitive and vulnerable spot in the superpowers' armoury. A nuclear-free Europe, or at least a nuclear-free zone (or zones) in Europe, looks like an idea whose time, at last, may have come. For it is no new idea, going back to the Rapacki Plan from Poland in the 1950s. And it is an idea that involves both unilateral *and* multilateral action on *each* side. Yet it has got to be taken beyond slogans by some very hard thinking and tough negotiations. To quote again the authors of *As Lambs to the Slaughter*, it involves deciding the basic question of what is Europe. As they recognize, the slogan 'From Poland to Portugal' will be criticized as grossly unbalanced by the West. 'It will involve removal of all NATO tactical and theatre weapons *and* the much longer-ranged French, British and American systems which are essentially part of the strategic arsenals, while leaving Soviet weapons untouched.'[4] But equally the other zone that is canvassed, from 'the Atlantic to the Urals', 'contains perhaps forty per cent of all Soviet ICBMs and the base for around sixty per cent of their missile- carrying submarines. In this case the balance, such as it is, has swung the other way and Soviet opposition will be fierce.' But this is no reason for abandoning the vision. It is a reason for requiring as much hard knowledge and hard thinking on the so-called Peace Movement's side as on the so-called strategists' side, and for real dialogue between them.

This is the lesson I believe to be drawn from the welcome offer by President Reagan of the so-called 'zero option' in Europe. First, it would never have happened without the groundswell of protest in Europe against accepting the new American weapons: it shows how public opinion *can* change things. Second, the initial Soviet response must not be regarded as their last word or proof of their perfidy. For what does the zero option mean? Not, as might be thought, no nuclear weapons on either side; but rather 'You dismantle the SS-4s and SS-5s and SS-20s you've installed and we won't introduce the others.' No mention of removing the forward based systems of nuclear bombers and submarines to which these were the response and which can hit the USSR itself, as the SS-20s cannot hit the USA. So a great deal of hard bargaining remains to be done. And the pressure must be to keep *both* sides to it, not to mention pressure on our own government and the French who have so far offered no independent initiative. So I hope that the upshot of the 1981 Reith Lectures and the Alternative Reith Lectures will be to bring both approaches closer together rather than farther apart.

One thing of which I am increasingly convinced is that both sides must get together to produce a strategy for alternative defence. There is no doubt that one of the dissuasive features of unilateralist propaganda, and indeed of the disarmament movement generally, is that it comes across to most people as purely negative. I was first appraised of this by a radical campaigner in the United States who sensed acutely the effect it was having. It makes the ordinary citizen feel he is just being left naked and defenceless. That is why another aspect of the current campaign in which I am interested is the Alternative Defence Commission set up by the Bradford School of Peace Studies to plan, to put it simply, for a better shield rather than a bigger sword, which need not threaten anyone or provoke escalation.

The real trouble at the moment is that we have a defence policy which we cannot implement without committing suicide, and therefore no credible defence policy at all. This applies both at the tactical and at the strategic level. At the battlefield level nuclear weapons are so implicated in a NATO response to conventional attack that it is impossible for us in the West to say that we will not be the first to use them. This is morally, ideologically and tactically a disastrous weakness, quite apart from being a most dangerous trigger to Armageddon, in blurring and lowering the nuclear threshold. We must extricate ourselves from this position with all deliberate speed.

At the strategic level, we are equally being propelled into a first-strike policy, and the shift is not being honestly acknowledged by our political masters. We are still assured that the only reason we have these weapons is deterrence, and that, of course, there is no intention of actually using them. But the counterforce rather than counter-city strategy, publicly acknowledged by Carter's Presidential Directive 59, but implicit well before that, has introduced a new and dangerous situation. It can be dressed up indeed as morally more acceptable, since the missiles are targeted not on civilians but on launching silos, though since these are in populated areas the destruction and fall-out would still be massively indiscriminate. But what is the point of hitting empty silos? You would have nothing to fire at, nor, since the other side is poised to do the same, to fire with, *unless* you strike first.

This point is powerfully made by Robert C. Aldridge in his book *The Counterforce Syndrome.*[5] Aldridge was intimately involved in designing new weapons systems for the US government and the technical sophistication of what he tells us is planned or possible reads like science fiction. He got out because he realized what he was being asked to design for. This was no longer to deter, so that the weapons would not be used, but to press ahead in the race to use them first. 'The only possible reason,' he says, 'for developing a counterforce capability is to acquire the capacity to launch an unanswerable first strike against the Soviet Union' – which involves knocking out *all* possible retaliatory second strikes. He believes that this could become a feasible reality by the mid-1980s – that is, for the United States; the Soviet Union has not a hope. The deadlines of the newer missiles, like the Trident and the cruise missiles, depend not on their size but on their pin-point accuracy. They are essentially first-strike weapons: for retaliation the old would be adequate to 'overkill' many times. And what, one may ask, does Britain want with an independent first-strike capability? Under what conceivable circumstances can we imagine it being used?

In fact the Trident programme for Britain seems about the most egregious abuse of public money that it is possible to conceive. One thing – and it is about the *one* thing – on which Mr Healey, Mr Benn, Mr Owen and Mr Steel are agreed is that they would cancel Trident. Under any conceivable alternative government it will go down the drain, and meanwhile contracts are doubtless being negotiated containing indemnity clauses against cancellation which will cost us millions – all for nothing. If Mrs Thatcher is *really* concerned to cut public expenditure, here is where she should start.

Moreover the qualitative advance in weaponry, which is even more significant than the quantitative (which is what SALT agreements cover), brings nearer and nearer the day when the only response for which there will be time is automatic 'launch on warning'. This is the final dehumanization of war, for computers do not have consciences and can be trusted not to hesitate. But unfortunately they cannot be trusted not to go wrong, and if the track record of the American ones which we know (or partially know) inspires little confidence, the potential reliability of the Russian ones sends shivers down the spine. Even within the present utterly mad system it is desperately important to withdraw from the position of forcing either first strike or launch on warning. Sheer prudential self-interest demands it.

What we urgently need is a defence policy which we could actually *use*. It is not within my technical expertise to propound this: that is why I am interested in the work of the Alternative Defence Commission at Bradford. The Max Planck Institute in Germany has also been putting some of the best minds in Europe to the problem – though both, typically, are under threat of cuts. Already interest has been expressed in army circles, which are the first to see the craziness of the present strategy. And countries like Austria and Sweden, Switzerland and Yugoslavia, who either cannot or will not have nuclear weapons, but who do not want the Soviets rolling across their land any more than anyone else, have been giving far more attention than we have to genuine *defence* policies. Simply competing in chariots, as the prophets would have put it, i.e., in tanks, would be impossible for them, or probably for NATO as a whole. But a large number of dispersed, light precision-guided missiles using the latest heat-homing and laser-beam technologies could inflict unacceptable losses on invading tanks and planes. They would be purely defensive, posing no threats to anyone else. They could not finally stop a determined invader but combined with real training in non-violent and guerrilla resistance, which must already have made the Soviets think twice about another Czechoslovakia or Afghanistan, they would be a powerful shield of freedom for any country not already disintegrating from distorted economic and social priorities aggravated by the arms race.

For this is the real danger. If you fear revolution look within. At the moment we seem to be going the best way to ensure that we are both 'red and dead'. There is no surer recipe for a Communist, or indeed for a Fascist, take-over, or ultimately for a North-South war, than to go on destabilizing our society and our world as we are doing. If the Soviets are forced to military intervention in Poland, which they can see would *solve* nothing, it will not be because they are on the march West (they have enough on their hands with their own decaying empire), but because they cannot tolerate a social situation which is dangerously subversive to their system. Such a move would be a sign of weakness rather than strength – and no less perilous for that. But for the West then to renege on arms control would be about the most stupid response possible. Yet it still looks the most likely response.

What should be our response, before it is too late? Surely a massive campaign of conscientization to bring people to the point of saying 'This is no way to live.' At the moment they go along like sheep (or is it lemmings?) because they believe, to coin a phrase, there is no alternative. They are told that the balance of terror has kept peace, the cold peace, for thirty-five years, and until we have put something else in its place it is dangerous to dismantle it or, like the CND, to undermine it. But meanwhile the arms race goes on escalating and the 'assurance' of mutual destruction looks as uncertain and as crazy as its acronym MAD. It is the new technological 'advances', if that is the right word, which are making the situation inherently unstable. We cannot just go on in the hole we have been in, even if it has hitherto brought relative security. I believe we must resolutely refuse to accept, as Professor Martin put in in his first 1981 Reith Lecture, that 'the best we can do is tidy up the hole and shore up its sides.' That is spiritual, and almost certainly physical, death.

Above all, we must recognize, as the Brandt Report said, that 'more arms do not make mankind safer, only poorer'.[6] And poorer means more destabilized. Look at the food shortages in the Soviet Union, the queues in Poland, the rumblings in southern Africa and central America, the unemployed and the rioters on our own streets. This is no way to go on. If this is what is meant by keeping the peace, then we must say as strongly as we can 'This is no peace.'

Earlier this year I stood in the extreme north-east corner of the state of Israel, within striking distance of the Sea of Galilee. Yet the last thing that would have come to mind were the lines of the well-known hymn,

O Sabbath rest by Galilee!
O calm of hills above

For this was the notorious Golan Heights, wrested from Syria by Israel in the six-day war and partly re-occupied by Syria in the Yom Kippur War, at fearful cost to both sides. The capital of the Golan is now a ghost town stranded in a demilitarized zone uneasily policed by the UN force, whose job is simply to keep the two sides apart. We were told that the lone Austrian soldier would be glad for a chat with anyone, but even he was not to be drawn out into the biting wind. So this was peace-keeping – the best that the human race can apparently do with all the international resources at its disposal. Never has the contrast between peace-keeping and peace-making struck me so forcibly.

I have come to be persuaded that the distinctively Christian contribution may not perhaps be at the moral level, let alone the technical. Most of what I have been saying so far could have been said by anyone, Christian or non-Christian. It has been concerned with the making and keeping of life human, and Christians claim to exclusive wisdom or prerogative in this, though I would hope they would respond to the *humanum* more deeply and broadly and unconditionally as a result of what they have seen in Christ and him crucified. Yet I believe they may have two distinctive – though not again exclusive – things to bring to the present situation, if they are true to the faith and the hope that is in them.

The first concerns what is involved in peace-*making*. The phrase is surprisingly rare even in the New Testament. In fact except in the beatitude 'Blessed are the peace-makers' it occurs only in one other context, where St Paul refers to God in Christ 'making peace by the blood of his cross'. That was the cost of the call to be God's son. And we should remember how the beatitude continues: 'How blest are the peace-makers, God shall call *them* his sons.' When Jesus said to his friends on his last night 'My peace I give to you, not as the world gives do I give you', he passed on this fearful call. For it is the fate of the peace-maker to be crucified, whether in word or in deed, as countless peace-makers of our generation, and not only Christians, have discovered, often at the hands of their own side. No one who is not ready for this need apply for the role.

Second, there is a perspective to the Christian life beyond even this. For the first time for two thousand years we live in a generation where many of the young do not expect to reach middle or old age. In fact, according to a BBC opinion poll taken in 1980 some fifty per cent believe the world will see a nuclear war by 1990. If so then my grandson born last year has but a half-chance of reaching the age of ten. But the first Christians too thought that they had but a short time to live, and they did not wring their hands or let it make them depressed or resigned. One of them wrote:

> Since the whole universe is to break up in this way, think what sort of people you ought to be. . . . That day will set the heavens ablaze until they fall apart, and will melt the elements in flames. But we have his promise and look forward to new heavens and a new earth, the home of justice.[7]

In fact the world did not end as the early Christians thought. And, pray God, that fifty per cent of the people in our poll will be wrong. Yet that now depends far more on us than it did on them; for we have it within our power to set in motion or to avert the ordeal which is to come upon the whole earth. But staring with clear eyes into the abyss delivered them from moral numbing. They had a hope, and it set them looking and working towards a new world which would be a 'home of justice', a world with its priorities right.

For the Christian, even the total annihilation of this planet is not the end of the world. And the perspective which this gives is vitally important, and vitally important to get right. For it might suggest that the Christian could regard this world as a write-off – and some indeed have drawn this conclusion. Yet, according to the New Testament, reflected classically in the second-century Epistle to Diognetus, the Christian style of life is marked by an extraordinary combination of detachment and concern. The Christian will care less for this world and at the same time care more for it than one who is not. He will not lose his heart to it, but he may well lose his life for it. Though difficult to define, this life-style is not I think difficult to recognize when authentically seen, even, or perhaps supremely, in so unpolitcized an example as Mother Teresa. And it manifests itself in that most distinctive conjunction of suffering and joy, of endurance and hope (very different from optimism, which is based on rosy prospects of which there are few around), and even of *hilaritas*.

How is one to come to terms with the fact that unless we in our generation solve the question of nuclear war there will be no other questions? Does one therefore allow oneself to think of nothing else, to become totally obsessed by it? I suggest not. For that is not only liable to become counterproductive ('he can talk of nothing else'). It is a neurotic reaction, making one part of the problem rather than of the solution. Rather it is because I am passionately keen to get on with the hundred and one other things – to write a book on the Fourth Gospel, to enjoy my grandchildren and our new home in the Yorkshire Dales in this still beautiful world – that I feel so concerned and committed.

That is the attachment. And the detachment can perhaps be caught in an answer Sister Rosalie Bertell gave to the question, 'But aren't you afraid what they can do to you?' 'Why should I be? There's nothing they can take. I haven't a job. I have no possessions.' Most of us cannot say that literally. But spiritually there is a freedom from this world which is the secret of freedom for it. And that is what the New Testament means by being 'risen with Christ'. It means walking with a lighter, less earth-bound step even in an unprecedentedly dark world.

The Church's Most Urgent Priority in Today's World

Given as the first annual McAndrew Memorial Lecture at Christ's Church Cathedral, Hamilton, Ontario, Canada, 3 October 1982

From time to time issues arise in the course of human history that confront the human race, and the church on behalf of the human race, with a magnitude that suddenly assumes overwhelming and urgent significance. It is a mysterious process, for they appear to come up like thunderstorms against the wind. Yet of course they do not come out of the blue. They have been there, gathering all the time, in fact for all recorded history. And they confront the church with implications of the gospel which again have been there all the time, accepted yet not really or fully faced. The triggers for these social shifts are usually equally mysterious. What is it that suddenly precipitates this particular issue to the fore at this moment? That is for the social historians —usually well in retrospect. But I want to speak as a theologian, which means as one who is concerned with prophecy, not in the popular sense of prediction, but in the biblical sense of discerning in the present the word of the Lord for today's scene.

To set things in perspective let me illustrate the process I have in mind from other relatively recent examples. For we can learn from them.

It so happens that the year 1982 is the two hundredth anniversary of the rise of the movement for the abolition of slavery. It was only ten years before that, in 1772, that Lord Mansfield had given the legal ruling that slavery could not exist in England. It took a further fifty years of campaigning before the act for the emancipation of all slaves in the British Colonies was finally passed in 1833, and another generation, and a bloody civil war, before slavery was abolished in the United States. Yet slavery had been part of the human scene since the dawn of history, and the recognition that 'in Christ' there could be 'neither slave nor free' since the first generation of the Christian church. Something happened to make it blow up then and for it to be the most urgent issue confronting Christians in their world.

In our century two other issues have followed in quick succession, and the gathering momentum of change means that neither is off the agenda before the next overtakes it. Racism and sexism complete the trio to remind us that in Christ, as St Paul also said, there can be neither Jew nor Gentile, male nor female. Yet for centuries we have been living with racism and sexism, in the world and in the church, often without even being aware of it (and that is particularly true until very recently of sexist language). Personal morality has happily co-existed with structural sin. It takes a long time for most people even in the church, perhaps particularly in the church, just to see that there is here an issue. And, looking back, we can see how we have all been unbelievably blind, both as individuals and still more as churches.

For in retrospect we can recognize that there is always a time-lag, between the first pioneers and pressure-groups and campaigns (whether of abolitionists, suffragettes, or liberationists) and the gradual and bitterly resisted absorption of these movements into the main stream of church leadership and church life. The decisive shift occurs only when the main body itself takes over and integrates into its system, usually slowly and often from the top downwards, policies which have hitherto represented a minority protest. One such moment in the Church of England, scarcely perceptible to the untrained eye, came in July 1982 when Graham Leonard, the Bishop of London, found himself as chairman of the Church's Board of Social Responsibility having to put to the General Synod a motion, which was passed (amid demurrers), for the total (if gradual) disinvestment of the Church of England in South Africa – in contrast with its previous policy of trying to use its investments as a lever for change. This may not sound very radical (or in itself be more than symbolic), yet it marked the watershed of a long campaign and even ten years ago would have seemed incredible as an official stance. Yet the campaign against apartheid and racial discrimination, thanks to the stature and the standing of its pioneers, like Trevor Huddleston and Ambrose Reeves, Martin Luther King and James Pike and now Desmond Tutu (all of whom were or are Anglicans except one), probably got absorbed into the mainstream of the church more quickly than most such movements (that against capital punishment is another contender). Yet the latest pastoral letter of the American Episcopalian Bishops, issued from the General Convention at New Orleans in the Fall of 1982, says that 'racism festers as unfinished business in the very house of God' – and certainly sexism does. The Church of England has yet to ordain or even receive its first woman priest and the Anglican Communion (or as far as I know any Christian communion) has yet to consecrate its first woman bishop. And, for all the theological smoke-screen, I cannot see how denying Holy Orders to an otherwise qualified person solely on grounds of sex is any different in principal from denying it solely on the grounds of colour or caste.

But I do not want to go on about these issues because I do not believe that any of them represents the church's most urgent priority in today's world – though they may have been even a few years back. For they have been overtaken by another which until recently we lived with in what already now seems astonishing complacency. And that is war.

War, like slavery and racism and sexism, has been ever with us and has been even more glaringly against the teaching not only of St Paul but of Jesus than the other three. Over the past fifty years successive Lambeth Conferences of the Anglican Communion have reiterated the statement with almost tedious regularity that 'war as a method of settling international disputes is incompatible with the teaching of our Lord Jesus Christ'. Indeed well before the Church of England declined officially to profit from apartheid, the Church Commissioners had a statutory ban on investments in armaments, drink and gambling.

Yet when it recently came to the crunch, and Britain did go to war to settle an international dispute arising out of the Argentinian occupation of the Falkland Islands, scarcely a voice of protest was raised from the official leadership of the churches (the Methodists and, as one would expect, the Quakers being honourable exceptions). The Bishop of London (and disappointingly Cardinal Hume) trotted out the old arguments for the 'just war', while the Archbishop of Canterbury took a long time to make, in the end, some rather good noises about what happens when the price of it becomes too high. But there arose no prophet prepared to be a troubler of Israel within the ranks of the establishment. When, *faute de mieux*, I found myself thrust upon the media, merely saying what Lambeth had said many times, I felt at first very isolated – until *all* the letters I got said with almost predictable regularity: 'Thank God someone has spoken up.' Now I have been as used as any to what Jim Pike used to call 'negative fan-mail', and its total absence on this occasion revealed to me an eerie vacuum. And the situation was made odder by the Pope, at the height of the Falklands campaign and amid the unrestrained jingoism of the popular press, receiving rapturous applause for saying that war was 'totally unacceptable as a means of settling differences between nations' and 'belonged to the tragic past', with 'no place on the agenda of the future'.

A similar schizophrenic situation obtains on the still more frightening front of nuclear warfare. The use of weapons of mass destruction, whether atomic, biological or chemical, has been utterly condemned by the Christian conscience in countless official state-ments of the church – from papal encyclicals downwards. Yet the threat to use them, which is utterly immoral if you mean it and dangerously foolish if you don't, underlies the entire policy of deterrence for keeping the peace with which the Christian churches have readily gone along. Deterrence means threatening, and meaning, to commit an act, either in deliberate first strike or, perhaps even worse, in blind retribution, which is irredeemably senseless and morally more obscene than anything Hitler thought up, the genocide not simply of one race but, for all we know, of all life on earth. To say that we must have these weapons to prevent their being used is absurd. There are better ways of doing that – like getting rid of them. No, we must have them, and ever increase them, in order, we are told, to protect our sovereignty or our freedoms, which is like protecting the privacy of one's room by threatening to blow up the whole house and everyone else's in sight. And this would rightly be deemed the thinking of a madman. Yet this is what we soberly commend to our children, through our votes and taxes, as the sole way to survival. No wonder they turn and protest.

Such weapons of mass destruction can never begin to meet a fundamental requirement of the 'just war', that of proportionality of response. Moreover there is wide agreement among any who think about it today that limited nuclear warfare could never pass this test either, since the possibility, not to say probability, of its escalating into the other is there from the beginning. Yet when I was in Germany recently talking to a thoroughly nice and intelligent chaplain to the British Army on the Rhine, he just took it for granted with everyone else that of course tactical nuclear weapons would have to be used, and used first by us. However, if I were even to raise this in a sermon or parish magazine where I live in the English countryside I should immediately be accused of 'talking politics' and listened to on little else. For merely to expose the basis on which the national consensus rests is deeply disturbing to church people. And if one takes part in a protest rally one is immediately aware of being in the alternative society: the main stream of the church, whether of leaders or led, is simply not there. One is out on a limb, not indeed as an individual (one is surrounded by tens of thousands) but as part of what has come to be labelled 'the peace movement'. For this is decidedly *not* the church, or vice versa. We are still here at the stage of campaigning against the main body, of both the nation and the church, of trying to get the majority of one's fellow countrymen or fellow Christians even to see the issue. Yet things are moving. The American Bishops in the letter I referred to went on to give a much more outspoken lead than anything I have yet heard in England. And a report due out shortly from a working party of the Church of England's Board for Social Responsibility[1] is calling for the unilateral renunciation at the very least of Britain's, literally incredible, independent nuclear deterrent – though the hasty disavowals prompted by its premature leakage to the press do not suggest that it will receive universal acclaim!

The question that concerns me is how and by what tactics one gets through to the rank and file of the main body, and not just to individuals and pressure-groups, that this is the most pressing priority for the church in today's world – while there is yet time. For this is by far the most *urgent* issue of any of those that I have mentioned. If we do not solve this issue, then there will literally *be* no other. Yet until very recently we have learned to live with the bomb, if not to love it, over more than a generation. We have adapted ourselves as a species, as Jonathan Schell puts it in his sobering book *The Fate of the Earth*,[2] reprinted from *The New Yorker*, to live with 'two souls', one for responding to the nuclear predicament, the other for getting on with life in its dailiness. And I confess that I have been as blind, or as numbed, as any. Even in my latest book, *The Roots of a Radical*, which was specifically concerned with the many frontiers of the church with the world, I realized that I had scarcely mentioned the issue of nuclear warfare, or indeed of war as such – till I added a hasty epilogue. For we lived through the 1960s and 1970s (the decades that concerned me in the book) with so many other issues that, by one of those mysterious processes I referred to at the beginning, that of peace, and our very survival as a planet, caught up on most of us unprepared. The pioneers of the 1950s had done their best to alert us – read for instance what Thomas Merton was saying twenty-five years ago – yet mysteriously the stream went underground for two decades. I have lately been trying to make up for lost time, though one has the uncanny sense of both preaching to the converted and talking in the wilderness at the same time.

But let me give you a picture – for most of us find it easier to think in pictures – which first came to me when I was listening in Cambridge to a Canadian, that very remarkable, because very unremarkable, nun, Dr Rosalie Bertell, who lives in Toronto. She has shown what one individual can do by sheer scientific and political foot-slogging to bring home the great danger we are in from the so-called 'safe' levels of radiation from working in and living around nuclear installations, even when nothing goes wrong. She was in charge of the so-called Tri-state project in the mid-West (the largest leukaemia study ever commissioned) and has recently finished a report for the West German government. Her research has led her to the conclusion that the exposure to 1 rem (the amount of radiation one receives from a heavy abdominal or spinal X-ray) is equivalent to one year of aging (not that we shall necessarily die sooner; we simply age earlier). But here I merely want to pass on one analogy she used. We often hear talk of our planet suffering from a terminal illness. Yet cancer is hardly the right analogy, except for what of it is self-induced – and that is rising the whole time. It is more like, she said, living with a drug-addict or alcoholic in the family. The strain begins to tell on everyone, till one reaches the point where one cannot cover up or carry on without the whole home disintegrating. And that is the effect of the arms race on the entire family of mankind. The drain is utterly debilitating. We have simply got to reach the point of saying, 'This is no way to live'.

A second picture I would give you is this. Two years ago I sold my house to a pilot of Laker Air Lines. Not long before the airlines' sad demise I was on one of its flights from London to Los Angeles, when I received a call from the flight-deck to meet the captain, who was a friend of his. I had never been in the cockpit of a jumbo jet before and I found it fascinating and not a little overwhelming. But what struck me most was that I could just walk in. 'Can anyone do this?' I said. 'Yes.' 'But what about hi-jackers?' 'Oh, we let them in and we give them this card.' On it were the answers in every likely language to any question a hi-jacker could be expected to ask. 'The only way with them,' he said, 'is to go along with them.' The sole alternative, adopted by El Al, the Israeli airline, was to have an armed guard on every plane. But the pilots' union would have none of it. It was simply too dangerous to risk a shooting-match in mid air. For one hole in the skin of the aircraft could bring down the pressure, if not the plane. That doesn't mean that you give in to them, or that no force would ever be used. In fact everything depends on a strict code of procedure for talking them down and keeping them talking, and on an agreement that no signatory country will offer them sanctuary. By this means the scourge of hi-jacking has in fact been considerably mitigated and the threshold of violence, till they start shooting their hostages, greatly lowered. The same applies to sieges by international terrorists, where the London police, for instance, have by non-violent means, except as a very last resort, built up a well-tried technique and an impressive record of success. (Contrast again the Israeli shoot-out at the Munich Olympics.)

I want to suggest that we are fast approaching the point at which on space-ship earth we find ourselves in the situation of that cabin when it is simply becoming too dangerous to start shooting. This is not because nations or groups show any sign of renouncing violence (very far from it) but because we cannot allow things to go on like this without mutual destruction. Until the day before yesterday the first thing you did in any international incident was to 'show the flag' or 'send in the marines'. And Britain did that at Suez, with disastrous results, and in the Falklands, with seeming success. The first instinctive response of Parliament was again to dispatch a 'task-force'. Of course, we were assured, it wasn't meant to be used (any more than 'the deterrent'). It was there to step up the pressure for a 'diplomatic solution'; but it soon became inevitable that it would be used, and used quickly. For you couldn't have it bobbing around the South Atlantic all winter. So Mrs Thatcher won her war and a lot of (temporary) votes and 'liberated' the one thousand eight hundred Falkland Islanders (at a cost of many more casualties on both sides). But for what? We are as far away as ever from winning the peace; in fact a good deal further. For except in close co-operation with Argentina there is simply no viable future for the Islands. Meanwhile the economic and political strains, between north and south, east and west, have been exacerbated and the only real beneficiaries are the manufacturers of Exocet missiles and the rest whose order-books are bulging. A great opportunity was lost of showing the world a better way. As Kenneth Greet, the Secretary of the Methodist Conference in Britain, said at its summer meeting, 'When the task-force sailed to the Falklands the clock was turned back fifty years.'

And this was just a 'little war', a supposedly containable 'just war' of the old sort. What the full implications will be of the other war launched when people's backs were turned (like Russia's Hungarian adventure at the time of Suez) is still too early to assess, though it already looks likely to bring far more wrath than peace. For Israel's invasion of the Lebanon is a classic instance of their same approach in the air. It started, you remember, as a preventive strike merely to clear terrorists from sniping range of Northern Galilee. 'Israel does not covet one single square inch of Lebanese soil,' said Begin on the first day of the invasion, and he probably meant it. But equally Levi Eshkol proclaimed on the opening day of the Six Day War, 'Israel has no intention of annexing even one foot of Arab territory.' And when one recalls the destablization of the entire world economy that has resulted from the Yom Kippur War (which of course Israel did not start – though those who live by the sword die by the sword), then it brings home the utter unrealism of even a conventional 'just war' in the twentieth century. The theory of that was that you could calculate a proportional, containable expenditure of force. But today there is simply no telling where the shooting will lead once it starts, and tomorrow when countries like Argentina and Brazil, not to mention those in the Middle East, have nuclear weapons, the danger to the cabin will become completely critical. It will be no use, like the nurse in *Mr Midshipman Easy* excusing her illegitimate baby , saying 'If you please, ma'am, it was a very little one' (perhaps it was symbolic that the Hiroshima bomb was nick-named 'Little Boy').

For once nuclear war starts, then beyond the first few exchanges it will be almost literally unstoppable. What is known in the jargon as C^3, the systems of Command, Control and Communications, are inherently more vulnerable than the weapons themselves. Quite apart from the effect of blast on fragile antennae, which have to be exposed in order to function, the radiation released by nuclear explosions, particularly the so-called EMP (electro-magnetic pulse), will cause widespread communications black-outs. A recent study from the International Institute for Strategic Studies in London, with the title *Can Nuclear War be Controlled?*, by Desmond Ball,[3] clearly points to the answer, No.

It is likely that beyond some relatively early stage in the conflict the strategic communications systems would suffer interference and disruption, the strikes would become ragged, unco-ordinated, less precise and discriminating, and the ability to reach an agreed settlement between the adversaries would soon become extremely problematical. There would be no way of halting, to one's own or the other side. The 'hot line' and everything else would be out of action.

If we are to stop the drift to holocaust, it has to be a great deal earlier. We have got to draw the line not merely below nuclear war, but now, I believe, below war. We must say, with the Pope, quite literally, that 'war has no place on the agenda for the future'. It is simply not one of the options open. That, of course, is easy to say. How do we learn to say it in a way that might persuade the world to take it seriously – and the church, the mainstream church as a whole and not just a minority within it, to back it loud and clear?

Let me give you first an example of how it has been done, of how a calamitous war has been stopped in its tracks by people of sufficient clout saying 'This is just not on'. The Suez folly was called off because the United States simply pulled the rug from under Eden and the British government. By intense diplomatic pressure and dire economic and financial threats, aided and abetted by a deeply divided opinion at home, the thing had to be called off and Eden had to go. If Reagan (abetted by the EEC) had been prepared to say the same thing to Galtieri and Thatcher and Begin, threatening instant and total cut-off of arms, trade and aid, something of the same might have happened. But of course these leaders are all birds of a feather and themselves believe in what I called the El Al solution. In any case this is the crudest possible peace-keeping mechanism and merely reinforces the philosophy of the big stick, even though, being made of wood, it is a great deal preferable to most else. And, let's face it, under any alternative at present available Galtieri would probably have 'got away' with his grab of the Falklands. That after all is how Britain acquired them in the first place; and they were and will continue to be geographically indefensible except at a cost Britain was not and in the future will not be prepared to pay. The real concern was, and must continue to be, not what piece of bunting flutters over these desolate moors (for as Schell says, sovereignty and war are two sides of the same obsolete coin), but the security and freedoms of the islanders. And for those who do not wish to stay under any other conditions than those they have known facilities for resettlement (willingly offered by New Zealand) would even at a million pounds a head for every man, woman and child, have been vastly cheaper than what we have had to pay in materials, let alone in lives.

But my point is that we must work for new structures to put in the place of the present ones, corresponding to those to which governments have been compelled by hi-jacking, when once it is recognized that you can't any longer start by shooting it out. It will be a long haul. But that same Methodist Conference in Britain surely gave a right lead by calling for a new level of commitment by the government 'to the search for other ways than the use of force to maintain international law and security'. The fact that the government shows no sign of listening – it is simply concerned with replacing the losses, to have more of the same, though with some pretty sober modifications – is no reason for giving up saying it. Rather I believe the churches, of all denominations and all nations, have to go on saying it, in season and out, as churches, together of course with masses outside their ranks, until governments are forced by their voices and even more by their votes to take notice.

How is this to happen? I believe there are several conditions. First, the base on which we take our stand has to be sufficiently broad not to allow pacifists and non-pacifists, unilateralists and multilateralists, to be divided and played off against each other by those who don't want any change. There are of course deep and genuine differences here; but the two witnesses in their manifold varieties must be seen as complementary, not as antithetical. In the time available you will never unite the main-line churches, whether at the level of the leaders or the led, behind a purely pacifist or unilateralist banner. That would condemn the churches to an indefinite future of minority protest. Each side must recognize and respect the role that the other has to play.

A second condition I would see of united and effective action is that there has got to be advocacy of an alternative defence policy. It is no use just talking of disarmament, and especially of unilateral disarmament (however necessary the latter is, in my judgment, to break the log-jam). For the effect will appear purely negative – that you are asking people to be stripped naked and defenceless. And this they will interpret as giving in to the hi-jacker or the aggressor and his blackmail, which experience rightly tells them only makes matters worse. And the powers that be will bounce them into huddling behind the bomb because they are persuaded that, to use Mrs Thatcher's refrain, 'There is No Alternative' (though if they actually had the bomb in their house they would run a mile – not that that would do them any good). The same applies to the 'necessity' for nuclear power to close the energy gap. In fact it has been shown that there are entirely credible alternatives, while nuclear power is beginning to look like an increasingly expensive and dangerous white elephant (which is why *no* new orders for nuclear power-stations have been placed in the United States since Three Mile Island, and several constructions abandoned at enormous cost).

One of the facts about the current situation, particularly in Britain, but in the West generally, is that we have a literally incredible defence policy, one that if it came to the crunch we could not implement without suicide, whether at the battlefield tactical level or at the intermediate and intercontinental strategic level. For at the former we cannot say that we will not use nuclear weapons first, because of our conventional inferiority; while at the latter the new counter-force rather than counter-city strategy, with the pin-point accuracy of missiles like cruise and Trident, makes sense only on a first strike, since there is no point in hitting empty silos. The whole policy of deterrence, based on 'mutually assured destruction' (suitably acronymed MAD), as a credible, stable and desirable condition is fast crumbling. And our leaders are not coming clean about this.

We must, I believe, put our efforts into replacing it with two things. First, positively and most importantly, a programme for what the Palme Commission Report (the successor of the Brandt Report) calls *Common Security*, such as has long existed between Canada and the United States and more remarkably since the Second World War between France and Germany (the major victory of the EEC). Similarly Western Europe and the Soviet Union are coming to be seen to have important common interests, notably in the gas pipe-line, which makes nonsense of the purely adversarial postures imposed by the doctrine of deterrence. That is why it is anathema to Mr Reagan. On this adversarial posture the best comment I heard comes from one of his most distinguished and intelligent compatriots, Mr George Kennan, their former Ambassador in Moscow:

> This tendency to view all aspects of the relationship in terms of a supposed total and irreconcilable conflict of concern and aims: these are not the marks of the maturity and discrimination one expects of the diplomacy of a great power; they are the marks of an intellectual primitivism and naiveté unpardonable in a great government. I use the word naiveté, because there is a naiveté of cynicism and suspicion just as there is a naiveté of innocence.[4]

Rather, as the Palme Report says,

> So long as (the nations) insist on trying to protect national interests unilaterally, behaving as if security can be gained at the expense of others, they will fail. The well-worn path of military competition is a blind alley; it cannot lead to peace and security.[5]

But, secondly, we must for the foreseeable future build up genuinely defensive, as opposed to merely deterrent, strategies which we could actually use, a better shield rather than a bigger sword. Thus modern weapons technology has made possible light, dispersible, highly mobile heat-homing anti-tank missiles of deadly accuracy which could inflict massive damage on an invader without posing any offensive threat. As Field Marshal Lord Carver has said, and as former Chief of the British Defence Staff he ought to know:

> For the shorter ranges, manportable weapons, capable of penetrating the thickest armour, can now be made available in quantity. They are not cheap, nothing is cheap, but they are very good value for money, and the operator does not need complicated and expensive training.[6]

Such weapons could not deter a nuclear first strike (which the Warsaw Pact, unlike NATO, has repeatedly forsworn). But they could, amid other measures, make an invading army think many times. There is a vast amount of work to be done here, at many levels, including serious training in non-violent resistance. That is why, unlike governments, which suspect and starve them, I believe we should back to the full such efforts as the Alternative Defence Commission set up in England by the School of Peace Studies at Bradford University (which even has a bishop on it) and similar thinking by the Max Planck Institute on the continent, exploring the so-called Ahfeldt strategy. For, let's face it, there has to be for most people, who will not be absolute pacifists, some equivalent to the final resort to limited and disciplined force which is required if and when the gunmen start killing their hostages. But until then there are many things to be learned, prepared and practised.

But finally, if there is to be a united and credible word from the church to this situation, as to the others from which I began, it must be distinctively Christian. There is an entirely proper place for what my friend Professor Rustum Roy of Penn State University, a distinguished scientist and lay theologian, calls an 'appropriate fear'; and unless we can bring people to this point of awareness we may not get them much further. That is the function of such apocalyptic warnings as *The Fate of the Earth*, which I would urge you to read if you need to be awakened from your dogmatic slumbers. Yet fear is a bad master and can lead to horrific consequences, as in a feature film recently shown by BBC television on 'the Survivalists' in the United States, where the last state was an utterly ruthless armed selfishness – all in the name of 'Jesus'.

We must preach the 'full gospel', which is not a gospel of fear. And that means, again, a number of things which I can only indicate here. It means, for those of us who can (and that includes any intelligent laity, such as we all are in this field), that we must do some hard and searching theological thinking. That has been hard to come by on this issue. There has been very little – in contrast for instance with the quantity, if not quality, of black theology and women's theology evoked by the challenges of racism and sexism. But I can recommend one book, by an American pupil of mine, which I believe cuts pretty deep and should stretch the church quite a bit, and that is by Jim Garrison, *The Darkness of God: Theology after Hiroshima*.[7] What, he asks, has the fact that *we* can now set off the doom that is to come upon all the earth done to our traditional thinking about *God* and all that the Bible knows as apocalyptic? He invites us to look into the darkness and to see in it the shadow-side of God, and in the rift in human history that Hiroshima has opened up, a window for our day into the searing but saving revelation of the crucifixion not only of humanity but of God. It is deep and dangerous stuff, and many may not be able to receive it.

But without an adequate theology of some sort we shall never be able to be peace-makers, not as the world knows peace but as Christ gives it. The world understands peace-keeping, even if, as the

Lebanon shows, it is pathetically inadequate at it. That is what UN forces exist to do, by keeping the combatants apart. But peace-making is concerned with bringing them together, by removing the enmity that stands between them. And that is an altogether more difficult and costly task. 'Blessed are the peace-makers.' Nothing could be more central to the distinctive gospel of Jesus or to the task of the church. And I find myself convicted that I only preached on that text for the first time last year. Yet it is also a surprisingly rare text. In fact there is only one other use of this Greek word *eirenepoio* in the rest of the New Testament, and that is where St Paul speaks (in Col. 1.20) of God 'making peace' through 'the blood of his Son'. And remember how the beatitude goes on: 'Blessed are the peace-makers: for they shall be called sons of God' (Matt. 5.9). That is the meaning and the price of sonship. And no one who is not prepared for that price need apply, as many of the peace-makers of our generation, Christian and non-Christian, have discovered, often at the hands of their own sides. The commitment of the church, the whole church, and not just of a 'peace movement' within it, to that gospel must search, and I am convinced may quicken it, more than any other in our day.

But let it again be the full gospel, not a 'single-issue' gospel, even this issue. For there is great danger, not only that we shall not be fired, but that having caught alight, we shall be fired by nothing else. And that can be disastrously counter-productive. We all know the people, the 'eco-freaks' and the 'nuke-niks', who can talk about nothing else – and they turn us off. This is the easiest issue in the world on which to become obsessive. Indeed, when the penny really does drop that if we do not solve this issue there will be no other, then it is difficult not to feel that nothing else is worth while. But it is precisely because I am passionately concerned for many other things that I know that I must give to this issue the most pressing priority. But not the only priority. It is not easy to get the perspective right. To focus the gospel on this issue may well be what the Spirit is saying to the churches in our day. To narrow it down to this issue is a neurotic reaction, making us more part of the problem than of the solution.

So let me end by a call not so much to lower our eyes as to raise our sights. I have a dream, as Martin Luther King might have put it, a dream of a mighty new initiative, which I hope could be led by the Pope himself, since on this he has already shown the gifts of a universal pastor not only to the church but to the world. But I trust he would be joined by the Ecumenical Patriarch and the Archbishop of Canterbury and the World Council of Churches and Billy Graham (who I know, unlike so many right-wing evangelicals, to their shame, is deeply concerned about this) and any one else you care to mention, together with the Dalai Lama, the Chief Rabbi and other leaders of world faiths (for this is certainly not an exclusively Christian concern). And I would hope there might be a summit (for you have to do these things these days if you are to have any chance of speaking, as the Gospels say Jesus did, to 'all the people'); a summit which would be not so much like a Vatican III as what my friend Murray Rogers, a great, because small-scale, peace-maker (first in India, then in Israel and now in Hong Kong) calls a Jerusalem II. The first Council of Jerusalem recorded in Acts 15 marked the break-out of the gospel from the shell of Judaism. The second, he believes, must see its break-out from the shell of Christianity as one religion among many. The preaching of peace, to them that are far off and to them that are nigh, and the abolition of war from all the earth, could be the one issue big enough, and urgent enough, not merely to requicken the church and its unity, but to take it out of itself to become the instrument of that universal vision glimpsed by the prophet, without which the peoples perish, where

> The wolf shall dwell with the lamb . . . and a little child shall lead them. . . . They shall not hurt or destroy in all my holy mountain; for the earth shall be full of the knowledge of the Lord as the waters cover the sea (Isa. 11.6–9).

Amen. So be it, Lord, beginning with me.

A Christian Response to the Energy Crisis

'Keynote address' to a conference on 'The Christian Dimensions of the Energy Problem', organized by the Roman Catholic Commission for International Justice and Peace at Brunel University, 23 April 1982.

Let me start with a text. It comes from Psalm 62.11: 'God spake once, and twice have I also heard the same, that power belongeth unto God.' Let me try to apply that to the form of power with which we are concerned: energy. And if it is not to be purely pious, it is necessary to unpack it a bit. As I see it, the text says at least two things.

The first is positive, that power, which is a function of matter, as everything from burning wood to releasing atomic energy brings out, is part of what God made, and 'Behold, it was very good.' The denial of the goodness of matter is Manicheanism, not Christianity. If Christians are wary, say, of atomic power, it is not because it is diabolic. The Book of Wisdom is quite clear on this: 'The creative forces of the world make for life; there is no deadly poison in them. Death is not king of earth . . . but godless men by their words and deeds have asked death for his company' (1.14f.). Science *per se* is also good, the expression of wisdom: 'He himself gave me true understanding of things as they are: a knowledge of the structure of a world and the operation of the elements.' And so the writer goes through the different fields of knowledge, and ends: 'I was taught by her whose skill made all things, wisdom' (7.17–22).

We may contrast the Prometheus myth of classical paganism, where fire is stolen from the gods and provokes their jealousy. In the Genesis myth what is condemned is the taking not of power but of the knowledge of good and evil into one's own hands, so as to become as gods, determining the moral values for oneself and running the show for one's own benefit.

This leads to the second and negative point, that if power belongs to God, it does not belong to us. It is not ours to own or dispose of. We are responsible to and responsible for it. This is the familiar role of stewardship, of man as the priest of nature. Man is given dominion over nature, yet this dominion is not absolute. The trouble is that, despite Genesis, which insists that the image of God is both masculine and feminine, the dominion has been interpreted in terms of a male chauvinist image both of God and of man. Man has raped the earth, and this generation has used up more non-renewable energy sources than all the others put together in the history of our planet. And having raped the earth, man is now preparing to rape sea and space.

A heavy bias is therefore now required in the opposite direction, from 'hard' to 'soft' energy policies. But we must be clear why. This is not because God made the countryside, and man made the town. God made all – not least the atom – and the pattern of the countryside is in fact almost entirely man-made. It is because, as the Book of Wisdom says, 'godless (or merely selfish) men by their words and deeds (and by their silent acquiescence) have asked death for their company'. It is because the use to which these beneficent powers have been put threatens death to the biosphere. As in the warning of Deuteronomy, 'If you are not careful to do all his commandments and statutes', then, among many other curses, 'the Lord will make the rain of your land powder and dust; from heaven it shall come down upon you until you are destroyed' (28.24). Indeed I would urge you to read the whole of that chapter, which is one of the longest in the Bible. It is not pleasant reading, and gives a grim picture of the final death-struggles of the family of man: 'The pampered, delicate man will not share with his brother, or the wife of his bosom, or his own remaining children, any of the meat which he is eating, the flesh of his own children. He is left with nothing else because of the dire straits to which he will be reduced' (28.54f.). Or take this for a profile of a devastated planet: 'Your life will hang continually in suspense, fear will beset you night and day, and you will find no security all your life long. Every morning you will say, "Would God it were evening!" – and every evening, "Would God it were morning!", for the fear that lives in your heart and the sights that you see' (28.65–67). If we do not get the balance of the eco-system right, then the

Bible, long before the atomic age, has no illusions about our power to destroy life on earth as we know it.

It is not (thank God) up to me to produce the formula for that balance – and it is incredibly delicate. But in case we should suppose that it is just a question of being 'even-handed' and pursuing a course of benevolent neutrality (and coincidentally leaving ourselves among the 'delicate and pampered'), let me say something of what I believe to be the in-built biases of the gospel.

The Christian way is not, as the Irishman described it, 'treading the narrow path between good and evil'. It is not being neutral between justice and injustice. And that means it is not being neutral between rich and poor, the power-ful and the power-less. There is a built-in bias in favour of the have-nots, as the Magnificat inescapably reminds us. This is not because material possessions are evil, any more than matter is evil, but because they have an unrivalled capacity to enslave and blind, and make it unbelievably hard for a rich man, or class, or nation, or group of nations, to enter the kingdom of Heaven. For no one doubts that it will be 'the delicate and pampered' who will be the last to share or to cede the energy resources of the planet.

The Christian dimension of the energy problem must begin there, with the re-evaluation of all power which Jesus introduced. You know, he said, that in the world power means one thing – lordship, sovereignty, getting and keeping control. 'But it shall not be so among you.'

That is the first bias that should come out of any distinctively Christian contribution to the equation; the bias in favour of the powerless, either because they have no natural resources or economic clout, or because they have not yet been born and will arrive to find the good earth already ravished. That may sound easy and pious to state, but try to introduce such a bias, or positive discrimination, say, into the Law of the Sea Treaty, so as to preserve the wealth still lying at the bottom of the oceans, which the UN has declared 'the common heritage of mankind', and you will find that it is even at this moment in grave danger of being stymied by the interests of international capitalism championed by the Reagan administration and abetted by Mrs Thatcher's. I am cynical enough, too, to disbelieve the argument for the West going nuclear in order to release the diminishing petro-chemical supplies for the rest of the world. Quite apart from whether nuclear energy, which only produces electricity, can in the short term (that is before the oil runs out) be a substitute for more than a small proportion of our really urgent needs for transport and space-heating, I believe that the scarce resources will in fact go irresistibly to the highest bidder. The only policy that will preserve these fuels for anyone is a drastic programme, led by the energy-guzzlers, to cut out inefficiency and waste, invest more in renewable resources and in the meantime rely more heavily on coal.

This brings me to what I believe to be the second bias of the gospel, not only in favour of the poor and power-less, but for conservation against consumption. This again is easy to say. But it makes a good deal of difference whether we start by asking what are our needs and what new supplies of energy are required to meet them (and our electricity targets have consistently been inflated) or whether we start by asking how we may reduce our requirements to match our resources. *Pleonexia*, constantly wanting more, *alias* 'growth', is one of the major New Testament sins. This does not mean that we should not be concerned that others should have more who have little or nothing. But so far our efforts to cut energy needs by putting research into redesigning wasteful machinery has been minimal compared with, say, the £2500 million for research and development on thermal reactors alone, whose contribution so far has amounted to supplying at most twelve per cent of our electricity or four per cent of all our useful energy (and many estimates are lower). A figure that has always stuck in my mind is that the same money put into conservation could save three times the energy that will ever be produced by a nuclear power-plant in its lifetime. But even supposing that figure was out by a multiple of three and the cost-effectiveness was exactly equal, I am still convinced that we should go for saving rather than generating (by whatever means). Yet, to take an example that any layman can understand, instead of guaranteeing, say, a ninety per cent subsidy for roof-insulation to required standards, this government has actually halved the subsidy to twenty-five per cent and abolished it altogether for council houses, despite the fact that it would soak up unemployment far more than any form of power-generation. Of course I am not naive enough to suggest that the energy-gap can be bridged by such programmes, or from renewable sources, alone. But I am saying that we ought to be pressing as hard as we can in the opposite direction to that in which the government is trying to lead us.

'Waste not, want not' is not just a Victorian moral platitude. It is a directive of the gospel. And I believe it makes surprising social and economic sense. Gerald Leach's *Low Energy Strategy for the United Kingdom*,[1] which claims to demonstrate 'systematically, and in detail, how the UK could have fifty years of prosperous material growth and yet use less primary energy than it does today' and the comparable American volume from the Harvard Business School, *Energy Future*, which argues that the US could use thirty to forty per cent less energy than it does 'with virtually no penalty for the way Americans live' may be overstated and at points vulnerable. But at least they have given the layman a conviction that there is an alternative and have delivered many of us from the stalking spectre of TINA ('There is no alternative'), with which 'they' are always trying to frighten us, whether in defence or economic strategy or energy planning.

Thirdly, I would say there was a bias of the gospel in favour wherever possible of decentralization, to bring things down to the human scale, to allow it to become visible that technology is for man, not man for technology. To me one of the hazards of any form of nuclear-powered society (and it would apply just as much to the more beneficent energy of fusion rather than fission, if and when we get there) is that it increases rather than decreases the tendency towards a highly centralized and highly vulnerable technology. In fact Aldous Huxley warned us as long ago as 1946: 'All countries embarking on a nuclear power programme will have to be totalitarian.' Or, in the words of a Bangalore physicist, 'Technology is like genetic material: it carries with it the code of that society.' The switches will need to be in the hands of an ever-smaller and more highly-guarded élite. To propound this as the path to self-sufficiency for the Third World, which above all requires labour- rather than capital-intensive programmes, would seem to me seriously irresponsible.

And all this is quite apart from the hazards to human survival. I cannot see how one can any longer blind oneself to the integral and inescapable (even if not necessary) connection between nuclear power and nuclear warfare, which to the layman looks as obvious as that between smoking and cancer. For what do oil-rich countries like Iraq and Iran want with nuclear power for their energy needs? And what is the real interest of Pakistan or Israel or South Africa or Argentina? And why is the United States wanting massive imports of plutonium, and why is Britain supplying it even if (so we are assured) it is not directly for weapons, and that at a time when (indeed because) the American civil programme is grinding expensively to a halt. No new nuclear plants have been ordered since Harrisburg and several cancelled at enormous cost. One more such near-miss, or one raid on a plant that, unlike the Iraqis', was already radio-active, would, I should have thought, be enough to make it politically impossible in any democratic country for the programme to continue – and where is your energy then? And all this is independent of how we are going to decommission these plants at the end of their working life or where we are to dispose of the waste – a problem which the Flowers Commission insisted *must* be solved first and has in fact been shelved. To a layman like myself it has come to look as if the nuclear lobby is losing the argument, even if with its massive investment and government backing it may still so far be winning the power-struggle.

But, and this brings me to my last point, I believe that discerning the signs of the times is an important part of watching for the kingdom of God. For the finger of God in history keeps moving on. No one who is not a prophet would claim to read the writing on the wall – and if he is a true prophet he will always confess that he may be mistaken. But I venture to think that there is a pattern in events, and that it is becoming more and more clear that, as I have argued at greater length elsewhere, we are living at the transition between what Alvin Toffler calls the second and the third waves in human history. The first was the agricultural; the second, which has lasted for the past four hundred years, the industrial; and the third, for want yet of a better name, the post-industrial, in which the sheer need for moving great masses of matter about, including ourselves to shop and work, may be appreciably less. Though more things may be electronic, the actual consumption of electricity could be no greater. It is of course a good deal easier to see second-wave characteristics and second-wave characters (of whom there are plenty in control of our priorities at the moment) than it is to discern precisely where things are going. Nor am I saying that any one wave with its presuppositions is nearer to the gospel than any other (though there are still some in the church who think the first wave was really the age of faith). But one Christian dimension of the energy problem is surely the spirit of prophecy, and we have to be open to the fact that what at present appear to be the big battalions may not have the future with them.

7

Religion in the Third Wave: The Difference in Being a Christian Tomorrow

Prepared for a Festschrift of honour Lloyd Geering,
Professor of Religious Studies at Victoria University of Wellington,
New Zealand.

Ten years ago I wrote a book with the deliberately ambiguous title, *The Difference in Being a Christian Today*. It was meant to cover both the difference in being a Christian rather than not and the difference in being a Christian today rather than yesterday – and the relationship between the two. Now I should like to look at the same correlation with regard to tomorrow.

It is perhaps significant that my first quotation ten years ago came from Donald Schon's *Beyond the Stable State*,[1] which he had recently given as a highly stimulating and provocative series of Reith Lectures on the BBC, describing how everything was gloriously cracking up, and the last from one by another American sociologist, Alvin Toffler, whose *Future Shock*[2] had just been published. The mood was the break-up of the old and the threat of the new. In a nasty word for a nasty thing, which we have got used to in the interval, it was a destabilizing situation, politically, culturally and spiritually. It is no wonder that the reaction of the 1970s was a strong yank of the tiller to starboard.

Then, a decade later, Alvin Toffler produced another book, *The Third Wave*,[3] which may in time prove equally symptomatic and perhaps prophetic. It clarifies the emerging pattern in what I think is a deeply *hopeful* way – which is neither the same as optimistic or utopian. It faces the future without shock because it detects a pattern that can perhaps help us to see where we are going. In all the bewilderment of the present confusion (and that remains on pretty well every front from the economic to the spiritual) it may help us to discern and detect what in it represents the death of the old, however seemingly big and powerful, and what the birth of a new future, however small and seminal. Above all it can allow us to recognize what – and who – in the present is reactionary and reversionary, clinging to the old assumptions and trying often desperately to keep them going, even though at the moment they are in possession and appear to represent the forces of stability and security. Discerning the pattern and direction of change we may be liberated to recognize the otherwise often bewildering and threatening shifts for what they are and to see what is detachable that looks so essential, in religion as in everything else. Otherwise the temptation will be to hold on to everything, in a spirit of fear and not freedom.

Operating on a large canvas with bold sweeps, Toffler detects three waves in the story of the human scene to date. The first is the agricultural, the second (which has only lasted for some three hundred years) the industrial, and the third, which is now upon us and is perhaps too new even to name, the post-industrial. It will not mark a return to what went before, yet it will be characterized by the end of most of the existing assumptions that have consciously and unconsciously shaped our priorities and judgments. It is producing and calling for a 'new man', which is neither the noble savage nor some projection of science fiction. In fact it is a good deal nearer what Ronald Gregor Smith depicted in his prophetic book of that very title, *The New Man*,[4] as long ago as 1956, in delineating the then still unfamiliar thought of Dietrich Bonhoeffer. Toffler himself does not pursue the analysis at any depth beyond the spheres of the economic and political, the psychological and the social (though that is a large enough canvas in all conscience). But he recognizes the implications for the 'whole man', and there are plenty of references to religion, though nothing very much more profound than allusions to 'a host of new religions' which he predicts. But he puts his finger clearly enough on the forces of reversion in the present religious scene. What he leaves to be explored is the pattern of tomorrow's spirituality and, to cite the title of an article by Charles Davis to which I shall return, 'our new religious identity'. What will mark the difference in being a Christian – or of having any distinctive faith – in 'the third wave'? On that he is not much help.

But what he does help us to do is to identify the forms and structures of religion, and of Christianity in particular, in relation to the three waves. So, taking off from hints he throws out, let me first indicate briefly the ways in which the pattern we have inherited, which to many seems so fixed and 'given', not least in religion, has been conditioned and shaped by the two 'waves' that have so far passed over us.

The first can for our present purpose (which is analysing the transition to the third) be noted very summarily, even though the pattern we have grown up with is even now more deeply affected by its forces (and particularly in so conservative an area of life as religion) than by the more dramatic impact of the second – if only because it was around so much longer. For this first, agricultural, wave goes back to the supersession of Cain, the nomadic huntsman, by Abel, the settled tiller of the soil. The 'acceptance' of the latter's sacrifice, in preference to the former's, marks symbolically the sanctification of the land by religion and its age-old link with the natural cycle of the agricultural year. It is epitomized within the Christian tradition by what Gregory Dix called 'the sanctification of time' in the church's calendar and the sanctification of place in the parochial system, which reaches back in England to Theodore of Tarsus in the seventh century, well before Britain became a single kingdom. It set a premium on 'the stable state' and in its mediaeval hey-day the virtues it extolled were the 'dependent' ones of poverty, chastity and obedience. Its glories were the cathedrals and monasteries of the land and the parish church within walking distance of every villager. The priest was priest to the whole parish (not just to the congregation) and to the whole man. It was a unified and unifying vision, which has proved astonishingly enduring. It is still what dominates the pattern of English landscape, and the structure of church government from its parishes and rural deaneries (observe still the name!), with dioceses and provinces, remains residentially based, and has not seriously changed in a thousand years. But, as does not require to be spelt out, it is obviously under massive strains and threats of irrelevance, not least in the inner city – if only because people do not live where they live: they largely just sleep where they live, and go home to subside and relax – or did until recently in the factory/office dominated situation. But it meant and has meant that religion became confined to this private sphere of their lives. Yet the values and assumptions of the first wave are not simply false: in fact they are likely to show every bit as much perdurance into the future as those of the second wave, and many have been seized on by the 'green' revolution. But they are just not enough, and no amount of nostalgia for the 'old-time religion' (mostly Victorian and 'second-wave') can bring them back or serve us for the future.

The second wave was born, spiritually speaking, with the Renaissance and Reformation. And we can now see that Protestantism and the Counter-Reformation had more in common than in what they fought over. The second wave was marked by the rise of national churches and later by world-wide associations of such 'churches' – in the new sense of 'denominations', though this word, like so much else in this field, was first used in this sense only in the nineteenth century. It was the period of the rise of the ecclesiastical 'isms', such as Presbyterianism, Quakerism, Methodism and Anglicanism (though interestingly the formation of the last word, unlike the others, which were coined in the seventeenth and eighteenth centuries, awaited the nineteenth century, which reveals again the persistence of 'first-wave' presuppositions in the *ecclesia Anglicana*). Even the Roman Catholic church, again with reluctance, comes to be seen as a church among the 'churches', as from the other end of the spectrum do sect-type Pentecostal movements. I once heard, in relation to South American Pentecostalism, the answer given to the question, 'When does a sect become a church?': 'When it installs a computer.' At any rate a marked characteristic of all 'second-wave' institutions is the pressure towards centralization, which peaked in modern papalism with Vatican I. Religion becomes 'organized religion' – a typically modern phrase – a separable area of life within an increasingly secularized society. The emphasis begins to fall on a clearer definition of doctrine and order and more streamlined structures and channels of communication, on what Schon called the 'centre-periphery' model common, as he said, to the Vatican and Coca-Cola, and issues in all denominations in a growth of ecclesiastical bureaucracy and synodical government. There is a creeping centralism, from the Methodism of Wesley's class meeting to the Central Hall, from the Anglican parson in his parish to the dominance of 'Church House' and the offices, to the growth (and reform – to make it more efficient) of the Curia.

Another feature that Toffler detects of all second-wave institutions is standardization. And this has been markedly characteristic of Christianity, both Catholic and Protestant, over the past three or four hundred years. Before that there was a wide variety of rites and uses, liturgies and translations. The standardization of the Vulgate and the Latin Mass and the elevation of a single, infallible

Magisterium in all matters of faith and morals is but the most conspicuous example. For every denomination became a 'little Catholicism' with its own Confession and Catechism, its standard version of the Bible, its common Prayer Book and its distinctive model of ministry, encapsulated, if it possessed the political leverage like the Church of England, in some Act of Uniformity (though ironically there has never been a less uniform church than the Church of England). But the undisputed dominance of what I was brought up to know as the Authorized Version (though ironically the King James Version was never actually authorized) and the Book of Common Prayer, unchanged for more than three hundred years, was, though my generation regarded it as normative, a very characteristic and peculiar feature of second-wave religion. Equally there was a steady standardization in the ministry, from the great variety of the primitive or even the mediaeval church to what Bishop Emrich of Michigan called the 'one-type soldier army', selected and tested by central councils and general ordination examinations. Ministers of religion even began more and more to look alike in the common, nineteenth-century, Roman collar, affected especially now by women priests needing to establish their identity in the clerical club. (In protest against the dog collar Alec Vidler used to exclaim, 'I don't want to be mistaken for a Jewish rabbi!')

But the standardization has been imposed not only on the clergy but the laity. In every tradition there has come to be a model of what all 'faithful churchmen' or 'good Catholics' or 'sound Evangelicals' should believe or do. There has been a 'royal road' of churchmanship, laymanship, mission, spirituality and prayer. The Protestant ethic and Catholic moral theology (the latter encapsulated in its hey-day in the imprimatur and the index and such almanacs as 'the Catholic doctor') have sought to guide and prescribe to 'the faithful'. And structurally that characteristic nineteenth-century proliferation, the parish organization, such as, in England, the Mothers' Union or the Boys' Brigade (each with its national and even international counterpart), has provided the pens where the sheep may safely graze and be fed, naturally, from above. And finally, between the 'denominations' organic union has seemed more and more to take on the aspect of organizational union and ecclesiastical merger, a closing of the ranks in face of the growing threat of secularism. For 'organized religion' is in deep trouble. Membership is static or slipping, ecumenism is in the doldrums, financing the established patterns of buildings and ministry has reached a critical point, code-morality is in the melting-pot and the royal road to spirituality and sanctity looks to many more to be what George Macleod once described his prayer-shelf as being, 'bankrupt corner'.

Not only are the internal walls of Christendom in disrepair but the ring-fences that marked off the distinctive Christian identity have been eroded. It is hard to believe now that when the second wave started the ecclesiastical scene was still set within the assumption of a static and self-complacent Christendom. For the Reformers, world-evangelism was already in principle complete. An adult baptism service was added only at the last revision of the Book of Common Prayer in 1661 in the hope that it might prove useful among 'the natives on our plantations'. That is the only reference in the book to the missionary task of the church. With the growth of Catholic triumphalism and Protestant particularism the centre-periphery model was simply stretched and expanded. Light was to be brought into the darkness along the paths providentially opened up by capitalist expansionism and gun-boat diplomacy. The conversion of 'the heathen' was to be accomplished on the imperial pattern and its high point and last fling was marked by the confident call, shortly before the First World War, in John Mott's phrase, to 'the evangelization of the world in this generation'. The goal was simple and compelling.

With this went the transition from the confident complacency of the eighteenth century (epitomized by Fielding's Parson Thwackum, 'When I speak of religion I mean the Christian religion, and when I speak of the Christian religion I mean the Protestant religion: and when I speak of the Protestant Religion I mean the Church of England') with its talk of 'our incomparable religion' (because in ignorance it neither received comparison or in importance was placed beyond it) to the nineteenth-century era of comparative religion – in which, however, one religion was still very much more equal than the others.

Indeed, corresponding to the creation of 'denominations' went, as Wilfred Cantwell Smith has shown, the creation of 'religions'. There was a spate of new 'isms', Hinduism, Buddhism, Mohammedanism and the rest, which were never so styled or seen as 'religions' by their practitioners but were creations of the nineteenth-century West. And once Christianity became a religion among religions, as Roman Catholicism became a church among churches, the relation between it and 'the rest' posed new problems, which were sorted out on much the same hierarchical model. Judaism and the other monotheistic faiths were nearer to the centre, followed by the other great 'world religions', the various primitive or tribal religions, tailing off into heathen darkness; just as within the Christian enclave Orthodoxy and Anglicanism were held to retain more 'marks of catholicism' than churches further gone from the supposedly pristine norms of faith and order. In the uneasy tension between co-existence and conquest perhaps the most subtle form of one-up-manship was, after calling the other world-faiths 'religions', to deny, with Karl Barth and Neo-Orthodoxy that Christianity was a religion at all, and so again to render it incomparable. (This corresponds to the official denial that the Roman Catholic communion is a church and cannot therefore join a council of churches.) But in any case it was very much a case of *Christianity at the Centre*,[5] to quote the original and now ironical title of a book by John Hick, who has since become the most outspoken advocate of the 'Copernican revolution', pleading for God at the centre with Christianity equi-distant with the rest and with no claim to unique status. It has been a case of 'if you can't beat them, join them', and the golden rule of the second-wave 'establish-ment' learned on the playing fields of Eton, 'Never chase a lost ball'. For not only is the age of 'effortless superiority' over; the entire centre-periphery model is in danger of collapse. Things that looked so certain are being shaken within the world and the religious scene. Both 'mission' and 'missions' are undergoing fundamental ques-tioning, the uniqueness of Christ is up for grabs, and we are urged to accept, from a Regius Professor of Divinity at Oxford, 'Christianity without incarnation'. At this point it becomes crucial to ask whether their is anything distinctive left, any difference in being a Christian at all.

Hence the reaction of the 'conservative churches', or of churches within churches, whether of evangelical or catholic stripe, is clear. It is: 'Strengthen the cords, harden the edges of doctrine and discipline; return to the fundamentals, know what you believe and where you stand.' It is as characteristic of the Papal hard line (especially on anything to do with sex) and the so-called 'new inquisition', as of the fundamentalist sects and charismatic cults. And it is as marked, if not more marked, in the militant revivalism of other faiths, not least in the Islamic revolution and religious Zionism. Toffler recognizes these responses for what they are — throw-backs desperate to retain second-wave assumptions by casting around them the defences of a laager mentality. But if we are not to go down that road, what is to be put in its place? On that he offers nothing so suggestive at the religious level as he does at others. And of course it is always easier to recognize (negatively) what is passing away, though it is important and liberating to see it as that. Otherwise we cannot be free to sit loose to it and, if necessary, let it go.

If there is one characteristic that Toffler sees of all third-wave trends it is 'demassification'. And that is as evident as it is elsewhere in all the signs of the times, morally and spiritually. There has been what Schon called a 'new ad hocracy', in ethics and liturgy, in structure and spirituality. There is no longer a single pattern of identity in churchmanship or ministry, or even in what it means to be a Christian. Distinctiveness is being marked, as I have long urged it should be, more in terms of difference for than difference from, centres rather than edges, of inclusiveness rather than exclusiveness. In terms of edges and boundaries 'the integrity of Anglicanism' (to use Stephen Sykes' title) or of any other 'ism' appears pretty chaotic. And for those in church or state who look to second-wave criteria there is indeed an identity-crisis at the religious as at every other level – only here it cuts more deeply and appears more threatening.

This is the point from which Charles Davis starts in the article I have already referred to, 'Our New Religious Identity'. He has been in some ways a paradigmatic figure of our times, exceptional only in articulating more clearly and courageously what is implicit in the religious situation in which many increasingly find themselves. When I first knew him he was a typical, though unusually intelligent, representative of the Roman Catholic church within the bounds of the old identities. He even looked, believe it or not now, what my old theological college principal used to call 'the latin type'. There were others within English Roman Catholicism at the time who were far more 'way out'. But he made the break. His book *A Question of Conscience*,[6] especially in view of the speed and the circumstances under which it was written, remains still, I think, a remarkable prophetic contribution to the new religious scene. Published some fifteen years ago, it seems now to belong to another age. Yet it was not the traditional break of someone who 'came out' by 'leaping over the wall' into another religious affiliation, or none at all. He has claimed to remain a Christian theologian, catholic in outlook, who yet identified with no other denomination and indeed has found himself freely crossing the frontiers into other religions and secular sociology. He writes in that article, which appeared in *Sciences Religieuses*:

> If someone now asks me whether I am a Catholic, I do not know how to answer. I know that I do not fulfil the requirements for membership laid down in Canon Law, nor do I give assent to all the Catholic dogmas. On the other hand, I meet acknowledged Catholics who do not take seriously the canonical conditions for membership and who sometimes believe fewer Catholic dogmas than I do. Moreover, I am openly made welcome as a communicating fellow Catholic by Catholic groups and individuals, clerical and lay, both in North America and Britain. That could not have happened a few decades ago. What criteria should I use to decide my possible Catholic identity?

And he goes on to ask, in the light of the symposium *The Myth of God Incarnate*, edited by a Christian theologian yet apparently denying the central Christian doctrine of the Incarnation as defined in the Church Councils, how one is to determine Christian identity today, which is in some ways more difficult than deciding whether a person belongs to a particular Christian denomination. And this is not just a problem of what he calls 'the seeming erosion of Christian identity in a secular culture'. It is the deliberate blurring at the edges of any distinctive Christian identity in relation to other religions. And in evidence he cites two leading Christian spirits of our times, both incidentally Roman Catholic priests:

> Raymond Panikkar declares that he is not only fully a Christian but also fully a Hindu. One could also argue whether the last teaching of Thomas Merton was Christian or Buddhist and perhaps conclude that he himself would not at the end have wanted to make that distinction.

Now these figures may be, and are indeed, exceptional individuals, but their following not least among the young shows that the questions they raise ring bells with many today. Previously our personal and social identity was bound up with particular roles, nationalities, social groupings or other institutions. They determined where we belonged, with what we 'identified'. But, Davis argues, we are moving to a post-conventional universalistic identity which (despite the evident casualties of a first generation) is not just rootless or eclectic, the equivalent of stateless citizens or wandering souls in search of a pabulum of religious *smorgasbrod* or spiritual syncretism. Nor are they candidates for Toffler's 'many new religions'. They are grounded, and yet not bounded. They have ceased to define their identity in terms of the old edges, their distinctiveness in terms of exclusivity or their name and nature as Christians by 'the fixed contents and norms of any one tradition or . . . permanent collective body'.

This is doubtless dangerous doctrine and can quickly fall over into irresponsible religious individualism. Yet the issue is fundamentally the one that the Christian church had to face at its very first and most critical Council described in Acts 15. Is being a Christian to be defined in that case over against Judaism, by its centre or by its edges, by the sole sufficiency of faith in Christ or by circumcision? What the Council did was to liberate those brought up as Jews to be Christians without having to be bound, or to disown their former pattern of life. And it liberated those brought up as Gentiles to be Christians without having first to become Jews, or to disown their own manner of life. There were limits, concessions to conscience for the sake of mutual peace. But these were quite flexible, and within ten years in the predominantly Gentile culture of Corinth St Paul was setting different 'edges' and drawing different guidelines, e.g., about meats sacrificed to idols, determined this time by sensitivity to pagan inferences (that Christians might implicitly be endorsing the reality of idols) rather than Jewish susceptibilities.

Yet the situation has moved on since the Council of Jerusalem sought to define the difference in being a Christian in the first century. It made the basic and courageous decision that to be in Christ one was not compelled to be circumcised in body. But Murray Rogers, a friend of mine who started as an evangelical missionary and who has since had more living experience than most in our time of intimate dialogue both with Hinduism in India, with Judaism and Islam in Jerusalem, and now with Buddhism and Shintoism in Hong Kong, has said this in an unpublished communication:

The spiritual, cultural and mental clothes in which the Lord Jesus Christ has been enwrapped for nearly two thousand years are no longer sufficient – if, indeed, they ever were. Until recently we Christians could truly agree that it was non-Christians who demanded this 'stripping'; but now it appears to be the inner dynamism of the Christian faith itself which demands a radical catholicity beyond anything previously imagined. Is the Christ, 'compelled' by the history of which he is Lord, to stay within the limits of the Mediterranean spiritualities? . . . Am I compelled to be spiritually a semite in order to accept the Christian message?

He was responding to a comment thrown out to him by Raymond Panikkar, that 'what we need is not a Vatican III – a Jerusalem II is far more urgent'. This must wrestle not simply with the terms of Christian identity within the church – which is stretching enough – but with the terms of Christian identity within the cosmos. For the Christ is bigger than any religion – even than Christianity – and he can wear the clothes of any religion. This is the true sense in which distinctively Christian faith and spirituality is not another religion among religions, marked off from them by defining who and what is in or out – any more than the distinctive Hindu ethos finds itself comfortable with this superimposed grid. There still are and will continue to be recognizably different centres – Christian, Islamic, Evangelical, Anglican and the rest. Such highly distinctive and to many no doubt exotic perspectives represented, say, by Aelred Graham's *Zen Catholicism* or Raymond Panikkar's *Intra-Religious Dialogue* or the Taiwanese theologian now with the World Council of Churches, Choan-Seng Song's *Third-Eye Theology* or Cantwell Smith's *Towards a World Theology*,[7] are certainly not marked by a desire for a mushy syncretism or dilettante eclecticism, and they are deeply rooted in their own traditions, Catholic or Reformed. Yet they may be symptomatic – like the spirituality of a Thomas Merton – of a free spirit abroad, for which supportive structures will still be needed for more than the rare individual with the power, for a time, to stand out. But they will not be the static, hierarchical and standardized structures of second-wave spirituality. Their shapes are already being thrown up from below and they are showing themselves scant respecters of traditional demarcations. They will certainly be small and fluid with strong, pluriform centres and very open-edged. But if the great church is going to be able to be permeated and transformed by them instead of simply being by-passed by them – as after all happened to an astonishing extent, despite the breaks, in the transition from the first- to the second-wave spirituality – then it is going to demand creative leadership of a major order. Winston Churchill once said, in relation to India, that he did not feel called to 'preside over the dissolution of the British Empire' (and this was perhaps his greatest limitation). And there is no sign that the present Pope feels called to preside over the dissolution of the Roman Catholic Church. Yet a similar creative transformation of second- wave structures may today be equally necessary. Perhaps Jerusalem II and Vatican III will have to happen together – and in a great deal less than another three hundred years, or even another thirty.

PART TWO

Sermons and Addresses

A Statement of Christian Faith

Four sermons preached in Trinity College Chapel, Cambridge,
10 February–3 March 1974

(i) The Human Condition

Where shall we start? Well, we can hardly do better than start where we are. And where we are is – incontestably – in a mess. Why what Mr Heath calls 'these self-inflicted wounds?' Why a strike that nobody wants, or an election that very few do? What is it that mixes everything we do in so much dirt? The preacher's answer is in no doubt: sin. And it is from sin and guilt that so much preaching of the gospel has started, particularly of the revivalist kind. And if people don't feel guilt, then induce it. That has been the well-tried formula.

Yet it was not Jesus's formula. He started not from man's despair but from the sheer undeserved graciousness of God, who sends his rain on the just and the unjust – though, as the verse goes on,

But chiefly on the just, because
The unjust steals the just's umbrella.

This, of course, does not mean that Jesus nursed any illusions about human nature. As St John pregnantly puts it, 'he knew what was in man'. Yet he said, 'If you, being evil, know how to give good gifts to your children, how much more will your heavenly Father. . . ?' For in truth man is a mixed-up kid. There is so much goodwill and idealism in all of us and nowhere more than in this country. Yet somehow 'the good that I will I cannot, and the evil that I do not will, that I do'; and, when it really comes to the crunch, whether as individuals or interest groups or nations, our deepest desires are ineluctably selfish.

Yet sin is not the first word – nor the last – that the Bible speaks about man. It is a fearful distortion of something much more primal; a twisting, a turning back and in upon itself, of the quest which man alone knows for something insatiably beyond, in a word, of the need for worship.

Now that sounds insufferably like sermon talk. So let me present it through another medium. I wonder if any of you have seen *Equus*, the play by Peter Shaffer (author of *The Royal Hunt of the Sun*, and formerly of this College). When I first heard about it I confess I felt no urge to see it. For it centred upon the gruesome story, based upon an actual case, of a highly disturbed young man who put out the eyes of six horses with a hoof-pick. But now I have seen it twice and read it three times. It contains some brilliantly sharp dialogue and beautiful acting. For any who thinks one is not taking sin seriously, it is as gory an instance of human depravity as any listed by St Paul in his catalogue in Romans 1. And as the layers of the boy's condition are stripped off by the psychiatrist it becomes clear that the analysis is the same. 'Their misguided minds are plunged in darkness . . . exchanging the splendour of immortal God for an image shaped like mortal man, even for images like birds, beasts, and creeping things.'

Alan, the boy, is the son of a timid religious mother and an old-fashioned socialist atheist, who tears from his bedroom wall a ghastly reproduction of Christ chained and flogged on the road to Calvary and stops him rotting his mind (as he supposes) on the telly. Replacing it is a picture of a horse with eyes staring directly at him and, now, the mindless chanting of TV commercials, as he invokes 'the hosts of Philco' and 'the hosts of Pifco', but above all the great god Equus, clothed with images from Job and Revelation, of fearful spiritual and sexual potency, who yet by watching him renders him impotent. This is his worship and the power of his being. 'Can you think of anything worse one can do to anybody than take away their worship?', says Michael Dysart the psychiatrist. For 'without worship you shrink, it's as brutal as that'.

Yet the irony of the play is that that the psychiatrist is 'the shrink' – the one who can take away his pain, restore him to 'normal', only by depriving him of a whole dimension of his being. 'Passion, you see, can be destroyed by a doctor. It cannot be created.' And he himself is a man alienated from his gods, the springs of his renewal – in his case the myths of ancient Greece. Yet, as he says in his curtain speech,

And now for me it never stops: that voice of Equus out of the cave.
– 'Why Me? . . . Why Me? . . . Account for Me!' . . . All right – I
surrender! I say it . . . In an ultimate sense I cannot know what I do
in this place – yet I do ultimate things. Essentially I cannot know
what I do – yet I do essential things. Irreversible, terminal things. I
stand in the dark with a pick in my hand, striking at heads!

I need – more desperately than my children need me – a way of
seeing in the dark. What way is this? . . . *What dark is this?* . . . I
cannot call it ordained of God: I can't get that far. I will however
pay it so much homage. There is now, in my mouth, this sharp
chain. And it never comes out.[1]

A way of seeing into the dark, the dazzling darkness of the human
condition. Perhaps that is as fair a way as any of beginning to
describe the Christian revelation. For a light has shone in the dark. It
does not illuminate in the sense of making all plain. In fact its first
effect is to deepen the shadows; hence the profundity of the ancient
myth of the Fall. Both the heights and the depths in man are more
than secular humanism allows. The Christian estimate of man is one
neither of shallow optimism nor of pessimism, but of what Tillich
called 'belief-ful realism'. The dimensions of it are strikingly
foreshadowed in that remarkable passage from the second chapter of
the book of Wisdom, with its dialogue between those who conclude
that life is surface only, a passing shadow and a reckless revel, and
the poor, honest man who by his very life-style questions all their
presuppositions. For despite appearances, says the writer, God has
made man the image of his own eternal self, and has set eternity in his
heart so that he cannot live without it. It is this exigency in man,
which refuses to let him close, which is his glory and his despair.

I think that if I were convinced by nothing more of the Christian
case – if I did not believe that the answer it gives was possible or
plausible – I should find it very difficult to get away from its diagnosis
of the question, the question posed by man and his condition. For
ultimately man is a question; a great contorted question-mark, as
this slow product of the evolutionary process raises himself in
agonized yearning so far above the rest of nature, yet twists and turns
back upon himself in flailing self-destruction. No estimate of man
that does not do justice both to his greatness and to his wretchedness
can begin to satisfy. But ultimately man is a question whose answer
lies outside himself. 'What is man?' asks the Psalmist; but goes on

'that thou art mindful of him?' That is his dignity and his terror. That is the divine dimension to his life that makes him a worshipping animal – for good or for ill.

Next week we shall be seeking to look across that invisible frontier by which all human life is bounded. For *what* we see meeting us across it, claiming us for its own, that chain of love or of fate that never comes out, determines who we are and the particular homage that life lays upon us.

What the boy Alan saw was dark and destructive both of himself and everyone else. Dysart may have envied him his virility compared with his own effete gods, with all his Homeric seas, his holy waters, 'stinking dead under three inches of sun tan oil!' Yet not all gods are better than no gods, and, as he confesses, he does not deal in replacements. Only the expulsive, redemptive power of a new faith can offer that. What the Christian faith offers as man's centre of gravity outside himself is a love that has made him for itself and will not let him go. And love makes us rather than breaks us because it is part of the very grain of things, of the way the universe itself is made. On the face of it it does not look like it. The *élan vital*, the evolutionary force, looks much more like the power of Equus than of Christ, and him crucified, whom the Christian faith calls 'the power of God and the wisdom of God'. Yet psychology has also shown us that man's primal need is to love and be loved. He is made for love and love makes him. And you learn to love, to accept yourself and others, not by being told to love but by being loved, by being accepted. Any modern study of disturbance, delinquency or depravity will point to its roots in deprivation of love, of real relationship. And this applies just as much to loneliness and frustration.

This basic need to be accepted and respected as persons runs right through the human condition. Any parent of a family will recognize the depth of outrage in the child's remark, especially in relation to the other children, 'It isn't fair.' And this, writ large, is the issue of 'relativities', and of the deeply ingrained sense of unfairness and inequality in our society – which *we* here may find it difficult to feel. After all, which of us, whether on salaries or grants, is actually getting our money docked to three days a week? There is still a great gulf fixed between the salaried person and the wage-earner. One of the cartoons recently that went nearest the bone was after the collapse of the rather absurd to-ing and fro-ing about counting in the miners' cleaning-up time. It was a picture of Mr Heath saying, 'So I wash my hands of the whole messy business', with the reply, 'Ay, and get paid for it too.' Here are the roots of the resentment, the insensitivity, the intransigence on both sides – which I fear the election will deepen rather than cure.

The human condition is of what Luther called 'the heart curved in upon itself', of man gone sour upon himself. His need is, quite simply, redemption from sin. And that, if we can speak it with compelling relevance, is, equally simply, the gospel.

(ii) The Divine Dimension

I spoke last week of man, the great question-mark of nature. Today I speak of God; and it would be easy to present him, simply, as the answer. But it would be truer to the Bible to speak of him first as the Questioner. 'Adam, Man, where art thou?' 'Cain, where is thy brother Abel?' 'Job, where wast thou when I laid the foundations of the earth?' Psalm 139 stands in a long line of witnesses to God as the disturbing presence, the hound of Heaven, of whom Gerard Manley Hopkins was to write:

Thou mastering me
God! giver of breath and bread . . .
Over again I feel thy finger and find thee.[2]

It is the question within, that comes nevertheless from without, of the Beyond *in* the midst. We can know this spiritual reality only as a dimension of our being. But it would be absurd to say that God was merely a dimension of human existence, that without us he would not be: just the opposite. That would be to confuse what Kierkegaard called 'subjectivity', the insistence that the truth (or at any rate any spiritual truth) must be true for you, existentially, with subjectivism, the view that it is true only for you. That is why I should prefer to speak of the reality of God, rather than either the existence of God or the experience of God. For 'reality' includes both the objective and the subjective.

Let us then start from this reality – if we can. For to speak of it, let alone to define it, is ultimately impossible. Such is the universal testimony of the human spirit. '*Neti, neti*', Not this, Not that, says the Hindu. 'The *tao* that can be spoken is not the eternal *tao*', says the wisdom of China. You must not take the 'name' of God upon your lips, says the Jew. One can speak of the Trinity, says St Augustine, solely *ne taceretur*, for fear that by silence one may seem to deny. 'That whereof we cannot speak' (to use Wittgenstein's phrase) is, in the famous image of Lao Tzu's, the hole at the centre without which there could be no wheel. It is the ultimate mystery, the abyss of all being, to which the mysteries point. 'Take off thy shoes from off thy feet' – and shut up!

No one who has not at some time sensed that mystery at the heart of things, of the 'inside' of everything, can understand talk of the divine dimension. You cannot prove it, any more than you can prove what it is to be caught by love or for a man to be overwhelmed, in Paul Gerhardt's lovely words, by 'joy of beauty not his own'. You may not be able to call this reality God, as the Taoist or the Buddhist cannot, or as Richard Jeffries the atheist naturalist and mystic of the last century could not, who had as acute and as painful a sense of what he called 'the Beyond' as anyone I know. But for the Christian these are all faces of God; some terrible, some beautiful, some loving.

But why have not such people been able to say, as St Thomas Aquinas so confidently ends his proofs, 'And this all men call God'? Because fundamentally, I believe, they have been saying to us Westerners, to us traditional Christians, 'Your God is too small.' The dictionary definition of God, as humanists do not cease to remind us, is of *a* supernatural Being or supreme Person, who 'has' a world. This is in fact a serious distortion of what careful Christian theology has taught; for it makes God a *primus inter pares* among beings. But this is undoubtedly the popular image of God, which to vast numbers of people today – Christian and non-Christian – seems parochially anthropomorphic, remote and incredible. It is no wonder that even Christian theologians – and not only Nietzsche – have begun in our time to talk of 'the death of God'. For *that* God has gone dead for vast numbers and seems an unnecessary hypothesis for many more.

Imagery is meant to aid the imagination but it is in constant danger, as St Paul warned the Athenians, of becoming an idol. Indeed the commandment which in English runs 'Thou shalt not make to thyself any graven image' is a warning against constructing any images of God, for mental images can be as dangerous as metal ones. Yet we all think in pictures (not least in a televisual age) and in fact the Bible abounds in images of God; as King, as the Rock, and above all in the New Testament as Father. Yet images constantly change, die and are reborn. Even father images signify something subtly different since Freud, and the King of Kings and Lord of Lords, the only Ruler of princes is scarcely a spiritual candidate today for 'Who governs Britain?' Yet merely to replace 'the Great White Father' by 'She's black' solves nothing. Our images of God – or rather the images through which God meets us, and which are 'given' rather than 'made' like some contemporary golden calf – are likely to be more diverse, transient and broken, though the archetypes constantly reassert their ancient power.

If there is a crisis of imagery today in every cultural field, there is a crisis too in God-talk or God-thinking (theo-logy). For the projection we have used for representing him on the maps of our speech- and thought-world have come to have a displacement effect, putting him, like the pole on Mercator's projection, off the edge, over and above the vital connections of life, in some supra-natural order which is no longer where men instinctively locate what is most real to them. So God, so far from being the centre, the *ens realissimum*, the most real thing in the world, comes in, if he comes in at all, as a sort of spiritual 'long-stop.' The fundamental aim of contemporary theology is not, as so many suppose, one of reduction, of cutting down the faith to what modern man can swallow, but of location, of so speaking of the transcendent and immanent God that modern man may recognize him as the Beyond in *his* midst.

In fact I believe that we must enter a protest against the reduction of God in so much popular Christianity to becoming incredibly humanistic and limiting to many of our generation most open to the Spirit, whether in East or West. For there is here a thirst for reality which is at the same time a protest against the limitation of any words, images or concepts. This does not deny the need for focussing, as in a burning-glass, the infinity of God. For the mystic's gift is precisely

To see a World in a Grain of sand . . .
And Eternity in an hour.
And Christians see in Christ supremely such a prism of 'the white radiance of Eternity'.

But what the mystic quest refuses – in every religion – is a 'still centre of the turning world' which is exclusive rather than inclusive. It is concerned with the All, and the All encompasses everything, the impersonal as well as the personal, darkness as well as light, evil as well as good. Here indeed we are at the ultimate mystery to which there are, in this age, no 'answers'. But one of the most damaging reductions of the image of God has been that of an all-good, omnipotent Being who is nevertheless reponsible for 'sending' or 'allowing' the most frightful evil. And it is the most sensitive whom it has most revolted. Here, for instance, is Philip Toynbee in his recent 'tract for the times' *Towards the Holy Spirit* (with, I fear, not a little ignorance, some arrogance, but yet genuine passion against what he thinks Christianity teaches – the other two Persons of the Trinity are deemed to be irrevocably 'out').

> Contemplate, for a moment, a single 'act of God': there has been an earthquake, and in a young family of three the father has been killed at once; the mother dies, in noisy anguish, during the next twenty-four hours; the child, pinned down uninjured between his dead parents, dies slowly of thirst during the next five days, while the bodies of his parents putrefy to each side of him.

Modern Christians have devoted a great deal of hard and painful thought, a great many contorted and embarrassed pages, to finding excuses for such behaviour on the part of their all-loving and all-powerful god.

> Love has finally banished the God of Love.[3]

I do not believe it has. But I do believe it has banished a God whose only face is love and whose other faces are projected on to a power of evil whom he either will not or cannot defeat. Jung accused Christians of having divided the God- and Christ-image, splitting off the dark, the 'shadow' side on to an irreconcilable counterpart, a devil or anti-Christ figure. For perfection or wholeness, he insists, is not the absence or the exclusion of evil but the integration of it into personal freedom and goodness. In the universe as in man there is much that is sub-personal and sub-moral in the God-given processes which has to be assimilated, taken up and transfigured into purposes of spirit. Jung pointed out that symbolically in the visions of Ezekiel and Revelation only one of the four faces of the living creatures round the throne of God is human. For God is in everything and everything is in God, impersonal as well as personal; not merely the obviously beautiful and good, the intentional and meaningful, but the waste and void, the nebulae, earthquakes, sunsets, cancers, tapeworms. As the second Isaiah makes him say,

I form light and create darkness,
I make weal and create woe,
I am the Lord, who do all these things.

If this is understood in terms of God deliberately devising suffering and calamity he becomes a very devil. But it is an insight and profound significance if we can see that none of these things can separate from God because they are not separate from God. They are all his faces. The real question is, how can he possibly be in them as love?

For the Christian no more than for anyone else is there love or intention, whether divine or human, in the ravages of a cancer or an earthquake. These are processes which in themselves are random and sub-personal – usually neutral but often anti-personal in their effects. That is why the whole of Jesus's ministry is set against such things when they stunt or destroy men and women – or rather to the victory of spirit over them, whether by cure or acceptance. Yet even at such points of what St Paul calls sheer purposeless 'vanity', God is to be found in them rather than turning away from them. Love is there to be met, responded to, and created through them and out of them. Meaning can be wrested from them, even at the cost of crucifixion. Literally everything can be taken up and transformed rather than allowed to build up into dark patches of loveless resentment and senseless futility. This is the saving grace: God is not outside evil any more than he is outside anything else, and the promise to which the men of the New Testament held as a result of what they had seen in Christ is that he 'will be all in all' *as love*. Over most of the processes of what Teilhard de Chardin dared to call this 'personalizing' universe it is still waste and void and dark. But, for the Christian, a light has shone in the darkness, indeed out of the darkness, in the face of Jesus Christ, which the darkness cannot quench. And that is the transforming factor. Henceforth, says St Paul, there is 'nothing . . . in the world as it is or the world as it shall be, in the forces of the universe, in heights or depths – nothing in all creation that can separate us from the love of God in Christ Jesus our Lord'.

Is man finally on his own, left to his own resources in an indifferent or hostile cosmos? That ultimately is the question of God. The Christian answers unequivocally, No! Through and out of everything 'God *is* love'. But while all remains so baffling and incomplete he can dare to say this only because of that 'transforming reality' in Christ, the *human* face of God, to which I turn next week.

(iii) The Transforming Reality

I led last week to the point at which 'the white radiance of Eternity', in Shelley's phrase, becomes focussed for the Christian in the person of Jesus Christ, the image, the human face, of the invisible God.

Let us be clear first of all that he is not the only or the exclusive image of God. Indeed by using this language of him, introduced in the Old Testament to describe Adam, the New Testament is deliberately applying to him the term which should be true of every man. For in this human figure is to be seen the true reflection of God which should be there in every human face – and which in different degrees still is. In so far as Jesus is unique as a man it is because he is normal – the 'proper' man – not because he is abnormal. That is a vitally important principle. And he is the definitive revelation of God – which in an evolutionary universe is less misleading than talking about the final revelation – not because there is no light elsewhere but because for the Christian he is the con-centration and the focussing of what is to be seen everywhere else, so that in his light we see light. Finally, to get the perspective right before we begin looking at the details, the Christ is bigger than the historical figure of Jesus of Nazareth. As St John's prologue insists, that thirty years of history is but the bringing to a fine point of the light and life of the eternal Logos, the self-expressive activity of God, first through nature, then through a people, and finally in a person. And the Christ does not come to an end with the life of Jesus. That is the significance of the resurrection, of the release of the Spirit, of the church as the present embodiment of Christ in the world, and of what can as yet only be spoken of in the word-picture or myth of the Parousia or presence of Christ coming into everything (seriously restricted by the non-biblical term 'the Second Coming'), whose function is to say 'You ain't seen nothing yet'. Indeed the phrase 'the revelation' of Christ, which we use (quite properly) of the Incarnation, the New Testament characteristically reserves for this final disclosure of God, and a world, in which there shall be no unChristlikeness at all. So let us never narrow the canvas. We are Christians, not just 'Jesus people'. That man is for us the irreplaceable centre, in which all things cohere, not the circumference.

Against therefore this cosmic background – which far transcends the scene on this little planet – what do we say? One way of putting it has been to say that into this world of sin and death God has sent his only Son from Heaven to rescue us from the power of Satan and bring us to eternal life. This is language which has inspired some of the greatest Christian poetry and art, and we shall be the poorer if we cannot make it our own. The trouble is that today it gives to most people, who do not live in this Miltonic universe, a seriously misleading image of the Christian faith – of a supernatural invasion or insertion into this world of a God-man (rather like a bat-man), who gets himself born, experiences our life as a human being, before taking off once again for another sphere. This is a parody, but I fear it is perilously close to what popular Christianity has seemed to convey: God taking a space-trip dressed up as a man – 'veiled in flesh the Godhead see'.

Now there isn't time in one brief sermon to sort out in this the wheat from the chaff (for any of you who are really interested in pursuing further most of what I am trying to say tonight I would refer you to my book *The Human Face of God*). So let's leave that picture for the time being and begin again at the other end.

And we can't do better than to start once more where St John starts. The Incarnation, as following his usage we have come to call it, is the ultimate embodiment in a single human individual of that clue to the universe as personal which all along has been coming to expression through the processes of nature and history. As far as heredity and environment are concerned ('according to the flesh', as the New Testament puts it), Jesus is the product of this process like every other member of the species *homo sapiens*: indeed he could not otherwise be its flowering and its crowning representative. As the early formula insisted, he is *totus in nostris*, wholly one of us, and that means in his origin as well as in his nature. He is not, for the Christian faith, a cuckoo inserted into the human nest. Perhaps, you may say, I protest too much. But protest is, alas, necessary because the other thing which the Christian faith has wanted to say of him at the same time has been allowed to undercut rather than supplement and interpret this insistence. And that is that 'according to the Spirit' he is not *just* the product and last term of the old but a new, divine initiative – yet an initiative of God working through the old, trans-forming it from within, rather than scrapping it and starting again.

This double conviction the New Testament writers sought to picture for their day by telling two stories about Jesus. The first – and it *is* the first, with pride of place in the opening chapter of the New Testament – is the story linking him, through the nexus of heredity, with the seamless robe of nature and history (though, as Matthew goes out of his way to insist by dragging four particular women into his genealogy, it is also pretty seamy). The second story, whether in terms of virgin-birth or pre-existence (and originally they were alternative and indeed incompatible myths), is the stress that the significance of Jesus cannot be exhausted in terms of heredity and environment. Who he is, where he comes from, is not to be explained merely in terms of Joseph and Mary or Nazareth: he comes from God, from Heaven. Now to us moderns this second story (in either form) is much more difficult, if not impossible, to hold together with his completely human origin (that he is totally 'of one stock' with us, as the Epistle to the Hebrews puts it) if we take the two as competing statements on the same level. But then exactly the same was true for our forefathers over Genesis and Darwin. We have come through to see that the statements of the first chapter of the Old Testament are not about the details of geology (with God making the rocks with fossils in them to look as if evolution were true) but interpretations of its significance: in this beginning, *however* science describes it, *God*. And we have lost nothing in the re-understanding, but rather gained. So too I think we shall come through to see that the statements of the first chapter of the New Testament are not about the details of gynaecology (or fiddling with the double helix to look as though Jesus's genes were not fakes) but profound re-interpretations of his significance – in this utterly human being, *whatever* his heredity (and we shall never know for certain), *God*. And this, I believe, will enable us to see still more strongly for our generation the wonder and the humility of the Incarnation.

But I must pass over this and much, much more, including the relation of the wonder of the transforming reality of the resurrection to the secondary questions of how physical or how psychological were the 'appearances' or precisely what happened to the old body: for these are questions about the chrysalis, not the butterfly. I want to concentrate rather on this transforming reality in relation both to the death of Jesus and to the present, shared life of Christ.

In Jesus. Christians see one man who represents both the self-expression of God to men – his human face – and the unique response of a genuinely human existence. This comes out in what the New Testament calls his 'obedience' – which is but the other side of its depiction of him as the one truly free man. There is nothing automatic or inevitable about this response, or it would not have been our freedom which he shared and transfigured. Indeed his will was brought into line with God's will only by an agonizing struggle. But there he stood – or rather hung – 'in that dark noontide hour' – alone and deserted. As in some spiritual Thermopylae, his body held the pass. 'Once, only once, and once for all', 'He only could unlock the gate', as the hymns say. He did what none of us could do. In that sense he stands alone, in our place. Yet also, as St Paul insisted, he stands for all, as our representative – not so that we do not have to die with him, but so that we can.

As with the Incarnation, so with the Atonement; so many traditional ways of stating it (and thank God no theory is orthodox) are today counter-productive. And none less than one which some, I think misguidedly, present as the only sound one, the penal substitutionary. (The New Testament never uses the word 'punishment' in relation to the death of Christ, and Christ the 'representative' is far more representative of its teaching than Christ the 'substitute'). But again I don't want to spend time sifting the wheat from the chaff in secondary ways of expression. Let us start again from the other end – not 2,000 years ago (though we shall always be brought back to that) but where we are.

Where we are is in a world, a network of personal and social relationships – sexual, psychological, racial, economic, power-political, and the rest – where redemption, reconciliation, yes, resurrection, are desperately needed. How can we live together in one earth, one nation, one household, indeed, in one self? Never have these questions pressed upon us more insistently, and never has the time – or the space – for their solution been more restricted.

For me (and one cannot but speak personally where, as St Paul says, 'the love of Christ leaves us no choice') the gospel is that into this reality which tears us all apart there has broken another at-one-ing, transforming reality which the New Testament speaks of as being 'in Christ'. If convention did not (properly) dictate that we should have one lesson from the Old Testament with its promise, like ours earlier (Isa. 41.1–9), of 'new things before they break from the bud', I should have chosen Ephesians 2 (as well as II Cor. 5) to convey the many-sided splendour of this new being in Christ as 'our peace'. For St Paul (to go no further afield) dilates upon this atoning, reconciling reality from every kind of stand-point – of Christ living in us and us in Christ, of being one with him as intimately as husband and wife, of being members of his body, partners in the company of the Spirit, sharing his very dying and rising through baptism and the eucharist. All these are ways of saying that our relation to Christ is not just to a dead historical individual, however inspiring, but to a present transforming solidarity. It is this in my experience that uniquely has power to enable one to forget one's selfish being, to take one out of oneself, to discover acceptance, forgiveness, release, in the freedom and service of others. 'Accept the fact that you have been accepted', that you can lift up your head and live. That is the joy of the resurrection in the fellowship of his sufferings. That is why the way in for most is through the common life or fellowship of the Spirit ('the go-between God', as John Taylor has called him), and from that to the grace of our Lord Jesus Christ 'who loved me and gave himself up for me', and, perhaps a long time later, to the almost unbelievable working in all things of the love of God as Father. Such is the effect of 'Christian lib': 'When anyone is united to Christ, there is a new world; the old order has gone, and a new order has already begun.' And yet, as we shall see next week, only begun.

(iv) The Liberating Hope

'What can I believe? What must I do? What may I hope for?' So Kant summed up the three-fold question of human existence. The last perhaps is the question least articulated today. I don't hear people asking me 'What may I hope for?' It would be interesting to consider why. Perhaps so many hopes have turned out to be dupes that people no longest have the courage even to pose it. Yet I suspect it is the greater inarticulate question. For no one can remain human without hope, and without vision the people perish. 'Hope springs eternal', we are told. Yet hope is in short supply. Most generations of the human race have grown up to believe that the world would go on much the same. In the last two or three hundred years each generation, including my own, has been brought up to assume without question that things (if not people) would get better. For the first time, this generation must know, if it is honest, that the conditions of life are likely to get rapidly worse. Here is a sentence from a book just published in America: 'The outlook for man, I believe, is painful, difficult, perhaps desperate, and the hope that can be held out for his future prospect is very slim indeed'.[4] Even the last six months have seen a dramatic shift in the scene, and in a bare ten years 1984 could well live up to its name. The very speed of change which before was so exhilarating has produced that distinctively modern disease 'future-shock' (though the capacity of the human frame to absorb it must never be underestimated).

This is not of course the first time in history that the outlook has seemed depressingly bleak. St Bernard's haunting hymn, 'Hora novissima, tempora pessima', reflects just such a mood. But it goes on: 'vigilemus', 'keep vigil' – for

The Judge is at the gate . . .
To terminate the evil,
To diadem the right.

And it has those triumphant lines which show John Mason Neale such a fine translator:

Send hope before to grasp it,
Till hope be lost in sight.

Yet its hope,

Resolving all enigmas,
An endless Sabbath-day,

is scarcely a credible solution for the three-day week or anything else! And all forms of Messianism, religious or political, are today distrusted.

The result is a deep-seated sense of pointlessness. St Paul described the Gentiles of his day as being 'without God and without hope in the world'. And today too for most people Godlessness takes the shape of hopelessness. They are indeed looking for hope without God. They are no longer saying, with Luther, 'Where may I find a gracious God?', but they *are* saying in some form 'Where may I find a gracious neighbour? How can we live together in one world? How can we make and keep life human? Yet despite all the secular strivings of our day, despite all the liberation movements, despite all the stirrings of the dispossessed, few are optimistic. For there are ashes in the mouth. Even, perhaps particularly, in the so-called 'new' world men and women are turning back in upon themselves. The search today is in the first instance a search for inner meaning and reassurance, for some aim in life and society that vanquishes 'vanity', the futility and frustration of feeling that your labour is empty, that nothing is worthwhile, that life is absurd. And this indeed is probably where for many today the rediscovery of God must begin.

One man who was dogged, like many another brooding Swede, by this interior quest for meaning was Dag Hammarskjold, the secretary-general of the UN. And on Whitsunday 1961, the year he died, he entered in his diary:

> I don't know Who – or what – put the question, I don't know when it was put. I don't even remember answering. But at some moment I did answer *Yes* to Someone – or Something – and from that hour I was certain that existence is meaningful and that, therefore, my life, in self-surrender, had a goal . . .
>
> After that, the word 'courage' lost its meaning, since nothing could be taken from me.

That is the distinctively Hebraic virtue of hope. Hope is subtly different from optimism. No one in his position could easily be optimistic. Yet it makes sense to say, 'I am not optimistic, but I have hope.' That, I take it too, is what men like Solzhenitsyn are saying to us. These are the truly liberated men, from whom nothing can be taken away. And this freedom goes with a strange combination of commitment and detachment. It means staying with causes and people long after most people are content to quit: what St Paul calls 'endurance'. But it means also not sinking your securities in anything that 'they' can take away. The man with such a hope knows that ultimately everything may, nay will, be taken away – 'goods, honour, children, wife'. He knows too that none of his hopes will be seen through to the end in this life or this world. Indeed, if in this life only he has hope, he is of all men the most foolish. For the cheques that he has drawn upon the future are such that cannot be cashable here. That is why hope is beyond optimism or pessimism. It does not go up and down with the market. It is the state of having nothing, and yet possessing all things. Yet it is not world-despising: it is the freedom, nay the compulsion, to give oneself to the world with an abandon of love and a concern for justice which comes of depending on nothing which it must give you. It is those who live such lives in whom the resurrection begun makes the resurrection credible.

For the Christian hope is distinctively one of resurrection, of eternal (or real) life rather than immortality or survival. And resurrection, as Harry Williams insisted in his *True Resurrection*,[5] is primarily a category not of the dead but of the living, not of life after death, nor simply of life before death, but of life over death, the deadness of mind, body and spirit. And after staying last week with a Christian with disseminated sclerosis I came away saying, 'I believe in the resurrection of the body.' Yet, as we have been reminded recently by two funerals in this chapel in as many weeks, the end of this present life *is* dissolution. And if we have no hope that reaches through beyond that, we deceive ourselves. But, says St Paul, 'We know that if the earthly frame that houses us today should be demolished, we possess a building which God has provided – a house not made with hands.'

This has usually been interpreted individualistically as a body waiting for us to pop on at the moment of death. But I am convinced that St Paul uses the present tense seriously. We have, as a present possession, an invisible solidarity which, despite the dissolution of the outer man, of everything that is seen, cannot be touched by death. This is the new body, the new humanity in Christ Jesus, entered at baptism, visible already in the transforming power of the Spirit, but yet to be completed in the reintegration of all things. Meanwhile we wait – and work – for God to make us his sons and set our whole body free, and for the taking up of all nature and all history into the liberty and splendour of the children of God. Compared with this vision of a new world, the puny, and unanswerable, question of 'What will happen to me when I die?' falls into its proper place. All we know, and all we need to know, is contained in the logic of the hymn: 'He changeth not, and thou art dear'. The love that has made us for itself is stronger than death and will never let us go.

To be with God forever: that, as Christian tradition has always insisted, is a sobering thought. For some it will be heaven, for some it will be hell; for most of us something of both. Yet I cannot believe in a God – certainly not the God and Father of our Lord Jesus Christ – who is content for any to live with him for ever and find it hell. He will take no man's choice from him, for a victory of love presupposes to the end the exercise of freedom in the other. Yet I am persuaded that he will, that he must, be all in all as love. That is the Christian hope – against all human desert or expectation.

The place and meaning, if any, of personal survival has become problematic for many today, dividing young and old alike. For some it means everything, for others nothing. Both, it seems to me, have got the New Testament wrong. If eternal life is the quality of relationship to God that Jesus and the Apostles affirm and Christian experience bears out, then it is inconceivable that it could be terminated by a bacillus or a bus. The taking up of the relationships, the texture, of this life into a life that is not flesh-bound (any more than that of the butterfly is bound, to the conditions of the chrysalis) is a corollary of the gospel: deny it and you have denied a dimension of the gospel. But it is not the centre of the gospel. The centre of the gospel is Christ and his kingship. And if we get bogged down in the questions of 'how?', 'with what body?', we shall deserve the answer of St Paul, 'You silly man!' The one thing we know, he says, is that it is nothing to do with resuscitation – the flesh-body disintegrates and nothing depends on it. Christianity is not interested in survival, physical or psychic. It is interested in the changing of the world at every level into a solidarity of spirit, a spiritual body. This does not mean the spiriting of it away, but the reduction of everything, by the power of him who is able to transfigure all, to the grace of our Lord Jesus Christ, the love of God and the fellowship of Holy Spirit.

The Meaning of the Eucharist

Five sermons preached in Trinity College Chapel, Cambridge,
18 January – 15 February 1976

(i) Hearing

Only twenty years ago the typical celebration of holy communion in the Church of England was something like this. At a minute or so to eight the priest emerged from the vestry, with or without a server, and took his place at the altar at the far end of the sanctuary. He stood with his back to the people, scattered among the pews of the nave, where they remained kneeling, head in hands, except for sitting for the Epistle, standing up for the Gospel, Creed and collection, and coming up to make their communion. The service consisted of a series of prayers led and lections read by the priest alone (though with no preaching of the word), apart from a few muted 'amens' and mumbled responses. After the service priest and people went home to breakfast in the respectful silence in which the whole had been most reverently conducted.

I have not the slightest wish to guy this, which was the spiritual food on which I was brought up and which had a devotion and sincerity about it which one often misses today. I start this way merely to indicate something of the revolution that has come over us in the past twenty years, whether we are high, low or middle stump, Anglican, Free Church or Roman Catholic (and the last have travelled further and faster than anyone). The change had begun earlier with the Parish Communion movement of the 1930s, 40s and 50s and in the Liturgical Movement in the Roman Catholic Church on the continent still earlier, and it was powerfully abetted by the rediscovery of the house-church and the worker-priest and a host of other things. But it has domesticated itself in all our traditions, with a vernacular liturgy in contemporary speech, with a celebration across or round the table, with full participation of the people male and female (except still at the altar), at a speed and with an acceptance that I for one would never have deemed possible. So much so that we are in danger of taking for granted in the next generation the teaching that went with it (or, one suspects, often failed to go with it). So this course comes as a sort of booster and refresher.

First, let us remind ourselves of something that the former rite much obscured, that the service falls into two distinct parts, the one focussed on word, the other on action, each with its own origin and structure.

The first part was what the early Christians called simply the 'synaxis', the meeting or coming together, from the same root as 'synagogue' or 'congregation', when used, not of the people as opposed to the priest, but in the sense of a meeting. And the form of the Christian meeting was modelled on the synagogue service in which Jesus shared. Its focus was not the altar (that for a Jew was in Jerusalem to which you had to go up at the Feasts) but what we should call the lectern and pulpit and prayer-desk. It centred on the word – its reading and exposition, its celebration in song and its translation into prayer. And the Christian version of it, whether in the ante-communion or in mattins or evensong or indeed compline, has naturally assumed the same shape. With whatever alternation, it includes preparation (as in the collect for purity or prayer of humble access), praise (as in the gloria and hymns), proclamation (in the readings and preaching of the word), profession (in the Creed), prayer (in the collect and intercessions) and penitence (in the confession and absolution). Unlike what follows, there is nothing peculiarly Christian about it, but it is linked with the action of the eucharist proper in the same way as the last discourses were linked in the Upper Room with what Jesus did at supper. They were there to interpret and draw out the meaning of it and all that it represented.

As the name 'synaxis' or 'congregation' implies, it is a shared activity of the whole people of God in which every member has a part, it is a 'breaking of the word' together, which at the Last Supper involved conversation (the root meaning of 'sermon'). In the way we here, like others, have come to do it we have made a token beginning of trying to express this dimension of it – by taking it all from the midst of the congregation, by sharing out the roles between clergy and laity, by saying or singing together everything that is not best spoken simply, and by corporate silence – to hear and sit under the word that can build us up as the holy common people of God.

Yet, as I have said, this is but a token expression. The size and formality of the congregation and the building are against it. Formality is fine in high places, whether in a congregation of the people of God or of the Regent House. But we should be impoverished if the only 'meeting' of the university were under the Vice-Chancellor in the Senate House. That is why so much of the renewal of the past twenty years has come from the discovery of what happens when you break down the parish communion, when you take the liturgy out of the glass case of the sanctuary. We too have found that, in the informality of the 'upper room' above Bob Reiss' on a Wednesday morning and more recently in the still greater informality of Philip Buckler's on a Friday evening. Particularly is this true of the liturgy of the word, which then becomes a much freer, open-ended period of listening and sharing, both in and after the service. So we shall be carrying over and taking further at those levels each week the theme of these five talks. Out of all this may there come a deeper hearing, and doing, of the truth which the Spirit is waiting to say to the churches.

(ii) Taking

Last week we concentrated on the liturgy of the word, with its focus on listening and responding to what is read and spoken. As I said, there is nothing distinctively Christian about it in origin or structure. But today we move to the eucharist proper, whose bone-structure is provided not by an alternation of readings and canticles and prayers (as in evensong or in what Free Churchmen irreverently call the hymn-sandwich) but by four actions, based on what Jesus did at the Last Supper, when he took and he blessed and he broke and he gave. These are nothing derived from the synagogue. Yet equally they are nothing simply invented or started then. After all we talk of it as the *Last* Supper. It was the climax of a series that stretched much further back. What Jesus did that night was to attach new significance to what they had often done and shared together before. And he did not tell his followers to do what they would otherwise not have thought of doing. He told them to do what they would go on doing anyhow with a quite fresh significance. For men have always eaten and drunk together and always will as a symbol of their deepest fellowship. What he did that night was to take this universal symbol of the common meal and make it the carrier of a new meaning and presence and power.

And that meaning can be described at at least three levels. In the first place he was simply acting out, as it were in dumb crambo, the significance of his coming death. 'Look', he said, 'this stands for me, my body, my blood. This is what they will do to me: they will take me and break me – yet through it they will but seal my dedication to the Father and the coming of his kingdom.' But, secondly, he was saying, 'This is what *I* shall do for you. No one is taking my life from me; I am laying it down of myself, to make possible a new relationship between man and God. This is my life – for you, the foundation of a new order built on sacrificial love: take it and divide it among yourselves.' But, thirdly, he was saying to them, 'This is what *you* must do, for my recalling, to be the pledge of my presence and the promise of my coming – into everything. Here is the workshop of the new world, whenever and wherever, even among two or three gathered in my name, the old is taken and blessed, broken and shared, until all life and all society is recreated in the kingdom of God.' At each of these levels the eucharist is both the presentation of the gospel and the power-house of the gospel – the focus and the fount of all Christian action in the world and for the world.

And the first act, which concerns us especially this morning, shows the starting point. Jesus took – just as he took this utterly natural and familiar action of eating and drinking to be the carrier of his supernatural meaning. He took bread and took a cup off the table, as they were having supper. The kingdom of God is created out of what lies to hand, just as Calvary and the resurrection were fashioned from the taking of a man led away like a common criminal. And so today communion starts from ordinary pieces of matter, sliced bread, a bottle of wine, bought in a shop and brought into church. We have come to speak of the bread and wine at communion as the elements – and they are quite elemental. As the *News of the World* would put it, 'All human life is here'. Yet it is *human* life – not just natural life, not simply wheat and grapes, like the water which is the raw material of baptism, but the gifts of God worked upon by the labours of man, symbols and samples of his life and leisure.

All that, with everything that goes into it and lies behind it, is taken – from off the table of the world. It is brought up, by lay Christians from the point where we enter chapel, with the money which represents our substance, and taken to be laid on the altar. And in this place we quite literally go up with it – for the communion cannot start till we are there. 'There are you upon the table,' said St Augustine, 'there are you in the chalice.' And it is fitting that we should gather round the new focus of this second part of the service, to participate in the action of which we all are the celebrants. The priest is the president, but we are the celebrants, the whole body of Christ offering itself in union with its head to be taken and blessed, broken and given for the world's redemption and renewal.

So the way in which we bring out the identification of ourselves with these elements, of that bread and wine with all other bread and wine, of this food with all other food, is very relevant to the reality of our Christian commitment. William Temple said that Christianity, the religion of the word made flesh, was the most materialistic of all the world religions. And the eucharist is the most materialistic action of the church. It is concerned with matter and with society, with the sharing of matter and the changing of society. The point from which it starts is with the taking of our common life – common in the sense of shared and common in the sense of ordinary. Take me, 'just as I am, without one plea'. There is indeed much that has to be blessed, much that has to be broken, before it, before we, can be used. But without the taking, without the willingness of one village girl to say, 'Behold the handmaid of the Lord', there would have been no Christmas Day and no new creation.

(iii) Blessing

Last week we focussed on the first of the four actions of Jesus on which the structure of this service is based, that of taking. In the Series 2 service it is accompanied by no words, though in Series 3 there is an offertory prayer, said together, to bring out its significance. But in both services it leads straight into what they have no doubt in calling the 'Thanksgiving'. This is the central prayer of the entire service – in fact in the early liturgies the only one – which also gave it its name. Indeed each of the familiar names for this service is taken from one of the three acts that follow: the communion from the last, of sharing; the breaking of bread from the third, the fraction; and the eucharist or thanksgiving from today's action of blessing. These names used to be badges of churchmanship, which merely shows how one-sided and myopic intelligent Christians can get. For all are essential scriptural emphases and 'the eucharist', the commonest name in the early centuries, is that today regularly used by New Testament scholars of whatever stripe. So let us explore its rich meaning.

We are here at one of the fundamental points of break-through in recent years. We used to speak of 'the prayer of consecration' and it was a mine-field of party strife. I remember sitting through hours of debate in the old Convocation and Church Assembly of the Church of England trying to get agreement on one word in the Series 2 service which would be acceptable to both Anglo-Catholics and Evangelicals. I voted for every alternative in the hope of getting a majority for something and passing on to more vital concerns of the kingdom. I can't even now remember what the word was. We shall all be using it this morning blissfully oblivious of battles long ago – though it is only in fact ten years.

All this was the back-log of mediaeval notions of consecration which not even Roman Catholics hold today. But the Reformers in reaction were just as much heirs of the same distortion. In fact the 1662 Prayer Book actually made it worse by cutting short the prayer of consecration immediately after the words 'This is my body', 'This is my blood', inevitably suggesting that the act of consecration was by formula – saying some magic words, accompanied by manual acts, over bread and wine and leaving it at that, without even a prayer to God or the Holy Spirit.

But the biblical and early Christian understanding was not of consecrating things but of blessing God for them and over them. 'Permit the prophets to offer thanksgiving as much as they desire' runs the first eucharistic rubric we have, and in our present service the prayer of thanksgiving is an extended blessing of God in thanksgiving for our creation and redemption. But it is also a prayer that these his gifts may be to us the body and blood of Christ, the means of contact between God and ourselves, the channels of his life-giving power released through dedication and death. This release must also involve breaking, as we shall see next week. But it starts with blessing, which means, in union with the self-dedication of Jesus, opening ourselves to and aligning ourselves with the sheer goodness and generosity of God, so that we can receive with thanksgiving everything he longs to give us and do through us. Sin is being closed to God, up-tight and possessive about the resources of this world. The values of our consumer society are almost exactly the opposite of this attitude of uncalculating openness to the divine generosity, with the blessed release it brings of being liberated from self and living in the right relationship to the good things of this world. Distribution and sharing, whether in this service or beyond, depend on thankfulness – 'freely have you received, freely give' – and that is what blessing is about.

And the word that best catches this eucharistic life-style is celebration. For despite what we have often made of it we still call this service a 'celebration'. And that note of eucharist has been recovered in our day, joyfully, exuberantly by the young, often on the fringes of the church. I have a button-hole badge from America (Roman Catholic in origin, I think) with the simple words 'Celebrate life'. And that doesn't mean treating life as one long party. For it isn't all bubbly. Our celebration centres after all on a death. In fact the most joyful eucharist at which I have recently been was at the funeral of a priest, as responsible as anyone in this country in our generation for liturgy coming to life both in the parish and in the house. It is the only funeral I have attended at which everybody communicated as the most natural way in the world of saying good-bye – and yet sharing in the bread of life that unites beyond death. And through the undisguised tears for this warm-hearted Christian there was the still more evident joy, culminating in a Sydney Carter song, dedicated to our dead friend, with its theme 'one more step along the road: keep on travelling on'. 'They shared their meals', says the New English Bible of the early Christians, 'with unaffected joy'; and that is an atmosphere you can still sense in the catacombs with their primitive eucharistic symbols. To catch something of it even in Trinity College Chapel on a cold day I am suggesting we go out of our 'celebration' this morning with another song of Sydney Carter's, 'Lord of the dance'. For we are here to celebrate, to make unforgettable, 'the life that'll never, never die', and with hearts up-lifted to say, 'Take my life, and let it be consecrated, Lord, to thee.'

(iv) Breaking

'He made himself known to them in the breaking of the bread.' Was there something 'distinctively Jesus' about the way he did it which was instantly recognizable by the disciples at Emmaus? We don't know. Yet this otherwise quite unremarkable action, to us the equivalent of cutting the loaf, became for the primitive Christians the title for the whole act, rather than the blessing of the bread or even the sharing of the bread or the communion. Yet ironically it was the bit of the four-action pattern that got lost, or rather absorbed, in later liturgies. In the 1662 Prayer Book service the moment of the offertory is obvious (though the 'taking' is most unfortunately isolated from the next action of 'blessing' by the long prayer for the church and all the penitential part), the prayer of consecration is obvious and the giving of communion is obvious. But the 'breaking' has been merged into the prayer of blessing. It is not an act we join in performing together now, but one of the gestures of the consecrating priest imitating what Jesus did over the bread and cup at the Last Supper. In the Series 2 service and in Series 3 and every modern rite, the fraction or 'breaking of the bread' has once again become a separate moment which words exchanged in dialogue help to make articulate. What then is its significance? There are two main emphases.

The first comes out in the textual variant in the words of Jesus at the Last Supper as recorded by Paul, 'This is my body, which is broken for you'. The breaking proclaims in the starkest way the death of Christ. Without the breaking the thanksgiving or eucharist would remain at the level of a harvest festival: indeed it is among many other things a weekly taking of and thanksgiving for the fruits of creation worked upon by the labours of men. But as I once heard someone say, 'The reason I like harvest festival is that it's nothing to do with sin', and that's the limitation of much harvest festival religion. But it could never be said of the Christian eucharist. For at its heart stands the block of sacrifice. There is no consecration or communion without fraction, no giving of life by Christ without the giving of his life. And if that had to be true of Jesus himself, it must be true of those who as his body now are called, as St Paul put it, to carry around in their bodies the dying of the Lord Jesus that his life also may be made manifest. There is so much in us that cannot of itself manifest Christ. So 'take my life and let it be broken, Lord, with thee'.

The sacrificial aspect of the eucharist has proved one of the most divisive in Christendom. Like the unprofitable arguments I referred to last week about consecration (transubstantiation and all that), the debate about 'the sacrifice of the mass' is happily now almost dead even among Roman Catholics. And the two debates are not unconnected. Indeed it was because (to use the technical jargon) the 'fraction' got absorbed into the 'anaphora', or offering of the eucharistic prayer, that notions of sacrifice and consecration got thoroughly mixed up and distorted, and the Reformers often made matters worse in their commendable efforts to mend them. Now the 'breaking' stands forth as the act of Christ, in his body and for his body, in which no Christian can fail to share as a contemporary reality, re-presenting the cross, if he is to follow him and share his risen life.

This leads into the second emphasis in the moment of breaking. 'We break this bread', says the president in the Series 3 service, 'to share in the body of Christ.' 'Take this,' said Jesus of the bread and cup at the Last Supper, 'and divide it among yourselves.' In the most elementary sense breaking, division, is necessary in order to share. But, mysteriously, sharing is also necessary to overcome division. Properly translated, it is, says St Paul, 'because of the one bread that we for all our multiplicity are one body – for we all partake of the one bread.' The Authorized Version (perpetuated unfortunately in the response in the Series 2 service), 'We being many *are* one bread, one body,' is really unintelligible if you come to think about it. We are not one bread. Rather it is because of the one bread that we are made, and constantly remade, one body. And this mystery of breaking and uniting is well captured in the Eastern Orthodox liturgy of St John Chrysostom: 'The Lamb of God is broken and distributed, who being broken is not divided, but unites them who partakes of him.' And the same note is struck in the beautiful prayer 'over the broken bread' in the earliest of all Christian liturgies, perhaps dating from the first century: 'As this broken bread was scattered upon the mountains and being gathered together became one, so may thy church be gathered together from the ends of the earth into thy kingdom.'

'Unless a grain of wheat falls into the earth and dies it remains alone. But if it dies it yields a rich harvest.' That is the meaning of the cross. The life of God can be given, can be shared, only if it is broken and poured out, shattered and spilt. We too, as Christ's body, can be used for bringing his life to the world only if we let ourselves be broken and spent with him. The new life is to be lived and a new world built only in the power of sacrifice, the incalculable power of his sacrifice. We come here to lay hold on that and let it take hold of us. We come not to get a jag of anaesthetic to put us on another week. We meet to bind ourselves in death and in life with him who came to cast fire upon earth. And that cannot stop here, in church. Once the fuse to a stick of dynamite is lit, you must throw it or be blown.

(v) Sharing

So we reach the last of the four great moments of this dramatic action – the sharing together in the bread and wine that Christ has taken, blessed and broken. 'Eat this'. 'Drink ye all of it' (not, as the Greek makes clear, 'all of it' but, as Series 3 says, 'all of you'). The ring of fellowship is closed as those whom Jesus has just called his 'friends' pass round the cup for the last and most intimate time. Yet this fellowship is not simply the old made more significant by circumstance. The purpose of this meal, says Jesus, has been to initiate a new covenant relationship, shortly to be sealed and ratified in his blood. Just as God's people of old were brought into being by the covenant sacrifice at Sinai, so this insignificant band of twelve working men was here being created the nucleus of the new people of God, whose life was to spring from his death. The Last Supper was the dress rehearsal for the first supper of the new age, when the risen Lord would eat the bread and drink the wine with them new in his kingdom, and life would begin afresh in the resurrection order brought into being by Good Friday, Easter and Pentecost.

The common sharing of the loaf and cup, made new by their association with his life, was what was to bind them together as the new community. 'Because of the one loaf, we who are many are one body.' The eucharist is that which creates and constantly recreates the Church. Because it is what enables us to partake of the body of Christ, it is what makes us part of the body of Christ. For the Christian life is essentially and inescapably a corporate life. It is one and the same Greek word *koinonia*, which we translate variously as participation, communion, fellowship, community. That is why St Paul says to those at Corinth whose individualistic behaviour shows they have 'no sense of the body', the church, that they can only eat and drink the Lord's supper to their own condemnation. For they are receiving, inviting in judgment upon themselves, the very thing their lives deny – the life of the one new man in Christ Jesus. For this reason breach of fellowship is *par excellence* what excommunicates

– for breaking *that* fellowship is dividing, dismembering Christ himself. And as St Paul said, and in saying it no doubt shocked and puzzled his converts, breach of fellowship included not only open animosity and conscious schism but sheer individualism, going it alone religiously, keeping yourself to yourself. There are no more 'holy solitaries', said John Wesley, than holy adulterers. It is impossible to have Christ without one's neighbour in Christ.

I have put this strongly, though no more strongly, I think, than the New Testament itself puts it. But, by way of balance, let me now make equally strongly a point which may appear the absolute opposite of it. I can put it most succinctly by pointing out that it was precisely at this place in the Prayer Book service, the moment when its essential corporate nature presses more inescapably than any-where else, that for the first and only time the words 'we' and 'our' gave place to the singular 'thee' and 'thy': 'The body of our Lord Jesus Christ, which was given for thee, preserve thy body and soul unto everlasting life.' 'Take and eat this in remembrance that Christ died for *thee*'. What we receive as we hold out our hands round the table is our *own* share in Christ's death and life, our own involvement in it, which can be ours and no one else's. It is a present with our own name upon it, from him who divides severally as he wills and knows his own by name. I remember how struck I was (it shouldn't have seemed odd) the first time I took part in a liturgy at which the words of administration were preceded, as is quite usual now in small groups, by the individual's Christian name: 'John, the body of our Lord Jesus Christ'; 'Mary, the blood of our Lord Jesus Christ . . . for you.'

Yet significantly that particular liturgy was devised precisely to bring out the social and corporate nature of this fellowship act. It is one of the deep mysteries of the truth as it is in Jesus that there is no contradiction or even antithesis here between the personal and the social. The collective may be the antithesis of the individual, but the communal is not the enemy of the personal. My personality is most whole, most free, most truly my own, when and as I come to find myself in Christ, which means, inextricably for the New Testament, in the body of Christ, the fellowship of the new humanity. What I receive in holy communion is something that makes me more fully and liberatingly a person than I can ever be left to myself. But it does it by making me a 'member', part of a body. What is 'given for me' is a share in a company, my share with my own unique name upon it, but something that will bear interest for me only as the company flourishes. One cannot have Christ apart from his body – that is the message of this whole service – and in practice the power of Christ in any individual's life will depend very largely on how dynamic is the Christian community of which he is part. Recognizing this, we meet here week by week to take to ourselves this transforming power of Christ in his church, to let our separate lives be knit up and restored as members of his body. United with him, as St Chrysostom said, 'we become one single body, limbs of his flesh and bone of his bone. This is the effect of the nourishment he gives us.' And because of this Augustine could say to his people: 'It is your mystery that you receive. You hear the words "The body of Christ" and you answer "Amen". Be therefore members of Christ, that your "Amen" may be true. . . . If you have received well, you are that which you have received.'

Last Sermons

(i) Where May I Find Him?

*An undated sermon, preached probably to
a university congregation, not long after the
publication of* Honest To God

I should like to begin with one of the most familiar and captivating stories from the Old Testament. You will find it in the third chapter of the first Book of Samuel, vv. 1–9:

Now the boy Samuel was ministering to the Lord under Eli. And the word of the Lord was rare in those days; there was no frequent vision.

At that time Eli, whose eyesight had begun to grow dim, so that he could not see, was lying down in his own place; the lamp of God had not yet gone out, and Samuel was lying down within the temple of the Lord, where the ark of God was. Then the Lord called, 'Samuel! Samuel!' and he said, 'Here I am!' and ran to Eli, and said, 'Here I am, for you called me.' But he said, 'I did not call; lie down again.' So he went and lay down. And the Lord called again, 'Samuel!' And Samuel arose and went to Eli, and said, 'Here I am, for you called me.' But he said, 'I did not call, my son; lie down again.' Now Samuel did not yet know the Lord, and the word of the Lord had not yet been revealed to him. And the Lord called Samuel again the third time. And he arose and went to Eli, and said, 'Here I am, for you called me.' Then Eli perceived that the Lord was calling the boy. Therefore Eli said to Samuel, 'Go, lie down; and if he calls you, you shall say, "Speak, Lord, for thy servant hears."' So Samuel went and lay down in his place.

I should like to treat this story as a parable of man in our day. It comes from a period when 'the word of the Lord was rare, and there was no frequent vision', and this seems to me true of our present situation. Yet there is also a great hunger for the word of the Lord, such as is described by the prophet Amos: 'Behold, the days are coming, says the Lord God, when I will send a famine on the land;

not a famine of bread, nor a thirst for water, but of hearing the words of the Lord. They shall wander from sea to sea, and from north to east; they shall run to and fro, to seek the word of the Lord, but they shall not find it'. My mail over the last eighteen months has been full of such spiritual Odysseys.

'Where may I find him?' This is a story of a child's awakening to an awareness of God, both simple and profound. It speaks of an openness to the mystery of life, of a childlike responsiveness to the tingling, teasing wonder of existence. The awareness comes to him through the known experience and the familiar relationship. He thinks at first that it can be identified with it. It is simply the voice of Eli that he hears. And yet he is brought to the recognition that it comes from beyond, and cannot be contained or explained within it.

What shines through this story is typical of the whole biblical awareness of God, as something both intimate and ultimate. It is totally personal, yet unconditional, transcendent.

Nothing could be further from the truth than that in *Honest to God* I wanted to cut out this dimension of the transcendent, to reduce our understanding of God to one of pure immanence, or to substitute some sub-personal pantheism. My God, the only God I am interested in, is the God of the Bible. It is the God of Abraham, Isaac and Jacob, the God of Augustine, Aquinas, Martin Luther, Karl Barth, and Martin Buber. I may not have quoted from them much, but these are the men from whom I have learnt. I don't want to deny anything in the biblical doctrine of God or the Catholic creeds. I am just as concerned with this utterly transcendent personal reality. The only question is how this can be expressed and made real and relevant for our generation.

For the trouble starts when we try to talk about this reality in such a way that we can share it. How are we to picture, communicate, describe, fix it, for ourselves and for others? If men ask, 'Where, how may I find him?', how do we speak of it?

There are various traditional ways of doing this. In the past they have been a help. In the present I suspect they are often as much of a stumbling-block as a help, though there is nothing whatever wrong with them if they *do* mediate the reality. My concern is for those for whom they do not – and evidently there are vastly more of them than we thought.

The first and obvious way to describe, to communicate, the presence of God is to represent him as being there, acting and speaking as though he were a human (though everyone knows, of course, that he is not). It is literally and actually God's voice that the boy Samuel hears. God himself comes down into the situation to speak or to visit. There was a strong conviction among the Hebrews that God himself could not be seen, though he could be heard. In this story he is actually represented as being personally present: 'The Lord came and stood there' (though Samuel could not see him). More often he sends his angel or works through some other intermediary. Or he causes things to happen to make his presence known, abnormal things beyond the occurrences of everyday experience. Signs and miracles have this function in the Bible – to describe acts of God.

All this is what I have called the *mythological* projection – the translation of spiritual reality into physical or quasi-physical description. It is a vivid way of saying that God is in this experience, or that in this experience we are aware of the numinous, the unconditional, the ultimate. It is entirely valid as a sign manual. One may illustrate the truth of it perhaps from the non-biblical myth of Atlas. The ancient myth of an old man supporting the world on his shoulders was a way of saying that the earth does not support itself in space. We also know that it does not: for us it is held in orbit by the sun's gravitational pull. The myth was saying something profoundly true. But such language today would not convey the truth to modern man. It would be much more likely to conceal it. So with Christian truth. The central affirmation is that in Jesus we see the clue to all life, the window through to ultimate reality. To say that he was the Son of a supernatural Being sent from heaven to earth may help to bring this home. But for many it transforms the whole of the biblical history into a fairy tale. Myth was a recognized way of expressing the interpretation, the significance, of the history. It turned the bare historical statement 'Jesus was born in Bethlehem' into the Christian doctrine of the Incarnation by describing it in terms of God sending his only begotten Son, to the accompaniment of angelic visitations, heavens opening, stars moving, etc. But for so many people today it simply succeeds in discrediting it as history. These things – the comings down and the goings up, the miraculous interventions – are described as though they were actual literal occurrences, and people just do not believe that these sorts of goings on take place. We can still use this language, but we must recognize what we are doing and distinguish much more rigorously than our predecessors just what we intend to be understood as event and what as myth, or theological interpretation in pictures. Most people today still take the biblical stories, for instance of the Ascension or the Second Coming, desperately literally, as things that could in theory be picked up on a television screen. They think that this is what they will have to swallow if they become Christians, and they find them frankly incredible.

The second way of trying to describe and communicate the experience of God is by use of the *supranaturalist* projection (I use the word in the sense of Mercator's projection and the rest – i.e., as a way of trying to represent a reality which exists on one plane in that of another). Let us start again from the Samuel story. God is not Eli, nor any other human person. But such a personal communication is intelligible only if he is a Person, a Being, up there or out there, from whom the message comes. The utterly personal reality of God in the human relationship and awareness is objectified, projected as the existence of a God as a super-Person living in a realm 'above' or 'beyond' this one. Statements about the experience (which is all we have evidence for) become statements about this Being – his existence, qualities and activities. God is thought of as a Person, a sort of super-Man, who lives in another world called heaven but who comes into this one and graciously makes himself known to us – supremely in the Incarnation (viewed as a sort of space-trip).

All this is a way of giving objectivity to the reality of the experience. The voice, as it were, must come from somewhere, unless it is an hallucination. So a divine super-world is constructed, inhabited by God and spirits – a duplicate of this one on a higher level. We are most familiar with this in the Olympian religion of ancient Greece. There is nothing distinctively Christian about it, though it may be characteristically Western. It is a way of giving reality to the spiritual experience of God in terms of the three-decker universe. Today its effect is to give it unreality. It makes God as incredible to millions as the man in the moon. Christianity comes to be discredited with it. People dismiss the experience because of the picture drawn, the model constructed, to give it expression.

Another way of describing and giving objectivity to the reality of God in human experience is to translate it into statements about the reality of God as he is in himself outside human experience. This could be called the *metaphysical* projection. It is a way of saying that what is intensely real for me is not real simply for me. These awarenesses, like those of the child Samuel, our deepest Christian convictions, tell us something about reality itself. And, indeed, the biblical writers and Christians ever since are convinced that they do. They are not something I invent or imagine, any more than Samuel did. Indeed I could invent a much more comfortable God to live with, and the same was true of Jeremiah or Job, or indeed of the boy Samuel himself, whose encounter with God when it eventually came through to him was utterly shattering to the relationship by which it was mediated. These awarenesses come to us with an inescapable givenness. The prophets are men who are seized by God, driven by the Spirit. So was Jesus, and so have Christians been ever since. Witness the opening lines of Gerard Manley Hopkins' 'Wreck of the Deutschland':

> Thou mastering me
> God! giver of breath and bread . . .
> Lord of living and dead . . .
> Over again I feel thy finger and find thee.

There is a terrible objectivity in all this. Nevertheless, all religious, all theological, statements are statements about this reality as it grips and holds me: they describe my existential relationship to it.

But the great temptation is to speak as though Christian doctrine describes not my engagement of the truth (statements beginning with 'I believe in . . .') but realities outside this experience altogether. This, for instance, has supremely overtaken the doctrine of the Trinity. As I see it, this exists to safeguard the conviction, that all the different aspects under which as Christians we know God are equally veridical, equally speak to us of the same ultimate reality. Not only the love of the Father, but also the grace of our Lord Jesus Christ and the fellowship of the Holy Spirit, take us through to the depth of reality which we can only speak of as God. This is the affirmation of Christians, as opposed to those who would say that in Christ or in the Spirit we have a merely human person or a merely human fellowship. It is indeed saying something about reality, about God – though always as he is known by us. But in the popular imagination the doctrine of the Trinity has been erected into a vast metaphysical construction. It seems to be describing a complicated mathematical entity, a sort of divine society or celestial triangle, to whose somewhat improbable properties the Christian is asked to give assent. And this is what theology is popularly supposed to be about.

But the demolition squad has been at work on such constructions. At the sophisticated level the linguistic philosophers are asking whether such statements have any meaning at all. But at the popular level there is an equal reluctance to credit any statement going beyond the evidence of our ordinary experience. The whole schema appears incredible. Dogma seems quite airborne and devoid of foundation. This generation is demanding the cash value of such statements in terms of our experienced relationships with other people and things. I personally welcome this test. Much of the relief felt in the reaction to *Honest to God* was because lots of people suddenly realized that theology was not about metaphysical entities beyond our ken but about ordinary experience in depth, at the level of ultimate concern. The trouble is that doctrines framed to define and safeguard the experience are as often today a barrier to it (this is particularly true, for instance, of doctrines of the Atonement). They make the whole thing seem unreal and remote. People think that they are being asked to believe in them for their own sake, and find this an impossible intellectual exercise.

There is a fourth way in which what was meant to channel the experience has in fact confined it and made it harder for many. The most effective way of fixing the encounter of faith with the living God is to put it in a box, enshrine it in religion. On the Mount of Transfiguration Peter sought to make three tabernacles, in order to hold the moment of faith, to fix it, and transmit it. To the question, 'Where may I find him?', the answer, if you want to be quite sure, is 'Within the religious system'. God is put in a house, in a sanctuary, a holy area of life. The assumption of most of our evangelism has been that there is a particular wave-band on which you can be certain to hear him if you tune in. There are different wave-lengths, high and low, broad and narrow, Catholic and Protestant – but this is the band. God may not get through very much in the secular areas of life, but he has his own channel – what the TV boys call the 'religious slot' – and it is within this that 'the ministers of religion', as we are called, operate.

In fact today the religious slot is being narrowed down and down. Except where it is artificially maintained by Act of Parliament (and even that may quite likely go) it has virtually disappeared from our society. Ancient man poured his libation to the gods before eating and drinking, and up till now it has always been assumed that a place must be left open for religion and the priest. To close the circle

without God was *hubris*, pride. But under the pressure of seculariz-
ation the circle of explanation and control in human affairs has been
virtually closed. The religious sector, representing the gaps in this
circle, which was the traditional way in for God, seems squeezed out
of modern life. Modern secular man lives his life without feeling the
need for leaving this space. The question is, Must he be induced or
worked upon to reopen it, to prize apart the ring, if God is to get
through? How is Christ to become Lord of a genuinely lay and
unashamedly secular world? Have individuals got to return to
attitudes they have abandoned and turn their back on this modern
world for an equivalent of mediaevalism?

The silent presupposition of all our churches is that unless we can
induce people to become religious first there is not much hope of
getting them to become Christians. But in fact I believe the
traditional way in often makes it more difficult for them to hear
rather than easier. They are not particularly drawn by religion or by
a desire to join a religious club. If they have to become religious first,
then they say, 'Thank you, this is not for me. I am not the religious
type.' If we make this a presupposition of accepting the gospel, then
we are in danger of imposing the condition of circumcision again in
modern form.

Remember that Jesus set no particular store by the religious sector.
The only figures from it in his parables are those of the Pharisee in the
Temple praying with himself, and the Priest and Levite passing by on
the other side. In contrast, as John Oman put it a generation ago,
'What a varied secular procession of kings and slaves, bailiffs and
debtors, farmers and fisher-folk, housewives and children, and all
their secular occupations, with more feasting than fasting, and more
marriages than funerals.' And George MacLeod has reminded us
that Jesus was crucified not in a cathedral between two candles but
on a cross between two thieves. His life and death were very secular
events. If he is to become Lord of this age we cannot insist that he
must enter it through the gate of religion. Before, that may not have
mattered as that gate was open. Now for many it is closed. They are
not coming to a commitment to Christ, to seeing him as the clue to
their world as individuals and as a society, because they are drawn by
hymn singing or church services. Localizing the holy in the sanctuary
in fact for many makes it more difficult to recognize. There are many
in our generation who are more likely to respond to the sacred in the
secular, the holy in the common (which is after all basically the

meaning of the *holy communion*), than in the distinctively religious. The coming of Christ into our world in such a way that he can be Lord of it is increasingly likely, I feel, to find the religious apparatus a liability rather than an asset. This certainly does not mean that there is not a place for a church in the New Testament sense of a dedicated nucleus pledged to Christ and his Lordship over the whole of life, shaping everything to his worth (which is fundamentally the meaning of worship). But I suspect that many of the religious trappings can go.

I desperately want to enable men, women and children to be open again to the reality of God. But unfortunately for most people today this three-letter word stands for that which is most unreal and remote in their experience, rather than for the most real thing in the world, the *ens realissimum*. 'We must realize', as Werner Pelz has said, 'that when we use the word "God" we are talking about something which no longer connects with anything in most people's life, except with whatever happens to be left over when all the vital connections have been made.' My concern is that he shall be seen once again in and through the vital connections rather than over and above them.

The trouble is that ways of helping have come so often to be more of a hindrance. People cannot hear the voices for the representation, the embodiment, of them, whether in mythological, supranatural-istic, metaphysical or religious forms.

There is, of course, no guaranteed answer to the question, 'Where may I find him?' But I believe that we must start where Samuel started – in the common, the familiar, the ordinary stuff of personal relationships – with an openness, a responsiveness, an awareness to the beyond in the midst, to the unconditional grace and demand which will not leave us alone. And if you ask, 'How will I recognize what it is like, what will it say to me?', then for the Christian the answer is that that word is defined and spelt out in flesh and blood in the life, death and risen life of the man Christ Jesus. We cannot command it. It is grace. It comes or it does not come. All that we can command is the receptivity, the integrity, the honesty to hear it. 'Speak, Lord, for thy servant heareth.'

(ii) Remember now thy Creator in the days of thy youth
(*Eccles. 12.1*)

A sermon preached in Trinity College Chapel, Cambridge,
22 November 1981

We have listened tonight to some of the noblest music of mortality: Psalm 90, the closing chapter of Ecclesiastes in the sonorous cadences of the Authorized Version, both spoken and sung, Tennyson's 'Crossing the Bar'. They all echo the nostalgic, *fin de siècle* beauty associated traditionally with this Sunday next before Advent. 'Too late have I loved thee, thou loveliness so ancient and so new, too late have I loved thee.' St Augustine's words touch and reverberate a chord deep in the sad heart of humanity. And this tragic sense of life has seldom been caught more hauntingly than by 'the Preacher', as the Authorized Version calls him, whose 'last sermon' we heard read this evening.

Who was he? We don't know. He gives us his reflections on life in the name of Solomon, 'King in Jerusalem', the traditional fount of all wisdom as David is the source of all psalmody. And he is content to shelter behind the role of 'Koheleth'. What this means is uncertain even in Hebrew. King James' men styled him 'the Preacher' (though he is surely no parson), the Greek translators of the Old Testament the *ecclesiastes*, or speaker of an *ecclesia* or assembly, rather like the Speaker of the House of Commons (it is certainly nothing churchy – Ecclesiastes is about the least ecclesiastical book in the Bible). The New English Bible in fact calls him the Speaker, the Good News Bible the Philosopher, as though he were the master or guru of a philosophical school, a Socratic-type figure. Perhaps the Teacher honoured by the Dead Sea sect of Qumran might be the nearest equivalent in Israel of the late third-century BC, which seems to have been his setting.

In any case his wisdom is timeless: he has seen everything – and seen through everything. There is nothing new under the sun, all is vanity, a chasing after the wind. There is no reflection on the rat-race which he cannot match with his mordant wit. The enjoyment of reading him, like reading Hardy or Housman, is the pleasure of biting on the tooth that hurts. But he ends, as the others do not, with a moving appeal to remember your Creator – before it is too late.

The magic of his imagery has left us one of the purple passages of the Authorized Version. One is tempted just to savour it for its literary beauty and to ask no questions. Yet the inwardness of it is entirely lost unless one grasps one clue which none of the traditional versions bring out and which escaped me for years. And that is that the imagery refers to the parts of the body, as age wearies them and the years condemn. The keepers of the house that tremble are the arms and hands. The strong men that are bent are the legs. The grinders that cease because they are few are the teeth, and those that look out of the windows and are dimmed are the eyes. The doors shut on the street are the ears grown deaf to the grinding at the mill or the sound of music. Yet even the chirping of a bird can waken the old, and he will be afraid of steep places or stairs and even crossing the street is full of terrors. The blossom whitening on the almond tree is obviously the hair, but the grasshopper becoming a burden is one of the many places where the Hebrew is very uncertain. 'The locust's paunch is swollen', says the New English Bible, but it may describe the old man hardly being able to drag himself along. 'Desire fails' seems to refer to the loss of taste and sexual appetite. For man is on his way to his 'long' or eternal home (I remember seeing an advertisement years ago in the subway at Harvard Square for 'Long's funeral home' and thought they had missed the perfect text!) and already the professional mourners are loitering in the street.

Remember, he says, before the silver cord is snapped and the golden bowl is broken, the pitcher is shattered at the fountain or the wheel broken at the well. The imagery is archetypal, and recurs in many traditions – of the thread of life cut by the fates, in Hindu body symbolism, in dreams (though Jung regrettably never commented on this passage), and interestingly in out-of-the body experiences, where a recurrent feature is of the sort of umbilical cord which still attaches the observing self to the physical body. When finally it snaps the flesh dissolves to dust and the spirit or breath of life returns to God who gave it.

The only translation I know which supplies the reader with the clue to the symbolism is that of the Good News Bible, for which I come to have an increasing regard especially in the livelier parts of the Old Testament (it is superb on Proverbs). Of course it has to sacrifice many overtones of the poetry, but here it is for the meaning:

So remember your Creator while you are still young, before those dismal days and years come when you will say, 'I don't enjoy life.' That is when the light of the sun, the moon, and the stars will grow dim for you, and the rain clouds will never pass away. Then your arms, that have protected you, will tremble, and your legs, now strong, will grow weak. Your teeth will be too few to chew your food and your eyes too dim to see clearly. Your ears will be deaf to the noise of the street. You will barely be able to hear the mill as it grinds or music as it plays, but even the song of a bird will wake you from sleep. You will be afraid of high places, and walking will be dangerous. Your hair will turn white; you will hardly be able to drag yourself along, and all desire will have gone.

We are going to our final resting place, and then there will be mourning in the streets. The silver chain will snap, and the golden lamp will fall and break; the rope at the well will break, and the water jar will be shattered. Our bodies will return to the dust of the earth, and the breath of life will go back to God, who gave it to us.

So what of its message today? First surely we must be grateful that this book got into the canon of scripture at all. It is deeply pessimistic and at times cynical, but a faith that is not broad enough to embrace such doubt and realism is worth little, especially in these times. 'Hora novissima, tempora pessima: The world is very evil, the times are waxing late.' So St Bernard in the twelfth century. Or, in modern imagery, the doomsday clock stands at four minutes to midnight. For the first time for two thousand years we have a generation of young people who must face the real possibility that they may not reach middle or old age: like the early Christians we must reckon with the expectation that we may have but a short time to live. And individually of course this has been the universal prospect of most of the human race till modern times – and still is. The patriarchs lamented that 'the days of their pilgrimage were few and evil'. The whole of Buddhism is built on the recognition that the primary fact of life is *dukkha*, suffering or unsatisfactoriness. And listen to Dr Johnson writing two hundred years ago before the advent of modern medicine:

A good man is subject, like other mortals, to all the influences of natural evil . . . He bears about him the seeds of disease, and may linger away a great part of his life under the tortures of the gout or stone; at one time groaning with insufferable anguish, at another dissolved in listlessness and langour.

And even with modern medicine the *memento mori* can strike with frightening swiftness. In my other parish, the village in the Dales I look after in the vacations, a girl of sixteen had not even been diagnosed as having cancer when I left at the beginning of term, and now she is hovering on the brink. As the Prayer Book says, 'In the midst of life we are in death'; or Browning:

> Just when we're safest, there's a sunset-touch,
> A fancy from a flower-bell, some one's death,
> A chorus-ending from Euripides.

'Ask for not for whom the bell tolls, it tolls for thee.'

But what is the corollary to be drawn? For the Preacher of Ecclesiastes it was 'Remember, remember' – before it is too late. For St Bernard 'Hora novissima, tempora pessima sunt, *vigilemus*', wake up and watch it. For the early Christians, in the words of one of them: 'Since the whole universe is to break up in this way, think what sort of people you ought to be, what devout and dedicated lives you should live! Look eagerly for the coming of the Day of God and work to hasten it on.' Think what to do with what remains to you of life – for what you put into it will be what you get out of it.

But let the last word be with St Paul to the young Timothy (II Tim. 3.10–15; 4.6–8). Here is a response very different from that of the tired cynic or even from Browning's Bishop Blougram teased by 'the grand Perhaps'. For he knows he is not on his own against the changes and chances of an alien universe. 'I know who it is in whom I have trusted, and am confident of his power to keep safe what he has put into my charge until the Great Day.' Hence the assurance of those final words: 'Already my life is being poured out on the altar, the hour for my departure is upon me. I have run the great race, I have finished the course, I have kept faith.'

If we can take aboard both the pessimism of the Preacher and the optimism of St Paul and what Paul Tillich called 'the courage to be' for living in between, then the dying cadences of the Sunday next before Advent will not have tolled for us in vain.

(iii) On Having a Critical Faith

*A sermon preached in Trinity College Chapel, Cambridge,
25 November 1979*

On Having a Critical Faith – that is the title of a book I read last vacation which has niggled at me ever since. It is the translation of a piece of writing by a German New Testament scholar which he says has meant more to him than any of his professional studies. It goes back, he tells us, to his student days and his dissatisfaction over the attitude of so many of his theological teachers. How could they go on working, day after day, when they could not even give a convincing answer to the insinuation that God is an illusion. 'I resolved either to find an answer of my own or give up theology altogether.'

So in a short book of a hundred pages he sets out to examine the arguments most commonly produced against the truth of Christian belief; first, that it is an ideology born out of social conflicts or psychological needs; second, that religion has no grounding in everyday experience and reality; and finally that the historical approach makes everything relative. There are good reasons, he concludes, for being a Christian. But this does not mean that Christianity can be defended in its traditional form. It will have to change if it is not to lose all credibility in the modern world.

I can gladly lend it to anyone who would be interested, but you may find it too conditioned by the German debate. In fact this is an exercise that probably has to be done afresh in every culture and every generation. Indeed it is something that each one of us has to do for ourselves over a whole life-time – facing faith with the question at every point, 'Is it true?' And it is a question that can easily be ducked or glossed over. Writing sixteen years ago now in *The Honest to God Debate*, David Edwards noted the various movements for renewal in the church which then and since have evoked hope and enthusiasm, and said: 'But they all share one defect: *they do not necessarily concern the truth of Christianity*,' and he added: 'A deeper renewal is needed, which may involve a costlier change.'

Professor Gerd Theissen, whose book I started from, ends with these words·

I am not interested in irrefutable assertions but in refutable truths. This question of the truth goes against much in life that is otherwise valuable. It causes resentment, at a time when agreement with others counts more than the corrections of the errors of yesterday and today. It is not legitimated by faithfulness to the tradition, but shows its faithfulness to the tradition by being open to cross-examination. But it is open to argument, even to argument from dogmatic traditions. It allows itself to be irritated by arguments, for it is based on the recognition 'that I may be wrong and you may be right, and by an effort we may get nearer to the truth'.[1]

That last sentence is a quotation from Karl Popper, whose influence can be recognized behind the words 'I am not interested in irrefutable assertions but in refutable truths'. For his great contribution has been to insist that statements can be scientific only if they are falsifiable. If nothing can be brought against a theory that could refute it, then it cannot be true.

And though the tests in the sphere of the spirit will not be those of the laboratory, of weighing and measuring, the same criterion must be accepted of religious statements. They must be prepared to stand up to the tests of argument, experience and history. In other words, we must be prepared to have a critical faith, ready always, as St Peter says, to give an answer for the hope that is in us.

This sounds so obvious as not to need stressing, especially, one would think, in a university. But criticism and faith have so often been seen as pulling in opposite directions, and not least here. Studying the Bible critically has been regarded as a threat to reading it faithfully. And being sceptical and believing appear to be opposites. Yet 'sceptical' simply comes from the Greek word meaning to look at carefully, 'all ways up' as we should say – hence to examine. And as Plato makes Socrates say, 'the unexamined life is not worth living'. And that sensitivity is one of the chief things we come to a university to sharpen.

There is truth that comes from the suspension of belief, but there is truth also that comes from the suspension of disbelief. Not that these are two sorts of truth; as though there were a dichotomy between the truths of science and religion. The same combined approach applies everywhere. As C. S. Lewis insisted, we have to be sceptical about scepticism itself – the attitude of mind that makes an 'ism' of disbelief, of never being able to come to a knowledge of the truth, any truth. In every aspect of life, in dealing with things or persons or in ultimate decisions about reality, our judgments will be a mixture of sifting scrutiny and a leap of faith. If we say, for instance, 'he is a man whose judgment I trust', that statement is built up out of all sorts of bits of empirical evidence, but finally it incorporates a commitment that can never be proved in advance. It is an act of faith, yet of critical faith.

In one sense a critical faith is one among many of the facets of faith we have been considering this term. In another and perhaps better sense it is something that should be built into every facet of faith. Faith has many faces, many expressions – mystical, worshipful, intellectual, practical, political. But in each of these if it is not fully and freely critical it can become unbalanced, dogmatic or fanatical – like so much Muslim faith in our modern world, which has never been prepared to submit itself or its Koran to criticism. This is what St Paul was concerned about in the congregation at Corinth (I Cor. 14.12–20). Many of them were what today we should call charismatics, men and women of ecstatic faith – and the last thing he wants to do is to quench the Spirit. But he insists that it must be brought to the double test of what is constructive of community and intelligible to others. 'Aspire', he says, 'to excel in what builds up the church.' 'I will pray as I am inspired to pray, but I will also pray intelligently.' 'Be as innocent of evil as babes, but at least be grown-up in your thinking.'

This does not mean that reason is a substitute for faith, or its basis. St Paul of all people is not arguing for a narrowly academic or dryly intellectual faith. The heart has its reasons too, and the basic meaning of faith for St Paul is an utterly personal union with Christ which comes through in every fibre of his being, so that, as he says, 'it is no longer I who live but Christ who lives in me'. But precisely because it is so whole it can never be less than whole, it cannot cut off or distrust any aspect of our nature, least of all what we are pleased to call 'the top storey'. Nor is a critical faith the opposite of a 'simple faith', especially for anyone who would call himself or herself a student. But a simplistic faith can never be profound; it is more like the faith Jesus designated as having no depth of root. And consequently it is very insecure, however seemingly certain and often dogmatic. It is those who most fear biblical criticism because it may weaken faith who, inadvertently, are often building up and abetting the most brittle faith. The churchmen, too, who rush to protect 'the faithful' (or should it be those of little faith?) against every wind of new thinking or doctrinal exploration are usually exposing their own insecurity.

Christians should be marked as men and women who have nothing to fear from the truth. It is not only that 'great is truth and it shall prevail' (and that actually comes from the Bible, the first book of Esdras, not from classical humanism). It is that for the Christian Christ *is* the truth, as well as the way and the life, and therefore everything true – whether it comes from science or art or history or other religions – must eventually lead *to* him not away from him.

Such is the trust, the deep trust of a genuinely critical faith. And it is profoundly liberating – 'the power', as the hymn puts it

. . . that makes the children free
To follow truth, and thus to follow thee.

(iv) Exploring Silence

A sermon preached in Trinity College Chapel Cambridge,
4 May 1980

Talking about silence – the ultimate absurdity. Professor C. E. M. Joad once said of freedom that it doesn't bear talking about – all the arguments turn out to be for determinism. And if that is true of freedom how much more of silence. The shortest sermon I ever heard was at a Roman Catholic mass on the feast of the Precious Blood. 'The less said about this,' began the priest, 'the better' – and left the pulpit. If I shut up now and left the next quarter of an hour silent, it would probably be the most memorable sermon I have ever preached. But I intend to resist the temptation. For, as Augustine said of the mystery of the Trinity, one must speak *ne taceretur*, lest by silence it should seem to be denied rather than affirmed.

So with silence. I want to affirm it, and simply to say nothing would be to leave the negative in possession. For the initial image of silence is undoubtedly negative. 'Abstinence from speech', 'absence of sound' are the first two dictionary definitions, and the roots of the words for 'silence' in the Indo-European languages are, I am told, from 'cease' or 'give up'. Of course absence of sound and cessation of speech can be a blessed thing, like the relief when a pneumatic drill stops or you walk out of a disco. 'Silence is golden', and the space from intrusion it represents (for we have no lids to our ears unlike our eyes) a rare blessing in the modern world. But there are many different kinds, many faces, of silence; and the first that comes to mind is negative.

It is the silence of *isolation*, and it is frightening. From all but the very nearest parts of our vast universe light reaches us but no sound. 'The eternal silence of these infinite spaces,' said Pascal, 'terrifies me'. And this sense has been greatly increased by the picture of modern astronomy with its ultimate horror of black holes into which even light is sucked. The ancients believed in the harmony of the spheres –

it was all like a great celestial concert, put on for the glory of God and the benefit of man. In the eighteenth century Addison tried to console himself in these words:

> What though in solemn silence all
> Move round the dark terrestial ball;
> What though nor real voice nor sound
> Amid their radiant orbs be found;
> In reason's ear they all rejoice,
> And utter forth a glorious voice.

Yet the infinite silences are still emotionally threatening. We live in a cold and eerie world, like a deaf child cut off from communication.

And this silence of isolation is close cousin to the silence of *alienation*. We are shut off because we can't or won't get through to people. There is the speechlessness of anger, resentment, estrangement. 'They haven't spoken to each other for years,' is the ultimate in separation. Yet in all our experiences there are what have been called 'dead, padlocked silences' masking the areas of unlove. To silence someone we say significantly 'Shut up!', go back into your shell. At the cosmic level too silence connotes alienation: 'Wherefore art thou silent?', says the psalmist to God, and another speaks of the dead as those that 'go down into silence', the final state of separation. *The Silence of God* is a title that speaks to many of our generation in face of Auschwitz and the rest. And there is a powerful modern Japanese novel simply called *Silence*, describing the drying up of the church's voice there in the sixteenth century under persecution and apostasy. Yet this silence of estrangement, which cuts us off from each other, is as much emotional as moral.

And it leads into the silence of *embarrassment* – of bewilderment ('I just didn't know what to say!'), or simply of boredom ('there was nothing to say'). And there's nothing like silence for revealing emptiness. But the silence of shyness can come out in the man of whom we say 'he has no small talk'. This can be painful to others, though we may secretly admire him as a strong silent man. The great Bishop J. B. Lightfoot was said to be a man of 'imperturbable silence' – and apparently quite content to be so. Yet taciturnity, like the word itself, speaks usually of sourness rather than joy. There is a withering portrait in the National Gallery which has as its title 'Aut tace aut loquere meliora silentio', 'Either keep quiet or say something better than silence'. And to me the most irresistible portrait in this college is that on the stairs of the Lodge of W. H. Thompson, Master here a hundred years ago, who looks as if he is uttering his most famous mot, 'None of us is infallible, not even the youngest.'

This perhaps provides a lead into the next sort of silence, the silence of *awe*. We talk of an awed or hushed silence. Chatter falls away. There is just nothing to say which is not trivial. We are in the presence. And this is an archetypal religious response: 'Woe is me . . . I am a man of unclean lips . . . for my eyes have seen the King, the Lord of Hosts.' Let every mouth be stopped. Let all mortal flesh keep silence. And this is the gateway to the positive, profounder meanings of silence. Yet it is still outside – at the threshold, where you leave your shoes.

For all these silences so far have this in common, that they are not shared silences – or if you experience them in common with other people (as in the tube) they only make you realize how cut off you are. They drive you in or back upon yourself, making for loneliness rather than solitude.

But now let us step across the threshold, into the silences that bring us closer to one another rather than further off – though again starting instinctively with the negative:

The silence of *sorrow*. This is a silence that comes from deprivation, yet because, or if, it is shared it is not empty. Indeed it comes often when we are too full for words, 'chockers'. There's just nothing you can say. I remember so well the first time I dined in Hall after the death of my mother. Fortunately high table in Trinity is a foot wider than that in any other college I know (sociologically very significant!), so that if you don't want to have to talk to anyone you needn't. And I remember feeling, Pray God no one starts a conversation. I was just too full. There is a time, said the Preacher of Ecclesiastes, to speak and a time to be silent, a time to embrace and a time to refrain from embracing. Yet deep down the silence of sorrow is a silence of sympathy, of simply being with and knowing when not to talk, and it can go powerfully with the silent hug and simply holding hands and not bottling it up. 'Drop, drop slow tears.' This is what Ivan Illich in an essay on 'The Eloquence of Silence' calls the silence of the *Pieta*, such as inspired our anthem 'Stabat mater dolorosa'. It is the silence of what Simone Weil called 'waiting upon God'.

And yet this silence of sorrow, as Mary Magdalene found at the tomb, can tip over by some magic into the silence of *joy*. Indeed we all know what it is to weep for joy. Again we are speechless, lost for words – not because we are empty, but because we are full. It's too much, we say. Shakespeare, as so often, got it right: 'Silence is the perfectest herald of joy; I were but little happy if I could say how much.' This is lovers' silence. They don't want or need to talk, but simply to be with each other. It is a silence of union, yet it preserves and cherishes the otherness of the other: 'two solitudes', as Rilke beautifully put it, 'that protect and touch and greet each other'. It is a silence that overcomes rather than simply denies separateness, creating and respecting the space of the other. And this of course is the image, the model, of what the religious imagination has always meant by resting in God, abiding, being at home. 'In thy presence,' says the psalmist again, 'is the fulness of joy.' It is a silence of plenitude, not emptiness. Yet finally it is but the gateway to another even deeper silence, not only of being with but of being in:

The silence of *interiority*. 'Go into a room by yourself,' says Jesus, 'and shut the door.' 'Be still, and know that I am God.' This is 'the secret place of the Most High', 'the still centre of the turning world'. And stilling, centring down has been the message of every mystical and religious tradition. At the heart of everything, said the Gnostics, is *Sige*, Silence; *Sunyata* or the Void, said the Buddha; the hole at the centre of the wheel, in Lao Tsu's vivid image: 'The eternal *tao* is not the *tao* that can be spoken. He who speaks does not know: he who knows does not speak.' Or listen to Ignatius of Antioch: 'He who truly possesses the word of Jesus is able also to listen to his silence.' Indeed he says the Word itself 'proceeds from silence', from 'the quietness of God'. This is the other side of the silence of God which seemed so threatening. The hymn speaks of sharing 'the silence of eternity, interpreted by love'. This is what transforms loneliness into solitude. It is what has been called the silence of availability – 'Speak, Lord, for thy servant heareth' – of concavity – 'Come fill the moment that without thee is empty'.

I have selected seven faces of silence, the silence of isolation, alienation, embarrassment, awe, sorrow, joy and interiority. But the number is as arbitrary as the colours of the rainbow; and I could have suggested others; for instance, the silence of Jesus before his accusers really fits none of these.

But I hope that I have indicated how silence embraces the whole gamut of the human experience. 'All human life is here', though not as a certain newspaper understands that phrase. For silence is the sacrament, the matrix, of existence at any depth. This is what the Quakers have been saying to us for three hundred years – and I wish we could learn from them that an act of worship begins when the first person arrives. Or perhaps you saw the three remarkable articles in *The Times* just after Easter by Bernard Levin on what he called 'An extraordinary journey into the interior', describing the vast gatherings in Poona of the Bhagwan Shree Rajneesh. The first thing that hit him was the colour of this sea of some one thousand five hundred people sitting on the floor. 'The second surprise is that there is *total* silence throughout this orange sea.' And the third surprise, he said, as the car bringing the Bhagwan approaches, is that 'mine is the only head that turns'.

That is a depth of silence of which most of us know little. We are nervously afraid of silence. Even in a retreat we have first to get over the hump of resistance to it. We don't know what we shall do with it, we have a horror of going blank. Or perhaps we fear what it may do with us. I have called this sermon 'Exploring Silence'; yet we hold back from the exploration because we sense that it also explores us, probes to the secret places, the empty places, we would rather not face. It 'sifts us', as the old Quakers used to say. It takes courage to lay ourselves open to the way of contemplation – and it takes training in our modern world merely to sit still, to switch off, to attend, to tune in, to overcome the 'static' by which our lives are surrounded. I am the last person to claim any expertise in this. The techniques of meditation are stranger to me than to many in your and my children's generation. I can only point you to others further along the way. Yet ultimately I *know*, as I am persuaded you know, that it is not in the storm or in the earthquake or in the fire, but in the still, small voice that the presence is to be found. And the final question, which we can only answer, as Kierkegaard put it, 'alone in the dark room', is whether we can stoop low enough to hear that voice.

(v) The Still Small Voice

A sermon preached in Trinity College Chapel, Cambridge,
10 May 1982

We have listened tonight to one of the great human stories of the Bible, indeed of all literature (I Kings 19.1–18). I find myself increasingly wanting to preach from the Old Testament. For it reminds us that any distinctively Christian gospel arises out of and is addressed to the big human questions, and it is diminished – usually individualized – if it is not seen as taking up and as it were using as its raw material the entire stuff of human existence. In the Bible, as in the *News of the World*, 'all human life is here'; and this story runs the gamut of the human condition. Let me draw out, the first two by way of context and the third by way of content, three dimensions of it: the physical, the psychological, and what I can only call the politico-spiritual.

We think of it, rightly, as the story of the still small voice. For that still pool of silence is its centre. Yet this gains its significance only from the context of almost breathless movement and the most intense expenditure of physical energy. Its background (and I should like to have had the whole of I Kings 18 read as well) is the highly dramatic encounter of the prophet Elijah with the massed prophets of Baal, who outnumbered him by eight hundred and fifty to one and had behind them all the backing of the court establishment and especially of Ahab's ruthless queen Jezebel. The sheer physical scale of the thing is exhausting if one has any idea of the terrain.

First, the protagonists are summoned to the top of Mount Carmel, overlooking the modern port of Haifa in the north-west of Israel. After an all-day struggle, which comes to its climax in Elijah's vindication, he orders them to be seized and taken down to the River Kishon in the valley below and there he kills them apparently single-handed. Then he climbs back to the top of Mount Carmel (I have only been up it in a bus and it is very steep!) to be given the vision of a tiny cloud no bigger than a man's hand coming up from the sea, which was God's sign to him that now, with the purging of the land, the three years' drought could end. So down he goes again to warn King Ahab to mount his chariot before the rains make the roads impassable, and then runs ahead of him all the way to the capital Jezreel – just about the distance of a marathon!

No sooner has he got there than he receives a message from Jezebel that he has twenty-four hours to flee for his life. So off he sets with his servant and doesn't stop until he gets to Beersheba, the most southerly city of Judah on the edge of the Negeb. And thence on the strength of a cake of bread and a jar of water he presses on, alone, for forty days across the desert to Mount Horeb or Sinai at the bottom of the Sinai peninsula. Then once again he is instructed to climb to the top of the mountain (some 8000 feet!) where he hears the voice of God – only to be told by it to go back through the wilderness to Damascus, the capital of Syria, this time well beyond the NE boundaries of Israel. Merely to read the itinerary is exhausting. They were giants in those days.

But with the physical swings and roundabouts go the highs and lows of the psychological journey. The encounter on Carmel had been but the culmination of three draining years of fraught and fugitive existence. The meeting with the King had reluctantly but deliberately been sought – 'Go and show yourself to King Ahab' – and the climax was heightened by provocation on the prophet's part. The test was made as steep as possible; three times his own sacrifice was to be soused with water. Would it catch? Would God vindicate him? There is a memorable painting of the scene at the top of Mount Tabor, the traditional site of the Transfiguration, where Elijah is poised looking up to heaven, at the moment when the fire or lightning strikes, with an expression of incredulous relief. He can only be described as whistling: 'Phew!! It worked!'

That was a 'high', and his manic behaviour afterwards was matched only by the depression that so rapidly followed it. Leaving his servant in Beersheba he went a whole day's journey into the wilderness – and you don't do that in your right mind if you expect to return – and in suicidal mood said, 'It's too much. Lord, take away my life. I might as well be dead.' And still forty days later in paranoid mood he is saying to God, 'I only am left and they seek my life to take it away'.

Then follows another mountain 'high', as Elijah is stripped of all his previous images of God and meets him in the pure mystical moment, what the psychologists would call the peak experience, of discerning his presence in the still small voice. But that insistently drives him back to the dusty and murky world of power-politics.

For here we enter the third dimension of this drama, which gives it its substance and its point. The physical and the psychological dimensions only prepare us for the real level of encounter. You could expect perhaps the physical and the psychological to be followed in a sermon by the spiritual, maybe passing through, but leaving behind, the political. But this is not what we find. For the whole fabric from which the story is woven is like shot-silk: politico-spiritual. And that is what prophecy is all about. 'You troubler of Israel', says Ahab when he meets Elijah. 'No, it is you who have troubled Israel', replies the prophet. The struggle between them is neither simply political nor simply spiritual, but both, going to the roots of the nation's life, to the gods, the values, it worships.

But within this public battle takes place the personal crisis for the prophet's soul. After that climactic spiritual struggle Elijah must have felt that he knew at last where God was. For out of the great ordeal on Carmel had he not shown himself in the lightning flash? 'The God who answers by fire,' he had confidentially said, 'he is God.' And after the second ascent of Mount Carmel, as the prophet crouched on the ground with his face between his knees and seven times sent his servant to look westward for a sign of rain, had not God answered in the deluging storm? And yet now on top of Sinai, the very spot where Moses had met Yahweh in the setting of lightning and thunder, he was to learn that God was in none of these, but in the merest whisper of a voice, at the still centre of the turning world.

Yet this was no quietist vision, pointing him away from the world. For what had the voice to say to him? Did it urge a mystical flight of the alone to the alone? No. Rather, 'return to the wilderness near Damascus, and then enter the city'. Become involved again. And more. Sow the seeds of a political coup. 'Anoint Hazael as king of Syria (Israel's great rival), anoint Jehu as king of Israel (to supplant Ahab) and Elishah to succeed you as prophet.' All of this represented a long view into the future. In fact Elijah himself had quite a time to go yet, Ahab was to be followed by two other kings first, and both Hazael and Jehu were actually put in by Elisha. And what a couple they were – typical junior officers in a middle-east military coup, seizing power by secrecy, suffocation and lies (you can read the unsavoury sequel in II Kings 8, 9) and letting loose the very blood-bath in Israel that Elijah was told to predict. And *this* was the message of the still, small voice! God is in everything, it is saying, even in the revolting Hazael from whom Elisha was to turn his face in horror and yet say 'the Lord has shown me that you are to be king of Syria'.

'Everything begins in mysticism and ends in politics.' So George McLeod of the Iona Community used to say, quoting Charles Péguy and urging us to picketing and to prayer. Unfortunately however he misquoted him. What Péguy actually said was that everything starts in 'mystique' and finishes in 'politique', by which he meant politicking. Yet misquotations can be inspired, and I think it puts a finger on the inextricably politico-spiritual dimension of biblical living. The mystical and the political are united in the prophetic: there is no either/or. The man of God (and that means every one of us) has to stand at the entering in of what the Upanishads call 'the cave of the heart'. But what he or she must expect to receive there is the call, as Kierkegaard put it, to a deeper immersion in existence – and human kind, as Eliot said, cannot bear much reality, whether inner or outer. The Transfiguration experience left the disciples bewildered both by the glory and by the suffering, and powerless to cope with the devils of the plain.

So let me leave you with one thought. The church, and individuals within it, will be prophetic – that costly and inescapable vocation – to the degree to which it is at the same time more deeply mystical *and* more deeply political. It loses its cutting edge and anything distinctive to say when it is too shallowly religious and too shallowly political, going along with the stream, declining in any profound sense to be the troubler of Israel, and sheering away from both the awe-ful and the awful, between whose poles the lives of Elijah and Elisha were set.

(vi) Evil and the God of Love

Reprinted by permission from To God Be the Glory *ed T. A. Gill, Abingdon Press 1973. It is included here as a companion piece to the last sermon which follows.*

God who searches our inmost being knows what the Spirit means, because he pleads for God's people in God's own way; and in everything, as we know, he co-operates for good with those who love God (Rom. 8.27–28).

Shortly after the Aberfan pit disaster in South Wales there happened to be a meeting of the Assembly of the Church of England. One of my fellow proctors overheard the remark of a charlady at Church House: 'They've come up to see what they can do for God.' You may smile, but still this is the public reaction in times of war or disaster. God gets his round of a bad press: How can he allow this – if he is both good and all-powerful? And Christians are supposed to be the counsel for his defence. It's up to us to justify the ways of God to man, to show how it's all in the plan, that everything is meant, however inscrutable his ways.

It's incredible to me that Christians have allowed themselves to be put in this box, without protest (echoing the words of J. Alfred Prufrock) that 'that is not what we meant at all'. For not only do I not want to defend such a God: if he existed he would be the very devil. The protest of the atheist is fully justified. Any human planner who foresaw (let alone intended) the slide of a coal-tip would evacuate the area beforehand. Indeed, it was the charge of negligence against the Coal Board that it didn't do precisely this. To believe in a God who deliberately allowed it to happen when he could have prevented it is morally intolerable, and no amount of juggling to show how it was or might all have been for the best can make it otherwise. If this is the problem of evil, then I have no problem, for I have no such belief. But the idea dies hard that this is what Christians are committed to – some Disposer supreme who like a super-computer arranges the lives of every individual, sending some cancer while others get a different packet, a celestial Mikado who sees to it that every accident is no accident but can show how each person who was killed in the collapse of the bridge of San Luis Rey (in Thornton Wilder's brilliantly told story) should have been, and equally that everyone who escaped should have.

I am sorry, but while I can sympathize with those who try this line of defence, I simply cannot believe it. It cannot, I think, be said too strongly that this is a conception of God which we must discard and disown, however much Christians have embraced it in the past and however much atheists and humanists insist that we must embrace it now. For it just does not correspond to anything which I, at any rate, know to be true. I remember having to write a letter to a priest in my diocese whose seventeen-year-old son, on his way to school, was knocked off his bicycle by the rear end of a turning truck, and killed. I felt agonizingly for him. His only boy was exactly the same age as my son, and I could hardly bear to think how I should have been feeling in similar circumstances. But I remember thinking how absolutely frivolous and irrelevant was the question some people ask, 'Why did this happen to me?' as if there were some hidden hand at work. Or, 'Why did God allow this?' as though one should give up believing in him because of it.

Whatever else was true, this was an accident, a ghastly accident, and the only conceivable culpability was either the driver's or the boy's or probably a bit of both. To bring in some intention on God's part in 'permitting' it, let alone 'visiting' it on this particular family, is, I believe, sheer blasphemy. And it's exactly the same with the accidents of nature – earthquakes, cancers, and the rest. The idea that there is any intention or plan about their incidence is, I am convinced, again sheer blasphemy. Nowhere in that great meditation on suffering and evil in Rom. 8 does St Paul suggest that these things disclose the purpose of God or that we cannot believe in him because of them. So far from revealing purpose or intention, their chief quality is what St Paul calls 'vanity' – meaningless, purposeless futility. True, he attributes this to Adam's sin, which we cannot, because we know that this random purposelessness was in the universe long before man's appearance on earth. But the Genesis myth says that also. It starts with a picture of waste and void, of sheer dark meaningless drifting, and it makes the astonishing statement 'In the beginning, in *this* beginning: God.' And still at this level, where cells divide and unite (millions of them, millions of times a second) and where some suddenly go berserk and become frighteningly beautiful and we call them cancerous – at this level which goes on the entire time beneath the tiny, tiny pinpoint of consciousness where categories of intentionality become relevant – at this level and in all this: God. These processes are all faces of God – nebulae, earthquakes, sunsets, cancers, tapeworms – some violent, some beautiful, some terrible, yet all subpersonal and not to be judged, one way or the other, by the wholly inappropriate categories of deliberation or purpose. Volcanoes and earthquakes build up to their point and place of eruption as a result of physical processes reaching back millions of years entirely unrelated to who, if anyone, may at that moment be living in their track. To suggest that there is any intention divine or human involved (apart from the consciously accepted risk, say, of living in San Francisco today) is as bad theology as it is geology.

The real point is this: given the meaninglessness, the literal senselessness of it all, which is as much a part of the evolutionary process for the Christian as for the non-Christian, is it possible to refuse to allow this, and a billion other subhuman faces of God, to separate from his face of love? Indeed, has he a face of love? Jung has pointed out that symbolically only one of the four faces of the living creatures round the throne of God in Ezekiel and Revelation is human. And this is a salutary reminder that for the Bible God is in everything and not merely in the obviously purposive, good, and meaningful. Thus Isaiah makes him say,

I form light and create darkness,
I make weal and create woe,
I am the Lord, who do all these things (Isa. 45.7).

Now if this is understood in terms of intentionality, of God deliberately devising suffering and calamity, he becomes, as I said, a very devil. But it is an insight of profound significance if we can see that none of these things can separate from God because they are not separate from God: for God is in them. The real question, as I indicated, is, How can he possibly be in them *as love*?

The first thing to be recognized is that, in any direct sense, he isn't. They are not loving. They are neutral, or destructive, or, in the case of human wickedness, morally evil – revolting and repulsive. And this is focussed for the Christian in the cross of Christ. Nothing apparently could be further from a face of love, as the crosses on each side of his bear out. It is a scene of utterly depersonalizing agony and futility – and that deliberately contrived by cruel and callous men – a scene which cries aloud for the response of Sydney Carter's song 'Friday Morning,' 'It's God I accuse.' What is the Christian's response? Not, as in the King James Version's unhappy translation of Rom. 8.28, that 'all things work together for good to them that love God' – that is to say that, if we can but see it, all things are for the best in the best of all possible worlds, and that therefore they aren't really evil. Nor that God deliberately works things thus by some super-computerized design, as if it were all in the plan. But rather (I am sure the New English Bible has got it right) that 'in everything . . . he [the Spirit] co-operates for good with those who love God'. That is to say, for those who make the response of love, in every concatenation of circumstances, however pointless, or indeed evil, there is to be met a love capable of transfiguring and liberating even the most baffling and opaque and downright diabolical into meaning and purpose. The problem of evil is not how God can will or allow it (that is not even touched on in Rom. 8), but its sinister power to threaten meaninglessness and separation, to sever and to sour, so that, in Sydney Carter's words, we lash out against 'the million angels watching, and they never move a wing' and are blinded from seeing God *in* 'the carpenter a-hanging on the tree'.

For the Christian no more than for anyone else is there purpose or intention in the ravages of a cancer. That is why the whole of Jesus' ministry is set against such things – or rather, directed to the victory of spirit over them. It is not the cancer or the paralysis, the haemorrhage or the schizophrenia, that represents God's will for persons, but precisely the transcendence of these blind, sub-personal processes, whether by cure or acceptance, in the power and freedom of a truly human life. Yet even at these points God is to be found in them rather than by turning away from them. Love is there to be met, responded to, *and created* through them and out of them. Meaning can be wrested from them, even at the cost of crucifixion. Literally everything can be taken up and transformed rather than allowed to build up into dark patches of loveless resentment and senseless futility. This is the saving grace: God is not outside evil any more than he is outside anything else, and the promise to which the men of the New Testament held as a result of what they had seen in Christ is that he *'will* be all in all' *as love.* 'We see not yet all things subject,' says the Epistle to the Hebrews. 'But we see Jesus.' In the mass of history and nature as we know it the personal outcome, the reduction of all things to the purposes of spirit, the vanquishing of 'vanity' by love, seems utterly remote and obscure. Over most of the processes of what Teilhard de Chardin dared to call this 'personalizing' universe it is still waste and void and darkness. But, for the Christian, a light has shone in the darkness, indeed out of the darkness, in the face of Jesus Christ, which the darkness cannot quench. And that, for St Paul, is the transforming factor. Henceforth 'there is nothing in death or life . . . in the world as it is or the world as it shall be, in the forces of the universe, in heights or depths – nothing in all creation that can separate us from the love of God in Christ Jesus our Lord.' And therefore, despite the fact that we ourselves as Christians are still groaning for God to make us fully his sons and set our whole body free, 'overwhelming victory is ours'.

It would be easy to close on that climax of pulpit oratory. And of course it is much more than pulpit oratory: indeed, it is the New Testament passage above all which I find myself going back to again and again. But on this of all subjects we cannot stay on the mountaintop of transfiguration: we have to come down and wrestle it through and sweat it out with the devils on the plain. And the place where the truest perception of such reality is to be found is likely to be not so much the pulpit as the novel. Read, if you haven't, *The Blood of the Lamb*, written by Peter De Vries, that brilliant *New Yorker* humourist, about the death of his own daughter from leukaemia; or Camus' *The Plague* – though both are agonizing protests against the traditional Christian answers. But read, I think, above all Petru Dumitriu's *Incognito*. I have quoted from this book before, both in *But That I Can't Believe!* (the title is taken from the same song of Sydney Carter's) and also in *Exploration into God*. But I make no apology for ending with it again.

It is an account of secular sainthood and makes no claim to be distinctively Christian, though it is obviously deeply influenced by Eastern Orthodox spirituality. Indeed, its very title is significant. It speaks of God dwelling incognito at the heart of all things, revealing himself in and through and despite the corruptions and inhumanities of life in our generation – and in particular those of the Stalinist Communism of the post-war Rumanian revolution with which the author was identified at both the giving and receiving end. I cannot here recount how he comes to the flash of recognition, at a moment of utter degradation and torture, that in the response of love and forgiveness the meaning even of this monstrous universe can disclose itself as something to which, however haltingly and obscurely, he must say, 'Thou'. It is the ability to take up evil into God and see it transfigured in the process, which is the most striking and most shocking feature of this theology. For Dumitriu no facet of experience can be excluded from the raw material of faith: all things, all events, all persons, are the faces, the incognitos of God:

> God is everything. He is also composed of volcanoes, cancerous growths and tapeworms. But if you think that justifies you in jumping into the crater of an active volcano, or wallowing in despair and crime and death, or inoculating yourself with a virus – well, go ahead. You're like a fish that asks, 'Do you mean to say God isn't only water, He's dry land as well?' To which the answer is, 'Yes, my dear fish, He's dry land as well, but if you go climbing on to dry land you'll be sorry.'[2]

It is not required to accept everything as it stands, but rather to 'vanquish lethargy' in the seemingly impossible response of love.

> What is difficult is to love the world as it is now, while it is doing what it is doing to me, and causing those nearest to me to suffer, and so many others. What is difficult is to bless the material world which contains the Central Committee and the *Securisti*; to love and pardon them. Even to bless them for they are one of the faces of God, terrifying and sad.[3]

Yet

187

. . . if I love the world as it is, I am already changing it: a first fragment of the world has been changed, and that is my own heart. Through this first fragment the light of God, His goodness and His love penetrate into the midst of His anger and sorrow and darkness, dispelling them as the smile on a human face dispels the lowered brows and the frowning gaze. . . .

Nothing is outside God. I have sought to love in such a fashion that love flowing out of me will spread as far as may be. I have tried to keep within the radiance of God, as far away as possible from His face of terror. We were not created to live in evil, any more than we can live in the incandescence that is at the heart of every star. Every contact with evil is indissolubly linked with its own chastisement, and God suffers. It is for us to ease His sufferings, to increase His joy and enhance His ecstasy. I made friends in the crowd, at meetings, in the sports stadium and coming out of the cinema, as a rule only for a moment, linked with them by a friendly exchange of words, a smile, a look, even a moment of silence. And in closer contacts my discovery spread slowly but constantly from one person to another, in that dense and secret undergrowth which is wholly composed of personal events.[4]

It is this fellowship of the 'secret discipline' of love that constitutes the invisible leaven of the kingdom of God.

For this fellowship, Dumitriu says, no labels are necessary, and any structure kills it. This is essentially a theology of the latent, rather than of the manifest, church. And we should listen to it as that, rather than criticize it for what it is not. There is nothing specifically, let alone exclusively, Christian about it. But there is one explicit reference to Christ on which it is fitting to end:

It was in that cell, my legs sticky with filth, that I at last came to understand the divinity of Jesus Christ, the most divine of all men, the one who had most deeply and intensely loved, and who had conceived the parable of the lost sheep; the first of a future mankind wherein a mutation of human hearts will in the end cause the Kingdom of God – the Kingdom, Tao, Agarttha – to descend among men.[5]

(vii) Learning from Cancer

A sermon preached in Trinity College Chapel, Cambridge,
on 23 October 1983

When I was last preaching here it was Trinity Sunday, and I knew I was going into Addenbrooke's the next day for an operation, which turned out to reveal an inoperable cancer. But I was determined not to give in and that I was going to keep my commitment to preach here tonight, if only to 'christen' this pulpit lectern that I wanted to bequeath as a belated thank-offering for what nearly fifteen years in this place has meant to me. So I thought I would use this opportunity to reflect with you on something of what these past months have taught me at greater depth.

Two years ago I found myself having to speak at the funeral of a sixteen-year-old girl who died in our Yorkshire dale. I said stumblingly that God was to be found in the cancer as much as in the sunset. That I firmly believed, but it was an intellectual statement. Now I have had to ask if I can say it of myself, which is a much greater test.

When I said it from the pulpit, I gather it produced quite a shock-wave. I guess this was for two reasons.

Because I had mentioned the word openly in public – and even among Christians it is (or it was: for much has happened in the short time since) the great unmentionable. 'Human kind', said Eliot, 'cannot bear very much reality.' It is difficult for me to comprehend that there are people who just do not want to know whether they have got cancer. But above all there is a conspiracy of silence ostensibly to protect others. We think they cannot face it, though in my experience they usually know deep down; and obviously it is critical how they can face other realities, and above all how they are told and who tells them (and of course whether they really need to know). But what we are much more likely to be doing is mutually protecting ourselves – and also that goes often (though less and less) for doctors. For we dare not face it in ourselves or talk about it at the levels of reality that we might open up.

But Christians above all are those who should be able to bear reality and show others how to bear it. Or what are we to say about the cross, the central reality of our faith? From the beginning Ruth and I were determined to know the whole truth, which after all was first of all our truth and not someone else's. And my doctors have been marvellously open, telling us as they knew everything they knew, which they are the first to say is but the tip of the iceberg. And incidentally they say how much easier it makes it for them if they know this is what the patient wants. Moreover they are fully aware in a place like Cambridge University that too many people know too much (or have access to such knowledge) for them to get away with fudging anything! So from the beginning we were in the picture as it was confirmed.

That does not make it any less of a stunning shock, and the walk from the specialist's consulting room to our car seemed a very long one. But knowing is all-important to how one handles it. For as the recent TV programme 'Mind over Cancer' has shown, the attitude one brings to it can be quite vital – though it is important not to give the impression that *all* depends on this, or that if you die it is because your attitude is wrong, any more than to suggest, as some Christians do, that if you are not cured it is because you have not enough faith. That just induces guilt. But it is equally important to say that 'cancer' need not mean death, nor to suggest that there is nothing you can do about it. In fact there are already numerous cancers that are not necessarily fatal. There are as many sorts of it as there are of 'flu or heart disease. To lump cancer together as a summary death-sentence is as unscientific as it is self-fulfilling. Whether we die of it or of something else is partly up to us. But all of us have to die of something; and by the end of the century, thanks to the elimination of so many other things, the great majority of us will die, in roughly equal proportions, either of cardio-vascular diseases, which still lead as killers but by preventive medicine are already dropping, or of cancer. And of course progress is constantly being made here too, though again there is unlikely to be a single 'cure' for cancer any more than for the common cold.

The shock-wave was also no doubt due to my saying that God was in the cancer. As I made absolutely clear at the time, by this I did not mean that God was in it by intending or sending it. That would make him a very devil. Yet people are always seeing these things in terms of his deliberate purpose or the failure of it. Why does he *allow* it? they say, and they get angry with God. Or rather, they project their anger on to God. And to let the anger come out is no bad thing. For so often diseases of strain and depression are caused by suppressed anger and hatred of other people or of oneself. So it is healthy that it should come out – and God can take it.

The other question people ask in such circumstances is 'Why me?' (often with the implication, 'Why does he pick on me?') or 'What have

I done to deserve it?' And this, deep down, is another good question to have out. 'Why have I got this? What is there in me that has brought it about?' To which the answer is for the most part, as in so much in this field, 'I don't know.' Certainly it is in my case. But the searching, probing and often uncomfortable questions it raises are very relevant, and can be an essential part of the healing. Sometimes there are direct environmental factors (such as smoking or asbestos or radiation) which we can recognize and, if we have the will, personal or social, do something about it – like diet in heart-disease or anxiety in duodenal ulcers. But usually it goes deeper and points inwards. The evidence mounts up that resentments, guilts, unresolved conflicts, unfinished agenda of all sorts, snarl up our lives, and find physical outlet. We do not love ourselves enough: we cannot or will not face ourselves, or accept ourselves. The appearance of a cancer or of anything else is a great opportunity, which we should be prepared to use. The psalmists of old knew this secret, and recognized God in it. 'O Lord, thou hast searched me out, and known me . . . Try me, O God, and seek the ground of my heart; prove me, and examine my thoughts. Look well if there be any way of wickedness in me.' 'So teach us to number our days, that we may apply our hearts unto wisdom.' 'I will thank the Lord for giving me warning' (and pain is a beneficent warning. One of the features of my sort of cancer is that one usually gets no warning till it is too late). For God is to be found in the cancer as in everything else. If he is not, then he is not the God of the psalmist who said, 'If I go down to hell, thou art there also', let alone of the Christian who knows God most deeply in the cross. And I have discovered this experience to be one full of grace and truth. I cannot say how grateful I am for all the love and kindness and goodness it has disclosed, which I am sure were always there but which it has taken this to bring home. Above all I would say it is relationships, both within the family and outside, which it has deepened and opened up. It has provided an opportunity for this and for my being made aware of it which might otherwise never have occurred. It has been a time of giving and receiving grace upon grace.

People sometimes say of a coronary, 'What a wonderful way to go', and as a process of dying for the individual concerned it must be preferable to much else. But it usually gives you no warning, no chance of making up your account. Still less does it allow loved ones to prepare. And preparing for death is increasingly recognized as a vital part of the process of grieving, of bearing reality, and of being restored to wholeness of body, mind and soul, both as individuals and as families.

But how does one prepare for death, whether of other people or of oneself? It is something we seldom talk about these days. Obviously there is the elementary duty (urged in the Prayer Book) of making one's will and other dispositions, which is no more of a morbid occupation than taking out life-insurance. And there is the deeper level of seeking to round off one's account, of ordering one's priorities and what one wants to do in the time available. And notice such as this gives concentrates the mind wonderfully and makes one realize how much of one's time one wastes or kills. When I was told that I had six months, or perhaps nine, to live, the first reaction was naturally of shock – though I also felt liberated, because, as in limited-over cricket, at least one knew the target one had to beat (and this target was but an informed guess from the experience and resources of the medical profession, by which I had no intention of being confined). But my second reaction was: 'But six months is a long time. One can do a lot in that. How am I going to use it?'

The initial response is to give up doing things – and it certainly sifts out the inessentials. My reaction was to go through the diary cancelling engagements. But I soon realized that this was purely negative; and I remembered the remark of Geoffrey Lampe, recently Regius Professor of Divinity at Cambridge, who showed us how anyone should die of cancer: 'I can't die: my diary is far too full.'

In fact 'preparing for death' is not the other-worldly pious exercise stamped upon our minds by Victorian sentimentality, turning away from the things of earth for the things of 'heaven'. Rather, for the Christian it is preparing for 'eternal life', which means real living, more abundant life, which is begun, continued, though not ended, *now*. And this means it is about quality of life, not quantity. How long it goes on here is purely secondary. So preparing for eternity means learning to live, not just concentrating on keeping alive. It means living it *up*, becoming *more* concerned with contributing to and enjoying what matters most – giving the most to life and getting the most from it, while it is on offer. So that is why, among other things, we went to Florence, where we had never been before, and to Switzerland to stay with friends we had to disappoint earlier because I entered hospital instead. I am giving myself too, in the limited working day I have before I tire, to all sorts of writing I want to finish. And if one goes for quality of life this may be the best way to extend its quantity. Seek first the kingdom of heaven – and who knows what shall be added? Pursue the wholeness of body, mind and spirit, and physical cure may, though not necessarily will, be a bonus.

Your Life in their Hands is the title of another TV documentary on doctors. At one level this is true, the level of physical survival (though it certainly is not the whole truth even of that). And my experience of the medical profession through all of this has been wholly positive. They have been superb in their skills and judgment and sensitivity – really listening rather than acting as gods who know the answers and treating you as the 'patient', the person simply on the receiving end. For the bigger men they are, and the more they know, the more they admit they don't know. Most of my month in hospital was spent simply in replumbing the stomach and getting it working again, and for this two operations proved necessary. In fact the cancer specialist did not arrive on the scene till towards the end, for there was nothing up to then that he could do. But when he did, he said: 'I know basically what your situation is; but before I say anything I want to hear how *you* feel about it.' How many professionals (and that includes not only doctors but lawyers and parsons) start like that? From the beginning I felt I was being asked to take my share of responsibility for my own health. And this was a point that came strongly through another series of BBC programmes this spring (and how fortunate we are compared with the TV of any other country I know!): *A Gentle Way with Cancer?* This was on the Bristol Cancer Help Centre, which is revealing and meeting an enormous need, and whose new building Prince Charles courageously opened the other day in the teeth of quite a bit of medical criticism. For this is alternative medicine, not opposing the profession and its techniques, but seeking to supplement them, at the dietary, psychological and spiritual levels (and the last level did not really come through the 'Mind over Cancer' programme. Yet spirit over cancer is every bit as important). And at all points it is important to see these as complementary. For there are many approaches – orthodox and non-orthodox medicine, unexplained gifts of healing (which are no more necessarily connected with religion than are psychic powers) and prayer and faith-healing. I am convinced that one must be prepared, critically and siftingly (for one must test the spirits at every level), to start at all ends at once and I have been receiving the laying-on-of-hands from someone in whose approach I have great trust, which for me is a large part of faith (and I have deliberately not taken up others). In fact in everything I am a great both/and rather than either/or man. In the pursuit of truth I cannot believe that a one-eyed approach is ever sufficient. In the pursuit of peace I believe in both multilateralism and unilateralism. And in the pursuit of health this is even more obvious. For health means wholeness. It is concerned not simply with cure but with healing of the whole person in all his or her relationships. Hence the high-point of the communion service, the gift of the bread of life and the cup of salvation, has traditionally been accompanied by the words, 'Preserve thy body and soul unto everlasting life', and it has ended with invoking 'the peace (the *shalom* or wholeness) of God which passes all understanding'.

Healing cannot be confined to any, or indeed every, level of human understanding or expectation. This is why too it shows up those twin deceivers pessimism and optimism as so shallow. In the course of nature, cancer-sufferers swing from one to the other more than most, as good days and bad days, remissions and recurrences, follow each other. But the Christian takes his stand not on optimism but on hope. This is based not on rosy prognosis (from the human point of view mine is bleak) but, as St Paul says, on suffering. For this, he says, trains us to endure, and endurance brings proof that we have stood the tests, and this proof is the ground of hope – in the God who can bring resurrection out and through the other side of death. That is why he also says that though we carry death with us in our bodies (all of us) we never cease to be confident. His prayer is that 'always the greatness of Christ will shine out clearly in my person, whether through my life or through my death. For to me life is Christ, and death gain; but what if my living on in the body may serve some good purpose? Which then am I to choose? I cannot tell. I am torn two ways: what I should like' – he says more confidently than most of us could – 'is to depart and be with Christ, that is better by far; but for your sake there is greater need for me to stay on in the body.' According to my chronology he lived nearly ten years after writing those words: others would say it was shorter. But how little does it matter. He had passed beyond time and its calculations. He had risen with Christ.

A Bibliography of the Writings of John A. T. Robinson

1945

'The Religious Foundation of the University', *The Cambridge Review*, 20 January

'Agape and Eros', *Theology* 48, 98–104

Thou Who Art: The notion of personality and its relation to Christian theology with particular reference to (a) the contemporary 'I–Thou' philosophy; (b) the doctrines of the Trinity and the Person of Christ, Cambridge University (unpublished)

1946

Review of J. L. Hromadka, *Doom and Resurrection*, and W. R. Matthews, *Strangers and Pilgrims*, *Theology*, 49, 149–50

1947

'The Temptations', *Theology* 50, 43–48 (reprinted in *Twelve New Testament Studies*, 1962, 53–60)

1948

'Hosea and the Virgin Birth', *Theology* 52, 373–375 (revised and expanded version reprinted in *Twelve More New Testament Studies*, 1984, 1–11)

1949

'Universalism – Is it Heretical?', *Scottish Journal of Theology* 2, 139–155

1950

Review of Oscar Cullmann, *Christ and Time*, *Scottish Journal of Theology* 3, 86–89

'The House Church and the Parish Church', *Theology* 53, 283–287 (reprinted in *On Being the Church in the World*, 1960, 83–95)

In the End, God . . . A Study of the Christian Doctrine of the Last Things, James Clarke

1952

The Body: A Study in Pauline Theology (Studies in Biblical Theology, no. 5), SCM Press

'The Theological College in a Changing World', *Theology* 55, 202–207
'The Social Content of Salvation', *Frontier*, November (reprinted in *On Being the Church in the World*, 1960, 23–30)

1953

Review of Rudolf Bultmann, *Theology of the New Testament*, Vol. I, *The Church of England Newspaper*, 27 February
Review of J. Marsh, *The Fulness of Time*, *Theology* 56, 107–109
'Traces of a Liturgical Sequence in I Cor. 16. 20–24', *Journal of Theological Studies* n.s. 4, 38–41 (reprinted in *Twelve New Testament Studies*, 1960, 154–157, with the new title, 'The Earliest Christian Liturgical Sequence?')
'The Gospel and Race', *The Church of England Newspaper*, 24 July (reprinted in *On Being the Church in the World*, 1960, 116–120)
Review of Oscar Cullmann, *Peter: Disciple, Apostle, Martyr*, *The Church of England Newspaper*, 7 September
'The One Baptism as a Category of New Testament Soteriology', *Scottish Journal of Theology* 6, 257–274 (reprinted in *Twelve New Testament Studies*, 1962, 158–175)
'The Christian Hope', *Christian Faith and Communist Faith* ed D. M. MacKinnon, Macmillan, 209–226

1954

Review of L. B. Smedes, *The Incarnation: Trends in Modern Anglican Thought*, *Theology*, 57, 147–149
'Our Present Position in the Light of the Bible', *Becoming a Christian* ed B. Minchin, Faith Press, 48–57
'Kingdom, Church and Ministry', *The Historic Episcopate in the Fulness of the Church* ed K. M. Carey, Dacre Press, ²1960, 11–12
'Trusting the Universe':
    (1) 'The Faith of the Scientist'
    (2) 'The Faith of the Philosopher'
    (3) 'The Faith of the Christian', *The Church of England Newspaper*, 17 and 24 September, 1 October
Review of J. Knox, *Chapters in a Life of Paul*, *The Church of England Newspaper*, 29 October
Review of J. Jeremias, *The Parables of Jesus*, *The Church of England Newspaper*, 26 November

1955

'The Parable of the Shepherd (John 10. 1–5)', *Zeitschrift für die neutestamentliche Wissenschaft* 46, 233–240 (reprinted in *Twelve New Testament Studies*, 1962, 67–75)
Review of E. Best, *One Body in Christ*, *Theology* 58, 391–393

Review of V. Taylor, *The Life and Ministry of Jesus, New Testament Studies* 2, 148–149

Review of J. Ferguson, *Studies in Christian Social Commitment, Journal of Theological Studies* 6, 336–338

1956

'The "Parable" of the Sheep and the Goats', *New Testament Studies* 2, 225–237 (reprinted in *Twelve New Testament Studies*, 1962, 76–93)

'A Tribute to C. H. Dodd – England's Greatest Biblical Scholar', *Church of England Newspaper*, 25 May

'The Second Coming – Mk. xiv, 62', *The Expository Times* 67, 336–340

'The Most Primitive Christology of All?', *Journal of Theological Studies* 7, 177–189 (reprinted in *Twelve New Testament Studies*, 1962, 139–153)

'The Historicity of the Gospels', in *Jesus Christ: History, Interpretation and Faith* ed R. C. Walton, T. W. Manson, and John A. T. Robinson, SPCK, 45–63

1957

Review of G. W. H. Lampe and K. J. Woollcombe, *Essays on Typology, Church of England Newspaper*

'Intercommunion and Concelebration', *The Ecumenical Review* 9, 203–206 (reprinted in *On Being the Church in the World*, 1960, 96–100)

'The Baptism of John and the Qumran Community', *Harvard Theological Review* 50, 175–191 (reprinted in *Twelve New Testament Studies*, 1962, 11–27)

'Preaching Judgement', *The Preacher's Quarterly*, September and December (reprinted in *On Being the Church in the World*, 1960, 135–147)

Jesus and His Coming: The Emergence of a Doctrine, SCM Press

1958

'Elijah, John and Jesus: an essay in Detection,' *New Testament Studies* 4, 263–281 (reprinted in *Twelve New Testament Studies*, 1962, 28–52)

'The Teaching of Theology for the Ministry', *Theology* 61, 486–495

1959

Review of J. Jeremias, *Jesus' Promise to the Nations, Journal of Biblical Literature* 78, 101–104

Review of W. D. Stacey, *The Pauline View of Man, Journal of Theological Studies* 10, 144–146

'The New Look on the Fourth Gospel', in *Studia Evangelica* ed K.

Aland, *et al.*, Akademie-Verlag, Berlin, 510–515 (reprinted in *The Gospels Reconsidered. A Selection of Papers read at the International Congress on The Four Gospels in 1957*, Blackwell, 154–166, and *Twelve New Testament Studies*, 1962, 94–106)

'The "Others" of John 4. 38', in *Studia Evangelica* ed K. Aland *et al.*, Adademie-Verlag, Berlin, 1959, 510–515 (reprinted in *Twelve New Testament Studies*, 1962, 61–66)

'Episcopacy and Intercommunion', *Theology* 62, 402–408 (reprinted in *On Being the Church in the World*, 1960, 101–109)

1960

'The Destination and Purpose of St John's Gospel', *New Testament Studies* 6, 117–131 (reprinted in *Twelve New Testament Studies*, 1962, 107–125 and in *New Testament Issues* ed R. Batey, 1970, 191–209)

Review of *The Biblical Doctrine of Baptism*, Commission on Baptism, Church of Scotland, Edinburgh 1959, *Scottish Journal of Theology* 13, 99–102

On Being the Church in the World, SCM Press

Christ Comes In, Mowbray

'The Destination and Purpose of the Johannine Epistles', *New Testament Studies* 7 (1960–1), 56–65 (reprinted in *Twelve New Testament Studies*, 1962, 126–138)

Liturgy Coming to Life, Mowbray (2nd edn with new preface 1963)

'Is Religious Revival on the Way?', *Church of England Newspaper*, 22 April

Review of J. Line, *The Doctrine of the Christian Ministry*, B. Minchin, *Every Man in His Ministry*, and L. Newbigin, *The Reunion of the Church*, *Theology*, 63, 422–424

'Taking the Lid off the Church's Ministry', *New Ways with the Ministry*, Faith Press, 9–21

'The New Look on the Fourth Gospel', *The Gospels Reconsidered* ed K. Aland *et al.*, Blackwell, 154–166

1961

'A New Model of Episcopacy', *Bishops: what they are and what they do* ed The Bishop of Llandaff, Faith Press, 125–138

1962

Twelve New Testament Studies (Studies in Biblical Theology, no. 34), SCM Press

'The Church of England and Intercommunion', *Prism*, no. 3, March, 3–15 (reprinted as Prism Pamphlet no. 2, London 1962)

'Resurrection in the NT', *The Interpreter's Dictionary of the Bible* (Vol IV), Abingdon Press, Nashville, 43–53

'Five Points for Christian Action', *Man and Society* 2, 13–15

'The Significance of the Foot-Washing', in *Neotestamentica et Patristica: Eine Freundesgabe, Herrn Professor Dr Oscar Cullmann zu seinem 60. Geburtstag überreicht*, E. J. Brill, Leiden, 144–147 (reprinted in *Twelve More New Testament Studies*, 1984, 77–80)

'Mirror to the Church' (review of Paul Ferris, *The Church of England*) *The Observer*, 4 November

'What I believe – and don't believe – about Christmas', *Sunday Citizen*

'The Tercentenary of the Book of Common Prayer,' *Portsmouth Diocesan Courier*, November

1963

'The Relation of the Prologue to the Gospel of St John', *New Testament Studies* 9 (1962–3), 120–129 (reprinted in *The Authorship and Integrity of the New Testament*, SPCK, 61–72 and in *Twelve More New Testament Studies*, 1984, 65–76)

'The Tercentenary of the Book of Common Prayer', *Parish and People*, no. 36 (Epiphany 1963), 15–19

'On Being a Radical', *The Listener*, 21 February (reprinted in *Christian Freedom in a Permissive Society*, 1970, 1–6)

'Our Image of God must Go', *The Observer*, 17 March (reprinted in *The Observer Revisited*, Hodder 1964, 42–47)

Honest to God, SCM Press and Westminster Press

'One Church . . .', *TV Times*

'That's What Love Will Do', *TV Times*, 5 April

'Why I wrote It', *Sunday Mirror*, 7 April

'Ascendancy', *Outlook*

The World That God Loves (pamphlet), Church Missionary Society (reprinted in *The Episcopal Overseas Mission Review* 10 [1965], no. 3, 2–7 and in *Christian Freedom in a Permissive Society*, 1970, 107–113)

'Keeping in Touch with Theology',*Twentieth Century*, Summer 1963

The Ministry and the Laity', *Layman's Church* ed T. W. Beaumont, Lutterworth Press, 9–22

'God and the Theologians: Reality and Revelation', *Encounter* 21.4 (October), 58–60

The Honest to God Debate ed John A. T. Robinson and David L. Edwards, SCM Press, 228–279

'Der Verpflichtung der Kirche gegenüber dem Menschen der Gegenwart', *Monatschrift für Pastoral Theologie* 52, 321–328

'The Place of the Fourth Gospel', *The Roads Converge: A Contribution to the Question of Christian Reunion* ed P. Gardner-Smith, Arnold, 49–74

Liturgy Coming To Life, (2nd edn) Mowbray

'The Four Stumbling Blocks', *The Friend*, 22 November

'The Great Benefice Barrier', *Prism*, no. 80, December, 4–13

'History or Myth?' (Adam and Eve – The Virgin Birth – The Resurrection), *Sunday Mirror*, 15, 22, 29 December

1964

'Our Common Reformation', *Catholic Gazette* 55, no. 1, January, 6–7

'My Kind of Chastity', *Tit-Bits*, 4 January

'Theologians of Our Time: C. H. Dodd', *The Expository Times* 75, 100–102 (reprinted in *Theologians of Our Time* ed A. W. and E. Hastings, T. & T. Clark, 40–46; and in *Tendenzen der Theologie im 20. Jahrhundert* ed H. J. Schultz, Kreuz-Verlag 1966, Stuttgart)

Christian Morals Today, SCM Press (reprinted in *Christian Freedom in a Permissive Society*, 1970, 7–51)

'Communicating with the Contemporary Man', *Religion in Television*, Independent Television Authority, 27–35

'Why I shall vote Labour and don't mind saying so', *The Sign*, 19 September

῍Η ἠθική κρίση καί ἡ ἠθική ἀξίωση, Εποχές (Athens) 18, October, 3–6

'Our Image of God must Go' in *The Observer Revisited*, Hodder

'Ascendancy', *Andover Newton Quarterly* n.s. 5, 5–9 (reprinted in *The Pulpit* 36 (1965), no. 5, 4–6; and, with the title 'The Ascendancy of Christ', *Pulpit Digest* 45 (1965), no. 321, 45–48)

'Towards a Genuinely Lay Theology', *British Weekly*, 26 November, 3, 10, 17 December

'Did the Miracles Really Happen?', *Sunday Mirror*, 29 November

'It's That Man Again', *Sunday Mirror*, 6 December

'Is there Life After Death?', *Sunday Mirror*, 13 December

'Curiouser and Curiouser: Reflections of a Bemused Suffragan', *Prism*, no. 92, December, 33–34

1965

'The Relation of the Prologue to the Gospel of St John', *The Authorship and Integrity of the New Testament*, SPCK (reprinted in *Twelve More New Testament Studies*, 1984, 65–76)

'Rocking the Radical Boat Too', *Prism*, no. 95, March 6–10

'Can a Truly Contemporary Person *not* be an Atheist?', *The Sunday Times*, 14 March (reprinted in *The New Reformation?*, 106–122)

The New Reformation?, SCM Press and Westminster Press

'Can Anglicanism Survive? Death and Resurrection', *New Statesman*, 9 April

'Ascendancy', *The Pulpit*, May

'The World That God Loves', *The Episcopal Overseas Mission Review*, Whitsun

'Living with Sex', *The Observer*, 13 June

' . . . And What Next . . .'? *Prism*, no. 101, September, 9–17

'God Dwelling Incognito', *New Christian*, 7 October

'Kann man heute kein Atheist sein?', *Kontexte* I

'Bearing the Reality of Christmas', *New Christian*, 16 December

1966

'Abortion: The Responsibility of Freedom', *Medical World*, January (reprinted in *Christian Freedom in a Permissive Society*, 1970, 52–58)

'Ministry in the Melting', *New Christian*, 10 February

'Religion without Dogma', *The Restless Church* ed W. Kilbourn, McClelland & Stewart

'The Real Purpose of Marriage', *Getting Married 1966*

Review of H. Gollwitzer, *The Existence of God as Confessed by Faith, Journal of Theological Studies* 17, 259–262

'Ascendancy', *New Christian*, 19 May

'C. H. Dodd' in *Theologians of our Time* ed A. W. Hastings & E. Hastings, T. & T. Clark

'Meeting Billy Graham', *The Bridge*, August

'Do We Need a God?', *New Knowledge* VII, 5

'Local Liturgy', *New Christian*, 14 July

'Pop Prayer', *New Christian*, 8 September

'Charles Harold Dodd', *Tendenzen der Theologie in 20 Jahrhundert*, ed H. J. Schultz, Kreuz Verlag, Stuttgart

Meeting, Membership and Ministry, Prism Pamphlet no. 31 (reprinted with revisions, in *Christian Freedom in a Permissive Society*, 1970, 152–166)

'Place of the Angels', *New Christian*, 20 October

Foreword to Richard H. McBrien, *The Church in the Thought of Bishop John Robinson*, SCM Press

'Why not *Abolish* Abortion?', *The Observer*, 23 October

'The Aldwych Liturgy', *The Guardian*, 3 November

'Stripping Down Christmas', *The Observer*, 18 December

'When did you last mention Hell to your Child?', *The Sun*, 23 December

Preface to W. Hamilton, *The New Essence of Christianity*, Darton, Longman & Todd

1967

'The Saint of the Secular', Dietrich Bonhoeffer, *Letters and Papers from Prison*, SCM Press

'Walls are Coming Down', *New Christian*, 26 January

'Abortion: The Case for a Free Decision', *Twentieth Century*, first quarter (reprinted in *Christian Freedom in a Permissive Society*, 1970, 58–67)

But That I Can't Believe! New American Library, Collins

'Opencast Theology', *New Christian*, 15 June

An Interview, *The Month*, September

'Mystique and Politique', *New Christian*, 21 September (reprinted in *Christian Freedom in a Permissive Society*, 1970, 83–88)

'Choosing the Priorities', *New Christian*, 5 October

'Is God Dead?', *The Guardian*, 19 October

Exploration into God, Stanford University Press and SCM Press

'On Being a Christian in a World Without Religion', *The Worth Record*, Summer

'Is God Dead?', *The Guardian*, 19 October

'About Christmas', *The Queen*, Christmas issue

Review of C. Davis, *A Question of Conscience, New Christian*, 30 November

'Christmas without Myth', *Together* for Methodist Families, December

'God and I', *Nova*, December

'Prophetic Ministry to the World', *Theological Freedom and Social Responsibility* ed S. F. Bayne, Seabury Press, New York (reprinted in *Christian Freedom in a Permissive Society*,1970, 123–129)

1968

In the End God (revd edn), Harper and Collins

'Le Mystère de la Mort de l'Eglise', *Christianisme Social*, no. 11–12

'Has "God" a Meaning?', *Question*, February

'On Staying in or Getting out', *New Christian*, 8 February and *The Christian Century*, 22 May (reprinted in *Christian Freedom in a Permissive Society*, 1970, 225–231)

'The Exploding Church', *The Observer*, 14 April

'For God's Sake Think', *Sermons from Great St Mary's* ed H. Montefiore, Collins

'Freedom for Ministry', *New Christian*, 11 July

Review of P. van Buren's *Theological Exploration, New Christian*, 25 July

'Church and Theology: From Here to Where?' *Theology Today*, July (reprinted as 'The Next Frontiers for Theology and the Church', *Christian Freedom in a Permissive Society*, 1970, 130–151)

'Towards Secular Ecumenism', *New Christian*, 3 October

'What's Ahead for Roman Catholics?', *The Critic*, October – November (reprinted as 'The Ecumenical Consequences of *Humanae Vitae*' in *New Christian* , October and in *Christian Freedom in a Permissive Society*, 1970, 114–122)

Review of G. Baum, *The Credibility of the Church Today*, 28 November

1969

'Man *is* what he is open to', *The Teilhard Review*, vol. 3, no. 2.

Review of D. L. Edwards, *Religion and Change, The Guardian*, 19 February

On Being the Church in the World (revd edn), Penguin

Review of R. P. McBrien, *Do We Need the Church?, New Christian*, 20 March

'Das Geheimnis des Todes der Kirche', *Evangelische Kommentare*, April

'Il faut bien qu'il y ait des scissions parmi vous', *Informations Catholiques Internationales*, June

'Obscenity and Maturity', *New Christian*, 24 July (reprinted in *Christian Freedom in a Permissive Society*, 1970, 68–82)

Interview, *The Times*, 22 September

     "   *Methodist Recorder*, 25 September

     "   *Church Times*, 26 September

'The Meaning of being a Bishop', *The Times*, 27 September

'Farewell to the Sixties', *The Observer*, 28 September (reprinted in *Christian Freedom in a Permissive Society*, 1970, 241–244)

'The Dramatic Dip', *New Christian*, 2 October

'Not Radical Enough?', *The Christian Century*, 12 November (reprinted in *Christian Freedom in a Permissive Society*, 1970, 232–240)

'Obscenity and Maturity' (a different article from that of 24 July) *Sunday Times*, December

1970
'God of the Right or the Left?', *The Times*, 3 January

Christian Freedom in a Permissive Society, SCM Press and Westminster Press

Introduction to J. R. Seeley, *Ecce Homo*, Dent

'Evil and the Love of God', *Expository Times*, 81, 240–242

'The Theological Excavator', *New Christian*, 28 May

'Christianity's "No" to Priesthood', *The Christian Priesthood* ed N. Lash and J. Rhymer, Darton, Longman & Todd

'The Destination and Purpose of St John's Gospel', *New Testament Issues* ed R. Batey, Harper & Row and SCM Press, 191–209

'In What Sense is Christ Unique?', *The Christian Century*, 25 November

Introduction to J. Hick, *Christianity at the Centre*, Herder & Herder

1971
Foreword to C. H. Dodd, *The Founder of Christianity*, Collins

'What is the Resurrection?', *More Sermons from Great St Mary's* ed H. Montefiore, Hodder

Review of E. Schillebeeckx's *God and Man*, *Journal of Ecumenical Studies*, Pittsburgh, 8, 166

'Dr John Robinson Explains', *Humanist*, April

'God and I', *The Beacon*, May-June

Christian Faith in a World without Religion, Aske Lecture

Lo Que Differencia al Christiano Hoy, La Aurora, Buenos Aires

'Nicht Radikal Genug?', *Warum ich mich Geandert Habe*, Kreuz-Verlag, Stuttgart

'The Battle for Soul', *The Guardian*, 25 October

'God without God?', *The Christian Century*, 24 November

'Not Radical Enough?', *Theological Crossings* ed A. Geyer & Dean Peerman, Eerdmans, Grand Rapids

1972

The Difference in being a Christian Today, Collins and Westminster Press
Review of Helder Camara, *Race Against Time*, *The Guardian*, 17 February
'Was Jesus Mad?', *Faith and Freedom*, Spring
'Sex and the Law', *The Guardian*, 6 July
Review of J. Wren-Lewis, *What Shall We Tell the Children?*, *Faith and Freedom*
'Need Jesus Have Been Perfect?', in *Christ, Faith and History* ed S. W. Sykes and J. P. Clayton, CUP
'The Place of Law in the Field of Sex' (abbreviated), *New Outlook*, 3
Foreword to F. Spicer, *Sex and the Love Relationship*, Priory Press

1973

The Place of Law in the Field of Sex, Secular Law Reform Society
The Human Face of God, SCM Press and Westminster Press
'Are you what they say you are?', *The Guardian*, 17 March
'Our image of Christ must change', *The Christian Century*, 21 March
'Evil and the God of Love' in *To God Be the Glory: Sermons in Honor of George Arthur Buttrick* ed T. A. Gill, Abingdon Press (reprinted in *Where Three Ways Meet*, 1987)
'The Use of the Fourth Gospel for Christology Today', *Christ and Spirit in the New Testament. . . Studies in Honour of C. F. D. Moule* ed B. Lindars, S. S. Smalley, CUP (reprinted in *Twelve More New Testament Studies*, 1984, 138–154)

1974

'The Place of the Angels', *A New Christian Reader* ed T. Beaumont, SCM Press

1975

'The Parable of the Wicked Husbandmen: A Test of Synoptic Relationships', *New Testament Studies* 21, 1974–75 (reprinted in *Twelve More New Testament Studies*, 1984, 12–34)
'Dying to Live', *South African Outlook*, June

1976

Redating the New Testament, SCM Press and Westminster Press
'Who Decides Whither?', *Crucible*, July–September
Review of E. Trocmé, *The Formation of the Gospel according to Mark*, *Heythrop Journal*, 17.4, 445–447
'As Others See Us', *Catholic Gazette*, November

Review of G. A. Wells, *Did Jesus Exist?*, J. M. Ford, *Revelation, Journal of Theological Studies*, 27, 447–449 and 468–470
Review of H. E. W. Turner, *Jesus the Christ, Virginia Seminary Journal*, Fall

1977
'Social Ethics and the Church', *The Month*, January
Can We Trust the New Testament? Mowbrays
'Look Back in Hope?', *Mowbrays Journal*, Spring
Review of D. E. Nineham, *The Use and Abuse of the Bible, Times Literary Supplement*, 8 April
'Reinvestigating the Shroud of Turin', *Theology*, 80, 193–197
Review of R. H. Gundry, *Soma in Biblical Theology, Journal of Theological Studies* 28, 163–166
Review of N. Perrin, *Jesus and the Language of the Kingdom, Theology* 80, 295
Review of B. Orchard, *Matthew, Luke, Mark, Ampleforth Journal*, Summer
On Being the Church in the World (3rd edn) Mowbrays
Exploration into God (2nd edn) Mowbrays
'The God of Hope and Man of Procrastination', *South African Outlook*, October
Review of *The Myth of God Incarnate* ed J. Hick and *The Truth of God Incarnate* ed M. Green, *Times Literary Supplement*, 25 November (reprinted in *Journal of Theology for Southern Africa*, December)

1978
Review of *New Testament Interpretation* ed I. H. Marshall, *The Churchman*, January
'Jesus the Jew: The Evidence of the Fourth Gospel', *Common Ground*, 1
Review of F. W. Dillistone, *C. H. Dodd, Theology*, 81, 148–149
Review of I. Wilson, *The Turin Shroud, Christian World*, 18 May
'The Unexamined Assumption of Christian Scholars', *The Times*, 24 June
'The Holy Shroud in Scripture', *The Tablet*, 26 August
'The Shroud and the New Testament', *Face to Face with the Turin Shroud* ed P. Jennings, Mowbray (reprinted in *Twelve More New Testament Studies*, 1984, 81–94)
'Due Process in the Ordination of Women Priests', *The Times*, 28 October
'If the Shroud were genuine what difference would it make?', *The Examiner*, Bombay, October-November

1979
Wrestling with Romans, SCM Press and Westminster Press
Jesus and His Coming (2nd edn) SCM Press and Westminster Press

Letter to Eberhard Bethge in *Wie eine Flaschenpost*
'Turning East', *Indian Journal of Theology*, January-March
Truth is Two-Eyed, SCM Press and Westminster Press

1980

'Has God a Meaning?', *Philosophy and Contemporary Issues* ed J. R. Burr and M. Goldinger (3rd edn), Macmillan, New York
Review of M. Hengel, *Acts and the History of Earliest Christianity*, *Theology*, 83, 218–220
Review of John Barnes, *Ahead of His Age: Bishop Barnes of Birmingham, London Review of Books*, 3–16 July
'Wann wurde das NT geschrieben?', *IBW* (Deutsches Institut für Bildung und Wissen) *Journal*, August
Interview in *Ship of Fools*, August
The Roots of a Radical, SCM Press and Crossroad Publishing Co (New York 1981)
Woman for All Seasons: A Julian Study, Julian Shrine Publications
Review of C. S. Song, *Third-Eye Theology*, *Ecumenical Review*, October
Review of D. Cupitt, *Taking Leave of God*, *Times Literary Supplement*, 5 December

1981

Preface to A. W. Robinson, *The Personal Life of the Christian*, OUP
Joseph Barber Lightfoot, Dean and Chapter of Durham
'A Unique Christ', *The Twentieth Century Pulpit II*, ed J. Cox, Abingdon Press
Review of W. Cantwell Smith, *Towards a World Theology*, *Times Literary Supplement* 4 September
'A Christian and the Arms Race', *New Society*, 26 November
'A Christian Response to the Arms Race', *The Guardian*, 24 December

1982

'A Christian Response to the Arms Race', *Debate on Disarmament* ed M. Clarke and M. Mowlam, Routledge & Kegan Paul (reprinted in *Where Three Ways Meet*, 1987)
'War is not an Instrument of Peace', *The Guardian*, 3 May
Review of R. Banks, *Paul's Idea of Community*, *Journal of Ecclesiastical History* 33, 322
'Did Jesus Have a Distinctive Use of Scripture?', *Christological Perspectives: Essays in Honor of Harvey K. McArthur* ed R. I. Berkey and S. A. Edwards, Pilgrim Press, New York (reprinted in *Twelve More New Testament Studies* 1984, 35–43)
Review of S. Laws, *Commentary on the Epistle of St James*, *Journal of Theological Studies* 33, 270–271
'Dunn on John', *Theology*, 85, 332–338

'The Church's Most Urgent Priority in Today's World', Christ's Church Cathedral, Hamilton, Ontario (reprinted in *Where Three Ways Meet*, 1987)

'What Future for a Unique Christ?', Divinity College, McMaster University, Hamilton, Ontario (reprinted in *Where Three Ways Meet*, 1987)

'A Christian Response to the Energy Crisis', Brunel University (reprinted in *Where Three Ways Meet*, 1987)

1983

'Zur Datierung des Johannesevangeliums': Eine Antwort an Prof. Josef Ernst, *IBW* (Institut für Bildung und Wissen), Paderborn, Germany, June

'Religion in the Third Wave: The Difference in Being a Christian Tomorrow', prepared for a Festschrift to honour Lloyd Geering, Professor of Religious Studies at Victoria University of Wellington, New Zealand (reprinted in *Where Three Ways Meet*, 1987)

1984

'Rudolf Bultmann: A View from England', *Rudolf Bultmann's Werk und Wirkung*, Wissenschaftliche Buchgesellschaft, Darmstadt, 149–154

'How Small was the Seed of the Church?', *The New Testament Age: Essays in Honour of Bo Reicke* ed William C. Weinrich, Mercer University Press, Georgia 1984, Vol II, 413–430 (reprinted in *Twelve More New Testament Studies*, 1984, 95–111)

' "His Witness is True": A Test of the Johannine Claim', *Jesus and the Politics of his Day* ed E. Bammell and C. F. D. Moule, CUP, 453–475 (reprinted in *Twelve More New Testament Studies*, 1984, 112–137)

Twelve More New Testament Studies, SCM Press

1985

The Priority of John, SCM Press and Meyer-Stone (New York 1987)

1987

Where Three Ways Meet, SCM Press

Notes

Preface

1. Eric James, *A Life of Bishop John A. T. Robinson: Scholar, Pastor, Prophet*, Collins 1987.

1. What Future for a Unique Christ?

1. *The Myth of God Incarnate* ed John Hick, SCM Press and Westminster Press 1977; *The Truth of God Incarnate* ed Michael Green, Hodder 1977; *Incarnation and Myth: The Debate Continued* ed Michael Goulder, SCM Press and Eerdmans 1979.

2. A Tale of Two Cities: The World to Come

1. Don Cupitt, *The World to Come*, SCM Press 1982.
2. Don Cupitt, *Taking Leave of God*, SCM Press and Crossroad Publishing Co 1980.

3. Interpreting the Book of Revelation

1. I. B. Beckwith, *The Apocalypse of John*, Macmillan, NY 1919; A. S. Peake, *The Revelation of John*, London 1920.
2. William Ramsay, *The Letters to the Seven Churches of Asia*, London 1904; William Barclay, *Letters to the Seven Churches*, SCM Press 1957.
3. Ronald H. Preston and Anthony T. Hanson, *The Revelation of Saint John the Divine*, Torch Bible Commentaries, SCM Press 1949; John Sweet, *Revelation*, SCM Pelican Commentaries, SCM Press and Westminster Press 1979.
4. Robert Law, *The Tests of Life: a study of the First Epistle of St John*, Edinburgh 1909.
5. Paul Tillich, *The Shaking of the Foundations*, SCM Press and Scribners 1949.
6. Preston and Hanson, op. cit., p. 102.
7. Ibid., p. 105.

4. A Christian Response to the Arms Race

1. Laurence Martin, *The Two-Edged Sword*, BBC Reith Lectures 1981, Weidenfeld and Nicolson 1982.
2. Paul Rogers et al, *As Lambs to the Slaughter*, Arrow 1981.
3. *The Guardian*, 28 October 1981.
4. *As Lambs to the Slaughter*, p. 259.

5. Robert C. Aldridge, *The Counterforce Syndrome: A Guide to US Nuclear Weapons and Strategic Doctrine*, Institute of Policy Studies, Washington DC., 1979.

6. *North–South: A Programme for Survival*, Pan Books 1980.

7. II Peter 3. 11–13

5. The Church's Most Urgent Priority in Today's World

1. *The Church and the Bomb*, CIO Publishing and Hodder and Stoughton 1982.

2. Jonathan Schell, *The Fate of the Earth*, Jonathan Cape and Pan 1982.

3. Desmond Ball, *Can Nuclear War be Controlled?*, Adelphi Papers No. 169, Institute of Strategic Studies, 23 Tavistock Street, London WC2 E7N.

4. 'On Nuclear War', *New York Review of Books*, 21 January 1982.

5. Independent Commission on Disarmament and Security Issues, *Common Security: A Programme for Disarmament*, Pan 1982, p. 100.

6. Michael Carver, *A Policy for Peace*, Faber 1982, p. 109.

7. Jim Garrison, *The Darkness of God: Theology after Hiroshima*, SCM Press and Eerdmans 1982.

6. A Christian Response to the Energy Crisis

1. Gerald Leach, *Low Energy Strategy for the United Kingdom*, Science Reviews 1979.

7. Religion in the Third Wave: The Difference in Being a Christian Tomorrow

1. Donald Schon, *Beyond the Stable State: Public and Private Learning in a Changing Society*, Maurice Temple Smith 1971.

2. Alvin Toffler, *Future Shock*, Bodley Head 1979; Pan 1973.

3. Alvin Toffler, *The Third Wave*, Pan 1981.

4. Ronald Gregor Smith, *The New Man*, SCM Press 1956.

5. John Hick *Christianity at the Centre*, SCM Press 1968; 3rd edn published as *The Second Christianity*, SCM Press 1983

6. Charles Davis, *A Question of Conscience*, Hodder 1967.

7. Aelred Graham, *Zen Catholicism*, Collins 1964; Raymond Panik-kar, *Intra-Religious Dialogue*, Paulist Press, NJ 1978, Choan-Seng Song, *Third-Eye Theology*, Lutterworth Press 1980; Wilfred Cantwell Smith, *Towards a World Theology*, Macmillan and Westminster Press 1981.

8. A Statement of Christian Faith

1. Peter Schaffer, *Equus*, Deutsch 1973.

2. Gerard Manley Hopkins, 'The Wreck of the Deutschland', *Poems of Gerard Manley Hopkins*, OUP 1918.

3. Philip Toynbee, *Towards the Holy Spirit*, SCM Press 1973, pp. 8, 10.

4. Robert Heilbroner, *Inquiry into the Human Prospect*, Calder 1975.

5. H. A. Williams, *True Resurrection*, Mitchell Beazley 1972.

10. *Last Sermons*

1. Gerd Theissen, *On Having a Critical Faith*, SCM Press and Fortress Press 1979, p. 99.

2. Petru Dumitriu, *Incognito*, Collins 1964; Sphere Books 1969, p. 403.

3. Ibid., p. 454.

4. Ibid., pp. 455, 427.

5. Ibid., p. 379.